Moral Dilemmas

PHILOSOPHICAL THEORY

SERIES EDITORS
John McDowell, Philip Pettit and Crispin Wright

For Truth in Semantics
Anthony Appiah

The Dynamics of Belief: A Normative Logic
Peter Forrest

Abstract Objects
Bob Hale

Conditionals
Frank Jackson

Reality and Representation
David Papineau

Moral Dilemmas
Walter Sinnott-Armstrong

Moral Dilemmas

WALTER SINNOTT-ARMSTRONG

Basil Blackwell

To Liz

Copyright © Walter Sinnott-Armstrong 1988

First published 1988

Basil Blackwell Ltd
108 Cowley Road, Oxford, OX4 1JF, UK

Basil Blackwell Inc.
432 Park Avenue South, Suite 1503
New York, NY 10016, USA

British Library Cataloguing in Publication Data

Sinnott-Armstrong, Walter
Moral dilemmas. — (Philosophical theory).
1. Ethics
I. Title   II. Series
170   BJ1012
ISBN 0-631-15708-5

Library of Congress Cataloging in Publication Data

Sinnott-Armstrong, Walter, 1955-
Moral dilemmas/Walter Sinnott-Armstrong.
p. cm. — (Philosophical theory)
Revision of thesis (Ph.D.) — Yale University.
Bibliography: p.
Includes index.
ISBN 0-631-15708-5
1. Ethics.   2. Dilemma.   I. Title.   II. Series.
BJ1031.S55 1988   87-29908
170 — dc19   CIP

Typeset in 11 on 13 pt Baskerville
by Times Graphics, Singapore

Printed in Great Britain

Contents

Acknowledgements

This book took much too long to write, but one advantage of taking so long is that I have many people to thank. The first version was my dissertation at Yale, so I take great pleasure in thanking my advisors, Bob Fogelin and Ruth Marcus, for their guidance and friendship through the years. Among so many other things, Bob Fogelin taught me about conversational implication, and Ruth Marcus taught me deontic logic and its problems. These are two of the basic methodological tools in this book.

After I left Yale for Dartmouth, Bernie Gert showed me how important it is to distinguish moral ideals from moral requirements, and he also convinced me that people rank moral requirements differently even under ideal conditions. This led to my distinction between overriding and non-overridden moral requirements, which is another basic theme in this book. Bernie, Bob and Ruth also provided careful comments on innumerable details of innumerable drafts. Without these three, this book would have been impossible.

Many other debts are also great. Melanie Blood, David Magilner, Ingrid Nelson, Joan Pepin and Bob Victor were students in an honours seminar where they read the first draft and wrote critical papers. The entire penultimate draft later received detailed comments from Chris Gowans, John McDowell and Philip Pettit. Each of these readers saved me from many errors.

Parts of the book also received help from Jay Atlas, Mark Bedau, Marvin Belzer, Michael Bratman, Hector Castaneda, Willis Doney, Tim Duggan, Stanley Eveling, Philippa Foot, Bart Gruzalski, Shelly Kagan, Isaac Levi, Judy Lichtenberg,

Barry Loewer, Al Martinich, Lynne McFall, Jim Moor, Michael Morris, Geoff Sayre McCord, Sally Sedgwick, Holly Smith, Scott Soames, David Solomon, Peter Vallentyne, Alan White, Bernard Williams, Crispin Wright and many people in audiences at Amherst College, Dalhousie University, Johns Hopkins University, the Northern New England Philosophical Association, and the Universities at Aberdeen, Edinburgh, Hull, Liverpool, St Andrews, Stirling and York. The many contributions of each of these careful readers and listeners are too numerous to list, but I thank you all very much.

I would also like to thank *American Philosophical Quarterly* for permission to reprint most of 'Moral Dilemmas and Incomparability' as parts of chapters 1, 2 and 3; *The Philosophical Review* for permission to reprint most of ' "Ought" Conversationally Implies "Can" ' as part of chapter 4; *The Canadian Journal of Philosophy* for permission to reprint most of 'Moral Dilemmas and "Ought and Ought Not" ' as part of chapter 5; and *The Journal of Philosophy* for permission to reprint part of 'A Solution to Forrester's Paradox of Gentle Murder' as part of chapter 5, and most of 'Moral Dilemmas and Moral Realisms' as part of chapter 7.

On the financial side, I would like to thank my parents and the Whiting Fellowship Committee for support at the beginning, and Dartmouth College for a Junior Faculty Fellowship in the final stages.

As always, my greatest debt is to my wife, Liz. She not only put up with me and this project patiently for many years, but she also provided much needed encouragement and gentle criticism. It is for these reasons that this book is dedicated to her.

Walter Sinnott-Armstrong
Dartmouth College

1

What Moral Dilemmas Are

Both classical and contemporary literature are filled with descriptions of situations that are supposed to be moral dilemmas or unresolvable conflicts between strong moral requirements. The best known examples are Greek tragedies, such as those about Antigone and Agamemnon, and Shakespearian tragedies, but many recent novels, such as *Sophie's Choice*, also hinge on moral dilemmas. These stories are so common and so realistic that they seem to show that moral dilemmas can occur.

This impression is also supported by everyday experience. Almost everyone has faced some situation where each of two incompatible alternatives is favoured by some strong moral requirement, but there seems to be no objective way to resolve the conflict. Such situations seem to be common not only for those who determine which people will die, such as doctors and military personnel, but also for anyone with divergent commitments – for example, to friends, family and country. All of this makes it a matter of common sense that moral dilemmas are possible and even actual.

Nonetheless, philosophers often deny common sense. Philosophers have denied that time is real, that anyone can know anything, that anyone has free will, that minds are distinct from bodies, and much else that seems to be common sense. They claim to have strong arguments that common sense is not always as reliable as it seems.

Similarly, most traditional moral philosophers deny that unresolvable moral dilemmas can ever really occur. They realize that they are denying common sense, so they give a variety of arguments against moral dilemmas. They assume that the purpose of a moral theory is to give a procedure for deciding what to do in every moral situation, so the best moral theory must show either that moral requirements never really conflict or that such conflicts are always resolvable by finding the one right action. This view is shared by most utilitarians and many of their rival deontologists, such as Aquinas and Kant. And this tradition is still alive today.

Of course, philosophers do not all agree about the possibility of moral dilemmas (or anything else). Even though traditional philosophers deny the possibility of moral dilemmas, other philosophers have recently rejected the philosophical tradition and argued that moral dilemmas are actual or at least possible. Sartre was one of the first to be so bold. Several deontic logicians later reached similar conclusions by very different methods.

These philosophers not only defend common sense but also claim that the possibility of moral dilemmas is important for several reasons. First, moral dilemmas force us to rethink the traditional view of the nature and purpose of moral theory and thus of the standards for deciding among moral theories. Traditional moral philosophers often assume that a moral theory must provide a complete moral decision procedure, but such completeness cannot be attained if moral dilemmas cannot be resolved. The recognition of moral dilemmas can thus prevent unrealistic expectations that distort moral theories and lead some to reject the whole project of ethics.

Some defenders of moral dilemmas also claim that the possibility of moral dilemmas refutes realism, objectivism, absolutism or rationalism in morality. Other moral philosophers have responded that moral dilemmas not only do not refute moral realism but actually support it. If either claim is correct, the possibility of moral dilemmas might solve one of the oldest and most important debates in moral philosophy.

The possibility of moral dilemmas also provides a new way to think about concrete moral problems. When a moral philosopher asks questions such as whether a preferential treatment programme is morally permitted, it is often assumed that there are only two alternatives. Either the preferential treatment programme is required, because the rights of those who benefit override the rights of those who are excluded; or the programme is not permitted, because the rights of those who are excluded override the rights of those who benefit. The recognition of moral dilemmas provides another alternative: neither right overrides the other, so the conflict is unresolvable. There is still much to be said about what can and should be done and felt in such situations, but this discussion cannot even begin until the possibility of moral dilemmas is admitted.

These philosophical implications and others make it important to determine whether moral dilemmas are possible. But moral dilemmas also have an intrinsic interest of their own. If moral dilemmas are as common as it seems, each of us will probably face some moral dilemma in his or her own personal life. We can deal with these situations better when they arise if we understand their nature and implications in advance. All of this makes it worthwhile to make the considerable effort that is needed to understand these complex situations.

1.1 THE STANDARD DEFINITION

The first step in understanding moral dilemmas is to determine what they are. This task is not as easy as it may seem, because many people have written about moral dilemmas, and they do not always agree about which situations are moral dilemmas. In fact, the opponents in a debate about moral dilemmas often seem to be thinking about different kinds of situation. Such verbal disagreements can be avoided only by carefully specifying which situations count as moral dilemmas and why.

The best way to find a definition of moral dilemmas is to look at the examples and definitions that are given by those who defend the possibility of moral dilemmas. Probably the best known example is given by Sartre, who reports that one of his pupils came to him in the following situation:

His father was quarrelling with his mother and was also inclined to be a 'collaborator'; his elder brother had been killed in the German offensive of 1940 and this young man, with a sentiment somewhat primitive but generous, burned to avenge him. His mother was living alone with him, deeply afflicted by the semi-treason of his father and by the death of her oldest son, and her one consolation was in this young man. But he, at this moment, had the choice between going to England to join the Free French forces or of staying near his mother and helping her to live. He fully realized that this woman lived only for him and that his disappearance – or perhaps his death – would plunge her into despair. He also realized that, concretely and in fact, every action he performed on his mother's behalf would be sure of effect in the sense of aiding her to live, whereas anything he did in order to go and fight would be an ambiguous action which might vanish like water into sand and serve no purpose. For instance, to set out for England he would have to wait indefinitely in a Spanish camp on the way through Spain; or, on arriving in England or in Algiers he might be put into an office to fill up forms. Consequently, he found himself confronted by two very different modes of action; the one concrete, immediate, but directed towards only one individual; the other an action addressed to an end infinitely greater, a national collectivity, but for that reason ambiguous – and it might be frustrated on the way. At the same time, he was hesitating between two kinds of morality; on the one side, the morality of sympathy, of personal devotion and, on the other side a morality of wider scope but of more debatable validity. He had to choose between the two.[1]

Although there is much uncertainty in this example, what is supposed to make the situation a moral dilemma seems to be that the boy ought to stay with his mother and also ought to join the Free French in England, but he cannot both stay with his mother and join the Free French in England.

A second example comes from classical tragedy. Agamemnon is the leader of the Greek troops who are going to attack Troy. On the way to Troy, the Greek ships are becalmed, and the high priest declares that no wind will arise until Agamemnon sacrifices his daughter, Iphigenia. All of the Greeks believe this prediction, so they believe that Agamemnon cannot lead his troops to Troy unless he kills his daughter. They also believe Agamemnon has a duty to lead his troops to Troy because of 'his responsibilities as commander, the many people involved, the considerations of honor, and so forth.'[2] This is supposed to be a moral dilemma because Agamemnon ought to lead his troops to Troy, and he also ought to kill his daughter, but he cannot lead his troops to Troy if he does not kill his daughter.

Many more examples have been given, but this is enough to show the general pattern. The standard definition of moral dilemmas seems to include all and only situations where (at the same time[3]) an agent ought to adopt each of two alternatives separately but cannot adopt both together.

One problem with this definition is that, in some moral dilemmas, it is unnatural to say that the agent *ought* to adopt each of two alternatives, because it is more natural to say that the agent ought *not* to do something. The agent still seems to be in a moral dilemma if he cannot do what he ought to do unless he also does what he ought not to do. However, such situations do fit the standard definition if the right alternatives are identified. When it is natural to say that someone ought not to do something, we can also say that the agent ought to adopt the alternative of not doing that thing. For example, when Agamemnon ought not to kill his daughter, he ought to adopt the alternative of not killing his daughter, and he cannot both adopt that negative alternative and also lead his troops to Troy. This might stretch common usage, but it allows a simpler definition to include various kinds of moral dilemmas.

1.2 'OUGHT'

Although the standard definition is standard, it is also vague in many crucial respects. Most importantly, the standard definition uses the term 'ought', but 'ought' is too dull a tool to use in an area where precision is crucial. Debates about moral dilemmas are usually formulated in terms of what agents ought to do, but this leads to confusion and misunderstanding unless the term 'ought' is explained very carefully.

A first dimension of vagueness in the term 'ought' can be brought out by comparing the following sentences:

(1) You ought to keep your promises.
(2) You ought not to kill innocent people.
(3) You ought to invest in IBM.
(4) You ought not to use a cannon if you want to kill him quietly.
(5) You ought to get 1023 if you add 345 and 678.
(6) The train ought to be here soon.

Many other examples could be given, but these suggest some of the variety of contexts or ways in which the term 'ought' is used.

Despite this variety, all such uses of the term 'ought' share something in common: they all indicate some kind of reason. In the most natural context, someone who utters (1) and (2) seems to claim at least that there is a moral reason to keep your promise and not to kill innocent people. In contrast, the most natural context for (3) or (4) is when someone claims not that you have a moral reason but that you have a prudential or self-interested reason to invest in IBM or not to use a cannon. Someone who asserts (5) need not claim that you have either a moral or a prudential reason to arrive at that sum. He probably claims only that you have an epistemic reason to get that answer. And the most natural use of (6) is to claim that the speaker has some epistemic reason to believe that the train will be here soon. Thus, even though these sentences use 'ought' to indicate different kinds of reasons, they all use 'ought' to indicate some kind of reason for someone.

This unity in variety makes it unclear whether the term 'ought' is ambiguous and has distinct senses or meanings. Many philosophers claim that 'ought' has several meanings. For example, Harman distinguishes the moral 'ought', the 'ought' of rationality, the 'ought' of expectation, and the 'ought' of evaluation.[4] This list is fairly standard, but it is not even supposed to be exhaustive (or exclusive?). If the term 'ought' has different meanings, it has very many such meanings with some overlap.

Other philosophers deny that the term 'ought' has distinct meanings. They claim instead that 'ought' is merely unspecific or vague about which kind of reason is relevant. 'Ought' is then supposed to be like 'child'. 'Child' refers to a boy child in some contexts and to a girl child in other contexts, but this does not show that 'child' is ambiguous or has different meanings. Similarly, the fact that 'ought' indicates different kinds of reasons in different contexts does not prove that it has different meanings.[5]

I will not try to determine whether 'ought' really does have distinct meanings, since this is not necessary in order to clarify moral dilemmas. Whether 'ought' is ambiguous or only unspecific, both sides agree that 'ought' always indicates some kind of reason and that it indicates different kinds of reason in different contexts. The standard definition of moral dilemmas sets up a context that is moral, so the relevant reasons are moral reasons. Consequently, to say in the definition of moral dilemmas that an agent ought to adopt each of two alternatives implies at least that there is a moral reason for that agent to adopt each alternative.

The vagueness of 'ought' allows us to generalize our definition. Any situation is a dilemma of some kind if an agent ought to adopt each of two alternatives but cannot adopt both. Non-moral dilemmas are, then, situations where an agent ought to adopt incompatible alternatives because of reasons that are not moral. There are many kinds of non-moral dilemma. When prudential reasons conflict, and the agent prudentially ought to adopt incompatible alternatives, the agent is in a prudential dilemma. When epistemic reasons conflict, and the agent or the speaker ought to believe incompatible alternatives, he or she is in an epistemic dilemma.[6] There might also be religious dilemmas when religious demands conflict, and legal dilemmas when laws conflict.[7] There might even be moral/prudential dilemmas when moral reasons conflict with prudential reasons (as in some cases of weakness of will), moral/religious dilemmas when morality conflicts with religion (as in Abraham's attempt to sacrifice Isaac),[8] and moral/legal dilemmas when laws conflict with morality (as in some cases of civil disobedience). All of these non-moral dilemmas are interesting, and it is also very interesting to compare and contrast them with moral dilemmas. Nonetheless, I will not discuss these other kinds of dilemmas except in passing. For the sake of simplicity, I will focus only on dilemmas where the conflicting reasons are purely moral.

1.3 MORAL REASONS

It is not very useful to explain 'ought' in terms of moral reasons unless we explain what moral reasons are. Part of the answer is that a moral reason to adopt an alternative is a fact about that alternative, a fact that the alternative has certain properties or consequences. Some might not want to identify a moral reason with a fact, but they can say instead that there is a moral reason to adopt an alternative if and only if the alternative has certain properties or consequences. Such changes would not affect my main points.

Not every fact about an alternative is a moral reason. A fact is a moral reason only when it is about properties or consequences that are relevant to morality. But this simple answer raises several issues.

One issue concerns what makes a reason a moral reason instead of a non-moral reason. Different positions on this issue can be represented by different definitions of morality. Morality has been defined in terms of universalizability (of several kinds), supremacy (whether the reason overrides reasons of other kinds), and/or some particular content or function (such as the welfare of others or social cohesion).[9] These different accounts of morality imply that different reasons are moral reasons and that different dilemmas are moral dilemmas.

A second issue concerns substantive ethics. Even if it is clear that someone puts forward a reason as a moral reason, an opponent can still claim that there is really no moral reason to do as he says. For example, someone can claim there is a reason for my wife not to get an abortion, and I can realize his claim is about a moral reason, if I know he thinks no other kind of reason is relevant here, but I can still deny that his claim is correct and that there is really any moral reason for her not to get an abortion. Different substantive theories about which facts really are moral reasons then imply that different situations are moral dilemmas.

The problem is that there is much disagreement about exactly which facts really are moral reasons. Almost all agree that death, pain, lies and promises are somehow relevant to morality. However, some theorists deny that the fact that an act would cause death is a moral reason not to do the act. They argue instead that there is a moral reason not to do such an act only if it would directly or intentionally cause death. Others claim that the fact that an act increases the risk of death is a moral reason not to do it, even if no death actually ensues, and even if the agent did not intend or even know that the act would create this risk.

Despite these disagreements, there is much agreement in some cases about whether there is a moral reason. For example, almost every moral philosopher agrees that the fact that an act would intentionally and directly cause death to another innocent person is a moral reason not to do it. This reason must be moral rather than some other kind, since there is supposed to be such a reason even when killing is not contrary to self-interest, law, religion, etiquette or aesthetics. Similarly, the fact that an act would intentionally and directly cause great pain or disability or loss of freedom to another innocent person is almost always seen as a moral reason not to do the act. Most philosophers also agree that there is a moral reason to keep promises and not to tell lies. Moral philosophers disagree about why these facts are moral reasons, but most agree that there are moral reasons in such cases.

This agreement allows me to do without any general definition of morality or any complete substantive moral theory. I will use examples where the reasons are moral reasons on any plausible definition of morality. Whenever differences among definitions of morality are relevant, I will say so and discuss the implications of different definitions of morality. I will also stick to examples where any plausible substantive moral theory must admit the moral relevance of the alternatives, and where the agent knows and intends (in the normal sense) the effects and properties of his actions. Since moral dilemmas do arise in such clear cases, the possibility of moral dilemmas can be shown without having to decide about more questionable cases. Even if a critic did deny what I take to be clear cases, I could always modify my examples to fit the critic's own theory, if it is plausible. Thus, when I make substantive assumptions about which facts are moral reasons, these assumptions are not essential to my arguments.

I still might seem to beg the question against emotivists and others who deny that any moral reasons are facts. However, this is to misunderstand my account. Emotivists can claim that, when someone utters a moral judgement, he or she expresses an attitude either toward an alternative because it has certain properties or consequences, or toward the fact that the alternative has these properties or consequences or toward facts of this kind. Even if moral judgements do not state facts, they can still express attitudes about facts. So my account of moral reasons is neutral among all plausible meta-ethical theories.

A final objection is that a moral reason cannot be a fact about an alternative, since there is no reason unless the agent also believes the fact about the alternative. However, there can still *be* a reason even when the agent does not *have* it. We can say there is a reason for John not to go on a certain road when its bridge is down, even if John does not know the bridge is down. This is why, if he asks, we tell him he ought not to take that road. We might not say John has a reason not to go on that road, but that is because having a reason implies believing the fact. And the same holds for moral reasons. If an agent promises to meet a friend but then negligently forgets her promise, there is still a moral reason for her to meet her friend.

Thus, there can be a moral reason even when the agent does not believe the relevant facts. Nonetheless, my account does not exclude the contrary view that reasons imply beliefs. As I use the terms, it is a fact about an alternative that its agent has certain beliefs. Whether or not these facts provide real moral reasons is a substantive question that I will leave open.

Opponents still might deny that a situation is a moral dilemma when the agent does not know there are moral reasons for the incompatible alternatives, possibly because such ignorance prevents some kind of anguish that might seem essential to moral dilemmas. I think such anguish is not essential to moral dilemmas, and neither is any belief in the conflicting moral reasons. Nonetheless, I will avoid such side issues by depending only on examples where the agent is aware of the morally relevant properties and consequences of the alternatives. This will also allow me to say either 'there is a moral reason for him' or 'he has a moral reason'. If someone still insists that a situation is a moral dilemma only when the agent has or believes in the moral reasons that conflict, she can add such a condition to my definition of a moral dilemma. This will not affect my main points.

1.4 REQUIREMENTS VERSUS IDEALS

Now that 'ought' and moral reasons have been explained, we can see that moral dilemmas cannot be defined simply in terms of 'ought' or moral reasons. The standard definition of moral dilemmas is inadequate, because not all conflicts between moral reasons are moral dilemmas. The first kind of exception arises because there are two different kinds of moral reason, which I will call requirements and ideals.[10]

A standard example of following a moral ideal is giving to a worthy charity. If I know that a particular charity is worthy, I have a moral reason to help this charity, since doing so will prevent the pain or death of some other people. This makes it morally good or ideal for me to help this charity. However, since the money or time that I give to the charity is my own, it would not be morally wrong for me to refuse to help this particular charity, and criticism and punishment would not be appropriate, even if I have no moral justification for refusing to help. It might be wrong for me not to give anything to any charity at any time, but this does not make it wrong for me to refuse to help in this particular case, if I do help in other cases.

Other moral reasons are very different. The other kind of moral reason includes obligations, duties and rights, but I will use the more general term 'requirement'. A moral reason to adopt an alternative is a moral requirement if and only if it would be morally wrong not to adopt that alternative if there were no moral justification for not adopting it. More precisely, there is a moral requirement to adopt an alternative if and only if it would be morally wrong not to adopt that same alternative in a situation that is similar to the actual one in all relevant respects except that, if there is a moral justification for not adopting it in the actual situation, there is no moral justification for not adopting it in the otherwise similar situation. For example, a moral reason to keep a promise is a requirement, because failure to keep a promise is morally wrong unless it can be morally justified. That is why we say one has a moral obligation to keep promises, but one does not have a moral obligation or duty to give to any particular charity (in the absence of any special commitment).

Negative moral reasons are similar. A moral reason not to adopt an alternative is a moral requirement if and only if it would be morally wrong to adopt the alternative in a situation just like the actual one except that there is no moral justification for adopting it. A moral reason not to kill is, then, a requirement, because killing is morally wrong unless it is morally justified. It is not wrong to kill if one has an adequate justification, but to kill without any morally relevant reason is wrong.

Basically the same distinction can be drawn in terms of liability to punishment. There is, then, a moral requirement not to adopt an alternative if and only if to adopt that alternative in an otherwise similar situation where there is no moral justification or excuse for adopting it would make the agent liable to punishment, where liability to punishment means that it would not be morally wrong to punish (even if punishment is impractical). This definition implies a moral requirement not to kill, if it is not morally wrong to punish someone who kills without any justification or excuse. Other examples force us to specify the relevant kind of punishment, since some kinds of violators might be liable not to legal punishment but only to social criticism. Promise breakers are not usually punished legally, but they are liable to verbal criticism. When the relevant kind of punishment is specified, this new definition in terms of liability seems to yield the same moral requirements as the original definition in terms of what is wrong. The reason is that who is liable to punishment of the relevant kind depends on what is morally wrong. In any case, however the distinction is drawn, there is an important difference between moral reasons like those to help charities and moral reasons like those to keep promises and not to kill.

It must be admitted that both definitions of moral requirements depend on intuitions about what is morally wrong. However, the necessary intuitions are about cases where there is no moral reason or justification at all for adopting the alternative (or not adopting it). This should secure more agreement about the relevant intuitions, because it avoids questions of whether a justification is adequate. This should also remove the need to specify exactly what it means to call something wrong, since, when there is no justification at all for acts like killing and breaking promises, such acts are wrong in the strongest way possible for that kind of act. In any case, I will again use only clear examples, and, if any is questioned, I can always substitute another example.

Utilitarians might object that both kinds of moral reasons concern maximizing utility. This might be true, but utilitarians can still accept the basic distinction. Mill distinguished what is wrong from what ought not to be done by pointing out that it does not always maximize utility to punish those who fail to maximize utility.[11] Utilitarians can, then, call a moral reason a requirement only if it maximizes utility to punish those who fail to act on it. Thus, even utilitarians can agree to some distinction between moral requirements and moral ideals.

Now that requirements and ideals have been distinguished, three kinds of conflict between moral reasons can be distinguished. (1) One moral ideal can conflict with another moral ideal, (2) one moral requirement can conflict with another moral requirement, and (3) a moral ideal can conflict with a moral requirement. All of these count as moral conflicts, but not all of them count as moral dilemmas.

The first possibility is when a moral ideal conflicts with another moral ideal. For example, moral ideals conflict if I can help only one of two worthy charities. People who defend moral dilemmas do not seem to have in mind such conflicts between moral ideals, since almost all of their examples include moral requirements. Furthermore, some people who deny the possibility of moral dilemmas explicitly admit that moral ideals can conflict. And both sides often describe moral dilemmas as conflicts of obligations or duties, which are kinds of requirement. For these reasons, I will not count conflicts between moral ideals as moral dilemmas. Conflicts between moral ideals are interesting, and they do exhibit much of the same structure as moral dilemmas, so many of my arguments will apply to moral ideal conflicts, but they are not my main concern.

The paradigm examples of moral dilemmas are conflicts between two moral requirements. These are the cases that both advocates and opponents of the possibility of moral dilemmas seem to have in mind. It is only when each alternative violates a moral requirement that the agent cannot avoid the negative repercussions of violating a moral requirement. This seems unfair to many opponents of moral dilemmas, and it seems to motivate much of the opposition to moral dilemmas. That is why I will count conflicts between moral requirements as moral dilemmas, if they meet the other conditions.

The third possibility is when a moral ideal conflicts with a moral requirement. For example, if I promise to go to your party, but later I am asked to work for a needy charity at the same time, my moral requirement to keep my promise conflicts with the moral ideal of helping the charity. Such situations could be called moral dilemmas, and they have much of the same structure as standard moral dilemmas. However, it is not clear that those who deny that moral dilemmas are possible want to deny that these conflicts are possible. Consequently, even if I show that such conflicts are possible, opponents can claim I have not shown anything they deny. To avoid this misunderstanding, I will not count such conflicts as moral dilemmas.

In sum, I will not count a situation as a moral dilemma unless one moral requirement conflicts with another moral requirement. This makes the claim that moral dilemmas are possible more controversial and more important. And if conflicts between moral requirements are possible, there is no reason to deny the possibility of conflicts between a moral requirement and a moral ideal or between two moral ideals.

1.5 OVERRIDING

Even when moral requirements are distinguished from moral ideals, moral dilemmas still cannot be defined simply as conflicts between moral requirements, because not all conflicts between moral requirements are moral dilemmas. The reason is that moral requirements vary in strength or importance. The standard example is that a moral requirement to keep a promise is not as strong as a moral requirement to save a life or not to kill, because it is wrong to kill or not to save a life if the only reason to do so is to keep a promise, since that reason is inadequate. None of this requires any mechanical or mathematical method of measuring the strengths of moral requirements. The point is only that some moral requirements override or are more important than others.

The strengths of reasons are hidden when moral dilemmas are defined in terms of 'ought', because 'ought' is vague in a second way. The term 'ought' can be used to indicate different relative strengths of moral reasons. Sometimes we say things like 'There are a hundred things that I ought to do tonight, but I can't do them all', even when we know that the reasons for some of the things are more important than the reasons for others. This use of 'ought' implies only that there is some reason for each thing that ought to be done, even if the reason is overridden. In contrast, I can also ask what I ought to do when I have some reason to do each of the hundred things. I am then asking what I have an overriding reason to do or which reasons override which. Thus, in different contexts, to say that an agent morally ought (or ought not) to adopt an alternative is to say either that

(MR) there is a (possibly overridden) moral reason

or that

(OMR) there is an overriding moral reason

to adopt (or not to adopt) the alternative. (OMR) is probably more common, but neither use is improper. The only way to determine which interpretation is correct in a given context is often to ask exactly what the speaker is claiming and what he or she is denying.

These two interpretations of 'ought' yield two interpretations of the standard definition of moral dilemmas. If 'ought' is interpreted by (MR), the standard definition makes moral dilemmas include all conflicts between moral reasons, even if some are overridden. But if 'ought' is interpreted by (OMR), the standard definition makes moral dilemmas include only conflicts between overriding moral reasons. In any case, neither interpretation of the standard definition is adequate, since moral dilemmas should be defined in terms of moral requirements rather than moral reasons.

Similar alternatives exist when moral dilemmas are defined by moral requirements. Moral dilemmas can be defined as conflicts between

(MRq) (possibly overridden) moral requirements

or

(OMRq) overriding moral requirements.

These definitions include different situations as moral dilemmas.

(MRq) would count a conflict between moral requirements as a moral dilemma even if one requirement is very much stronger than the other. Such conflicts will be called 'resolvable'. In one example, someone promises to hold a weapon and return it when his friend asks for it, but his friend asks for the weapon when the friend plans to use it to kill his wife. Lemmon calls this situation a moral dilemma, even though he recognizes that the moral requirement not to return the weapon and thereby aid the murder is stronger than the moral requirement to keep the promise.[12] Thus, Lemmon seems to use something like (MRq) to define moral dilemmas, since his example would not be a moral dilemma on (OMRq).

However, Lemmon's usage is unusual. Conflicts between moral requirements do not usually count as moral dilemmas if one requirement overrides the other. Many of those who deny that moral dilemmas are possible do not deny that moral reasons or requirements can conflict.[13] Furthermore, most defenders of moral dilemmas want to claim more than just that moral requirements can conflict.[14] This possibility would not have many of the crucial implications that they claim for moral dilemmas. For these reasons, (MRq) is not adequate to define moral dilemmas. Resolvable conflicts between moral requirements are still interesting and important, and I will discuss them below, but they will be called 'moral requirement conflicts' rather than 'moral dilemmas'.

Once (MRq) is rejected, it might seem that the only alternative is (OMRq). (OMRq) implies that moral dilemmas are possible only if there can be an overriding moral requirement for an agent to adopt each incompatible alternative. This is clearly impossible. What makes a moral requirement overriding is not just that it is stronger in some respect than what it overrides. Instead, a moral requirement is overriding only if it is stronger overall than any conflicting moral reason (including any moral ideal). A moral requirement can be stronger in one respect while weaker in another respect than a conflicting moral reason. But moral requirements cannot be stronger overall than each other. The reason is that, if one requirement overrides another, and the other also overrides the former, then the former must override itself; but this is impossible.[15] In other words, overriding is transitive and areflexive, so it must be asymmetric. This shows that moral dilemmas would be impossible if they were defined by (OMRq).

However, this does not show that moral dilemmas are impossible. Philosophers who defend the possibility of moral dilemmas do not define moral dilemmas according to (OMRq), so they do not claim that situations of this kind are possible. They are not always clear about this, but some do admit it is not possible that an agent *must* adopt incompatible alternatives, and they seem to use 'must' so that an agent must do something only if not doing it violates an overriding moral requirement.[16] In any case, to ascribe an absurdity lacks charity when more coherent interpretations are available. Thus, any argument that rules out only conflicts between overriding moral requirements misses its target if it is supposed to refute those who claim that moral dilemmas are possible.

This misunderstanding seems to occur because many opponents of moral dilemmas assume that, if moral dilemmas cannot be defined by (MRq), they must be defined by (OMRq). However, (OMRq) is not the only alternative. If moral requirements conflict, but neither moral requirement overrides the other, then neither is overriding, but also neither is overridden. Such situations do not fit (OMRq), but they are also very different from conflicts where one moral requirement overrides the other. To capture these situations, moral dilemmas can be defined as conflicts between

(NOMRq) non-overridden moral requirements.

This definition includes less than (MRq) but more than (OMRq).

The difference between definitions (OMRq) and (NOMRq) is often overlooked. For example, McConnell writes, 'It is obvious that, if there are genuine moral dilemmas, then the "oughts" that conflict must be strict or absolute ones, and not merely prima facie ones.'[17] Similarly, Conee says the alternatives in moral dilemmas must be 'absolutely, unconditionally, and not merely prima facie morally obligatory'.[18] These phrases are not clear, but to say the conflicting moral requirements must be 'strict' and 'absolute' suggests that they must be overriding. In contrast, to say the conflicting reasons are '*not* merely prima facie' and are '*un*conditional' suggests that they must be '*non*-overridden'. Thus, McConnell, Conee and others seem to conflate two different levels of reasons or requirements that are not prima facie. We will see that the main arguments against moral dilemmas depend on this confusion between overriding and non-overridden requirements.

However, most defenders of the possibility of moral dilemmas have in mind conflicts between non-overridden moral requirements. For example, Nagel writes, 'the strongest cases of conflict are genuine dilemmas, where there is decisive support for two or more incompatible courses of action or inaction . . . . [When] each [choice] seems right for reasons that appear decisive and sufficient . . . either choice will mean acting against some reasons without being able to claim that they are outweighed.'[19] Many others have also argued that a lack of ranking among the alternatives is enough to make a moral conflict into a dilemma.[20] And most of the examples that are given by defenders of the possibility of moral dilemmas fit under (NOMRq). Thus, their claims are captured by (NOMRq) rather than (OMRq).

This definition also has other advantages. (MRq) makes the possibility of moral dilemmas too weak to be controversial, and (OMRq) makes it so strong that it is absurd. (NOMRq) steers a middle path which is controversial but not absurd. Furthermore, (NOMRq) is precise enough to make sense of the complex issues that surround moral dilemmas. I will also show that (NOMRq) gives the possibility of moral dilemmas at least some of the important implications that have been claimed for moral dilemmas.

For these reasons, the best definition of moral dilemmas is (NOMRq). On (NOMRq), a moral dilemma is defined as any situation where there are non-overridden moral requirements for an agent to adopt each of two incompatible alternatives.

This occurs when moral requirements conflict but neither is overridden by the other (or by any other moral reason).

When moral dilemmas are defined by (NOMRq), it is crucial to specify when one moral requirement overrides another. I have already said that one moral requirement overrides a conflicting moral requirement if and only if the former is stronger overall in some morally relevant way. In such cases, there is no adequate justification for violating the overriding requirement, so such violations are morally wrong and imply liability to punishment. However, in a moral dilemma neither moral requirement is overriding in this way, so there is an adequate moral justification for violating either moral requirement, namely, it must be violated to avoid violating the other moral requirement, which is also not overridden. Thus, it is not morally wrong to violate either moral requirement in a moral dilemma, since I reserve 'wrong' for the strongest possible criticism in the relevant kind of situation.

Another way to look at the strengths of moral requirements is in terms of rankings. One moral requirement is stronger than another if and only if the former can be ranked higher overall in some morally relevant way. It is important to realize that not every kind of ranking shows that one moral requirement is morally stronger or overriding.[21] Someone might rank one moral requirement above another simply because the former is in her self-interest. Someone might decide that one promise is more important than another simply because she wants to break the former. An agent might even flip a coin in order to decide what to do. There need not be anything wrong with making and acting on such non-moral rankings. Nonetheless, non-moral rankings do not resolve the moral conflict or show that it is not a moral dilemma. In order to show that, a ranking must be morally relevant and have all of the essential features of morality. If morality must be impartial or supreme or universalizable or objective, a ranking must be so too in order to resolve a moral conflict and keep it from being a moral dilemma. Moral philosophers disagree about what is essential to morality and thus about which rankings are morally relevant and which situations count as moral dilemmas. I will say more below, but here I need not determine which features are essential to morality. Whatever counts as moral, only a moral ranking can show that one moral requirement overrides another or that a conflict between moral requirements is not a moral dilemma. Thus, on (NOMRq), a moral dilemma occurs exactly when moral requirements conflict, but neither can be ranked lower in any morally relevant way.

So far I have discussed only the strengths of moral requirements, but to say that a moral requirement is overriding is not just to say that it is stronger. Even if one moral requirement is morally stronger than another, the former does not override the latter unless the two moral requirements conflict. For the sake of simplicity, I will also call a reason overriding if it does not conflict with any other reason. But one should not forget that, when moral requirements do conflict, whether one is overriding depends in part on the moral requirements for incompatible alternatives.

In sum, then, a moral dilemma can be defined as a situation where moral requirements conflict and neither is overridden in any morally relevant way. The relations between moral dilemmas and related situations can be represented in the following diagram:

What conflicts?
    /\
Nothing   Reasons → Conflicts
      /\
   Non-moral   Moral → Moral conflicts
        /\
     Ideals Requirements → Moral requirement conflicts
          /\
      Resolvable   Unresolvable → Moral dilemmas

This terminology is not supposed to capture all common or proper usage. The point is only to distinguish situations in ways which will be useful and which will not beg any questions against any plausible moral theory from utilitarianism to absolutism.

It is still worth mentioning two ways in which my definition might stray from common usage. First, my definition counts situations as moral dilemmas even when the conflicting moral requirements are trivial, but it might seem odd to call a trivial situation a moral dilemma. Nonetheless, the structure of moral dilemmas is the same whether a lot or a little is at stake, so my definition does capture the features that determine whether moral dilemmas are possible. If a critic still insists that moral dilemmas cannot be trivial, I could ensure this by adding restrictions to my definition. These restrictions would not affect my main points.

It might also seem common to call a situation a moral dilemma when an agent is very unsure about what ought to be done. And agents are almost never certain that neither moral requirement overrides another or that their situation is a moral dilemma on my definition. However, it would be too easy to show that moral dilemmas are possible if uncertainty were enough for a moral dilemma, and it would be too hard to show that moral dilemmas are possible if certainty were required for a moral dilemma. Furthermore, the structure of a moral dilemma remains the same whether or not the agent is certain about the conflicting moral requirements and their rankings. For these reasons, I will not build certainty into my definition of moral dilemmas. When an agent is not certain about her moral requirements or their rankings, the agent is not certain whether she is in a moral dilemma, even if she does have a moral problem. Of course, she still might or might not be in a moral dilemma, depending on whether it is really true that moral requirements conflict and neither is overridden.

1.6 ALTERNATIVES

So far I have discussed only the moral terms in the definition of moral dilemmas, but there are also problems with the non-moral terms. In particular, we need to determine what an alternative is and when an agent can adopt one. My arguments below will not depend on how I analyse these terms, but a few comments will add some precision.

Although I refer to alternatives, it is more common to say that what an agent ought to do is an act, so an agent in a moral dilemma ought to do two acts but cannot do both. However, the term 'act' does not accurately describe what agents ought to do in most cases.[22] If I ought to buy milk today, the action sentence 'I buy milk today' would be true no matter where or how or when today I buy milk. However, an act of buying milk at 3.00 p.m. at one shop with a cheque would not be identical with an act of buying milk at 4.00 p.m. at another shop with cash. These acts are distinct because they occur at different times and places, and because I might have to decide which act to perform, and I might do both. Thus, the sentence 'I buy milk today' does not say that I do any particular act but only that I do some act of a general kind, namely, some act of buying milk today. Similarly, the moral judgement 'I ought to buy milk today' does not say that any particular act ought to be done but only that I ought to do some act of a general kind.

This implicit generality of action sentences can be captured with an existential quantifier over acts. A sentence like 'I buy milk today' can be symbolized as '$(\exists x)(Mxi \ \& \ Tx)$', and this can be read as 'There is some act of buying milk by me and it occurs today.' A moral judgement like 'I ought to buy milk today' can then be symbolized as '$O(\exists x)(Mxi \ \& \ Tx)$'. These predicates can be analysed further, but the existential quantifier will remain.

This analysis also fits negative action sentences. The sentence 'Agamemnon does not kill his daughter' does not claim that there is any particular act of killing his daughter that Agamemnon did not perform, but instead that there is not any act of killing by Agamemnon of his daughter. This can be symbolized as '$-(\exists x)Kxad$'. Similarly, the moral judgement 'Agamemnon ought not to kill his daughter' does not say that there is a particular act of killing his daughter that Agamemnon ought not to do, but rather that Agamemnon ought not to do any act of killing his daughter. This can be symbolized as '$O-(\exists x)Kxad$'. This is fulfilled even if Agamemnon tries to kill his daughter but fails, so a more complicated analysis is needed to capture the judgements that he ought not to try (or intend) to kill her and that he ought to refrain from killing her; but the existential quantifier will remain.

This analysis shows why it is inaccurate to say that someone ought to do an act, so it also creates a need for new terminology. Many expressions, such as 'course of action', could be used, but I will refer to alternatives. As I use the term, someone ought to (or can) adopt an alternative if and only if a true judgement can be formed by attaching the operator 'ought' (or 'can') to an action sentence which says that person does some act of the relevant kind. For example, I ought to adopt the alternative of buying milk if I ought to do some act of buying milk. Judgements that someone ought not to adopt an alternative are similar except that the moral operator is attached to an action sentence that is negative. The same form applies to judgements about moral reasons and requirements both to adopt and not to adopt alternatives. This account of alternatives might stretch common usage, since it allows different alternatives to be compatible, but it will prove useful.

This account simplifies the definition of moral dilemmas by allowing negative as well as positive alternatives. This leaves three kinds of moral dilemma. Positive/positive moral dilemmas include moral requirements to adopt positive alternatives, such as occur if Sartre's student has a duty to help his mother and a duty to go to England (to do an act of each kind). Positive/negative moral dilemmas include a moral requirement to adopt one alternative and a moral requirement *not* to adopt another alternative. One example is that of Agamemnon, if he has a duty to lead his troops to Troy and a duty not to kill his daughter, but he cannot lead his troops to Troy without killing his daughter (cannot do an act of one kind without doing an act of the other kind). Third, negative/negative moral dilemmas include a moral requirement not to adopt one alternative and a moral requirement not to adopt another alternative. An example occurs if someone has a duty not to lie to a friend and a duty not to hurt him but cannot avoid hurting him except by lying to him (cannot avoid an act of one kind without doing an act of the other kind). Although these cases can be distinguished, they are all situations where an agent has moral requirements to adopt incompatible alternatives.

Another advantage of my account is that it allows us to define moral dilemmas in terms of only two alternatives. In some situations, there are moral requirements to adopt each of three or more alternatives when the agent cannot adopt all of them. However, there is always some subset of the alternatives which the agent cannot adopt together with the rest of the alternatives. The situation can then be redescribed as a moral dilemma with only two alternatives by treating the subset as one alternative and the rest as a second alternative. My account allows a disjunction or conjunction of alternatives to be described as a single alternative, because moral operators can yield true judgements when they are attached to conjunctions and disjunctions of action sentences. The situation is then a moral dilemma if and only if moral requirements to adopt two of these complex alternatives conflict without either being overridden. Thus conflicts with more than two alternatives can still fit under my definition of moral dilemmas.[23]

This reduction is not so easy when there is more than one agent. Sometimes two (or more) agents have non-overridden moral requirements to adopt different alternatives, but it is not possible for both (or all) agents to adopt their respective alternatives. Marcus cites the classical tragedy of Antigone as an example.[24] Polyneices was a traitor, so, in order to preserve the peace, King Creon decrees that nobody shall bury Polyneices. Antigone is Polyneices' sister, and she thinks her brother will suffer in the afterlife if she does not bury him. Antigone seems to have a moral requirement to bury her brother, and Creon seems to have a moral requirement to stop her, but Antigone cannot bury her brother if Creon stops her. Such interpersonal moral dilemmas need not create difficult moral choices for either agent, so they seem very different from moral dilemmas of a single agent. Interpersonal moral dilemmas do reduce to single-agent moral dilemmas if there is a moral requirement for one agent not to prevent another agent from fulfilling his or her moral requirements. However, this principle is questionable. In any case, I will avoid such complications by not counting interpersonal conflicts as moral dilemmas unless they can be reduced to single-agent moral dilemmas. Interpersonal moral dilemmas are still interesting, but I do not want my arguments to depend on them.

1.7 'CAN'

The last important part of the definition of moral dilemmas is the judgement that the agent cannot adopt both alternatives. What an agent can do determines which situations count as moral dilemmas. However, 'can' is vague in much the same way as 'ought'. Sometimes I cannot go to a party because I lack the physical means. In other cases, I physically can go, but I psychologically cannot bring myself to face the host. I also say that I cannot go when I have to prepare a lecture, or when I promised to stay home. In all of these cases, the reason why an agent cannot do something is that doing it would violate or be contrary to a law or rule of some kind. This might show that 'can' has separate meanings or just that it is unspecific. Either way, various laws or rules determine what someone can and cannot do in various contexts.

The crucial question is what kinds of law or rule show that an agent cannot adopt both alternatives in a moral dilemma. There are many possibilities. The clearest case is when the agent physically cannot adopt both alternatives, such as when someone promises to be in different places at the same time.

Another clear case is when the agent morally cannot adopt both alternatives because there is an overriding moral requirement not to adopt both alternatives. For example, if someone promises to mow two yards by sundown, she has a moral requirement to mow each yard by sundown. But suppose a suicidal friend leaves a message that he will kill himself if she does not come and talk to him at 4.00 p.m. If she goes to talk to him at 4.00, she will be able to mow either one but not both of the yards by sundown. If she does not talk to her friend, she physically can mow both yards. Nonetheless, it would be natural for her to say she cannot mow both yards by sundown, because she cannot do so without violating an overriding moral requirement to help her friend. And such a situation seems to be a moral dilemma, even though she physically can keep both promises. This makes it reasonable to use the term 'can' in the definition of moral dilemmas so that an agent cannot do what violates an overriding moral requirement.[25] Such situations can also be seen as conflicts among three alternatives where one overrides the other two, but this will not help the agent decide which of the other two to adopt, and it will not keep the situation from being a moral dilemma.

A trickier case occurs when the agent physically and morally can adopt both alternatives but lacks the necessary knowledge. A neat example occurs in Shakespeare's *Measure for Measure*. Angelo, the deputy of the duke of Vienna, condemns Claudio to death for fornication. Claudio's sister Isabella then pleads with Angelo for her brother's life, and Angelo tells her that he will not let her brother go unless she has sex with Angelo. But Isabella is a nun, so this would violate her vow of chastity. There is supposed to be a moral requirement for her to save her brother and a moral requirement for her not to break her vow of chastity. These requirements conflict if Isabella cannot save her brother without breaking her vow. But this is not clear. The Duke has returned to Vienna, and at one point he stands right next to Isabella. If she tells him her story, he will let her brother go. But she does not recognize the Duke, since he is disguised. Thus, she has the opportunity and physical ability to save her brother without breaking her vow, but she lacks the necessary factual knowledge. This makes it natural to say that she cannot save her brother without breaking her vow. And this suggests that, in contexts of moral dilemmas, an agent cannot adopt both alternatives if she lacks the knowledge needed to adopt both. However, it is not clear whether others would count such cases as moral dilemmas.

Other cases of ignorance are also unclear. Often an agent could adopt both alternatives if he knew how to do something that he does not know how to do, or if he used some ingenuity and thought quickly enough. Other agents might be able to think up some compromise and some way to get everyone to agree to the compromise. However, there are also cases where the agent cannot figure out any such escape in time. Whether we say the agents in such cases cannot adopt both alternatives seems to depend on how much ingenuity and time are required, and whether we think normal people would figure it out in time. This often leaves it unclear whether an agent can adopt both alternatives.

Many other cases could be discussed. What if the agent physically can adopt both alternatives but psychologically cannot bring himself to do what is necessary to adopt both alternatives? What if the agent physically and psychologically can adopt both alternatives but only at great personal cost? Does it matter how strong the conflicting moral requirements are? It is not clear whether to count these kinds of situations as moral dilemmas.

Fortunately, such borderline cases do not affect the main arguments about whether moral dilemmas are possible, so I can leave somewhat vague exactly what an agent can and cannot do. My definition of moral dilemmas is then vague, but this is better than arbitrary stipulation. Anyway, my arguments will depend only on clear cases where the agent physically or morally cannot adopt both alternatives, and no compromise is possible.

Nonetheless, two special cases deserve mention. First, when promises conflict, the agent could escape the moral dilemma if one of the promisees agreed to cancel the obligation. However, if he cannot think of any moral way to get either to release him, then the agent cannot avoid breaking one of the promises, so he is in a moral conflict or even dilemma. The fact that the agent could escape if one promisee *did* agree to cancel does not show that he can avoid violating one of the promises when neither promisee *does* agree to cancel. And, when I say promises conflict, I assume that neither promisee either does or would agree to cancel the obligation.

Another special case will be created when I argue below that an agent can have a non-overridden moral requirement to do what he cannot do. This creates problems for my definition. For example, suppose I have a non-overridden moral requirement to meet you at your office tomorrow, but I cannot do so. Then I cannot both meet you there then and also visit my parents next year. I could do both if I could meet you at your office, but I cannot do both of two things if I cannot do one of them alone. But then, if I also have a non-overridden moral requirement to visit my parents next year, this situation would count as a moral dilemma if the definition required only that the agent cannot fulfill both non-overridden moral requirements. However, defenders and opponents of moral dilemmas are not thinking of situations like this. In standard moral dilemmas, the agent can adopt each alternative separately even though he cannot adopt both together. Consequently, the definition of moral dilemmas should exclude such cases by requiring that the agent can adopt each alternative separately.

1.8 THE FINAL DEFINITION

I can now give my final definition of moral dilemmas. A moral dilemma is any situation where at the same time:

(1) there is a moral requirement for an agent to adopt each of two alternatives,
(2) neither moral requirement is overridden in any morally relevant way,
(3) the agent cannot adopt both alternatives together, and
(4) the agent can adopt each alternative separately.

I will usually refer only to clauses (1) to (3), but (4) is also met in the central cases that I and others discuss. The central cases will also be situations where the conflicting moral requirements are not trivial and where the agent believes that (1) to (4) are met, although the agent might or might not be certain about this.

This definition is only supposed to capture the clear cases that most philosophers on both sides have in mind when they discuss moral dilemmas. It is not intended to include every situation that is interesting or that could legitimately be called a moral dilemma. Many borderline cases share many logical features with standard moral dilemmas, so the arguments below do apply to these borderline cases. However, if any argument depended on borderline cases, it might establish the possibility of some situations, but an opponent could still respond that these situations are not really moral dilemmas. Such responses might be inadequate, but it would be complicated to show why. I will avoid such complications by restricting my definition and discussion to cases that would clearly be moral dilemmas.

Some opponents still might respond that I do not defend what they deny. A main complaint might be that I define moral dilemmas in terms of moral requirements instead of what agents ought to do. However, the term 'ought' is the source of much confusion in the literature on moral dilemmas. My definition of moral dilemmas in terms of moral requirements is an improvement, because it captures what is meant by others' judgements in terms of 'ought', but it also provides needed precision, as I will show below. Another advantage of my definition is that it captures what is interesting and important about moral dilemmas. When I discuss the implications of moral dilemmas, I will show that the importance of moral dilemmas is due to the features that are essential to moral dilemmas on my definition. This will justify my definition of moral dilemmas.

1.9 POSITIONS

So defined, almost everyone admits that some situations appear to be moral dilemmas. But the issue is not about appearances. The issue is whether or not there really are or can be situations that fit the definition of moral dilemmas.

Several positions are available. One position is that moral dilemmas are both possible and actual or, in other words, that there not only can be but are situations that are moral dilemmas. Another position is that moral dilemmas are not even possible. An intermediate position is that moral dilemmas are possible but never actual, or that they can occur but never do.

The intermediate position is implausible. There is tremendous variety and multiplicity to the situations in the actual world that appear to be moral dilemmas. There is also plenty of time in the past and future for moral dilemmas to arise. These are strong reasons to believe that, if moral dilemmas can occur, at least some do or did or will occur. Religious philosophers might respond that God prevents moral dilemmas from ever occurring even though they are possible.[26] But such arguments are not persuasive, if only because they depend on an assumption that God exists and controls everything. This dependence does not refute these arguments, but it does give my reasons for not considering them in detail. In the absence of such a God, it would be an extremely unlikely coincidence if moral dilemmas were possible, but this possibility were never actualized. That is why I will assume that the only plausible alternatives are that moral dilemmas are not possible and that they are both possible and actual.

Even among those who deny that moral dilemmas are possible, there are many possible positions. The definition of moral dilemmas shows what these options are, because it determines what must be true for a situation to be a moral dilemma and also what must be denied by opponents who deny that a situation is a moral dilemma. These opponents will be discussed in detail later, but it is worth listing the main opponents now, in order to show how many different philosophers deny the possibility of moral dilemmas.

Some opponents admit the possibility of moral requirement conflicts but not moral dilemmas. They admit that moral requirements can conflict, but they claim that one of the conflicting moral requirements always overrides or can be ranked higher in some morally relevant way.

Another kind of opponent claims that not only moral dilemmas but even conflicts between moral requirements are impossible. They might also deny the possibility of conflicts between moral ideals or between a moral ideal and a moral requirement, but the most common claim is that moral requirements cannot conflict. Opponents who make this claim need to show something about the structure of morality that prevents moral requirements from conflicting. There are several ways to do this.

A monistic position is that moral dilemmas cannot arise, because morality can be reduced to a single principle. If moral dilemmas arise only when different moral principles conflict, then a moral theory with only one basic principle might seem to avoid all moral dilemmas and even conflicts. A related approach is to reduce morality to the maximization of a single value. If there is a moral requirement to adopt an alternative only if that alternative maximizes a certain value, and if conflicting alternatives cannot each maximize that value, then there cannot be moral requirements to adopt conflicting alternatives. There can still be a disjunctive moral requirement to adopt either one alternative or the other, if this is necessary to maximize the relevant value, but there is still no non-disjunctive moral requirement to adopt each alternative by itself. This argument might be one reason why utilitarians often deny that moral dilemmas are possible.

Other opponents are pluralists, so they admit morality has more than one basic principle or value. Pluralists can still avoid moral requirement conflicts and dilemmas if they arrange their moral principles and values in certain ways. One way to rule out moral requirement conflicts is to claim that all moral requirements are negative in the sense that they say what not to do instead of what to do. If all moral requirements are negative, it might seem that an agent can always avoid violating all moral requirements simply by not doing anything, and thus not doing anything there is a moral requirement not to do. A similar claim is that moral requirements forbid alternatives only when they cause harm intentionally. This might seem to allow an agent in a moral dilemma to adopt either alternative without violating any moral requirement as long as his only intention is to avoid the other alternative and not to cause any harm. Yet another way to avoid moral requirement conflicts is to insist that, whenever moral principles seem to conflict, the situation is really an exception to one of the principles, so there is no moral requirement to adopt one alternative. A final way to avoid moral requirement conflicts is to insist that, when moral requirements seem to conflict, one is merely prima facie, but merely prima facie moral requirements are not really moral requirements at all, so moral requirements never really conflict.

Each of these opponents tries to show that a moral theory *can* avoid moral dilemmas. The same opponents also give arguments to show that morality *must* be constructed in this way, because the definition of moral dilemmas implies a contradiction.

One such argument applies the premise that 'ought' implies 'can'. In a moral dilemma, the agent cannot adopt both alternatives together, so it is not true that the agent ought to adopt both alternatives together. But the agent ought to adopt each alternative separately, so the agent ought to adopt both alternatives together. These consequences contradict each other.

Another argument applies the principle of closure, that, if an agent ought to do one thing, but he cannot do it if he does something else, then he ought not to do that other thing. This implies that an agent in a moral dilemma both ought and ought not to adopt each alternative. This not only seems very odd but also conflicts with the common principle that 'ought' implies 'permitted', where an agent is permitted to do what it is not the case that he ought not to do. Opponents again conclude that moral dilemmas are impossible.

There are also many other arguments. Some opponents claim that a moral theory that yields dilemmas cannot serve a purpose of moral theories, such as to give a complete moral decision procedure. Others argue that agents can make choices in moral dilemmas, so the basis for their choices must give some way to resolve the conflict. Others argue that moral dilemmas would be unfair, because the agent could not avoid the negative repercussions of violating some moral requirement. All of these arguments provide rationales for denying that moral dilemmas are possible, and they make it difficult to defend that possibility.

Nonetheless, I oppose all of these arguments and positions. My own position is that moral dilemmas are both possible and actual. However, my argument for this position will be somewhat indirect.

I will not argue directly for the actuality of moral dilemmas. In order to show directly that moral dilemmas actually occur, I would have to give an actual example and argue that it really is a moral dilemma. However, all actual situations are so complex that what seems to be a moral dilemma might not really be a moral dilemma, because there always might be some way for the agent to fulfil both requirements or some morally relevant way to rank the requirements.

In order to avoid such difficulties, I will argue primarily for the claim that moral dilemmas are possible. The possibility of moral dilemmas is easier to establish than their actuality, because there is no need to rely on actual examples. I will discuss both actual and fictional examples which seem to be moral dilemmas, but my arguments will not depend on any particular example. If any of my examples is questioned, I can always modify or replace it without essentially affecting my arguments that moral dilemmas are possible.

Nonetheless, I will argue for a strong kind of possibility. Sometimes we call something possible simply because it is not contradictory and it makes sense linguistically. For example, it is possible in this weak way for water to boil at 90°C (even at standard pressure), since the laws of nature might change. However, we can also say that something is possible in a stronger way: it is possible for water to boil at 90°C, even in this world with the same laws of nature, since it does so when the pressure is low enough. I want to show that moral dilemmas are possible not only in the weak way but also in something like the stronger way. My thesis is that moral dilemmas are compatible with morality, including any defensible moral intuitions and any reasonable view of the definition and purpose of morality. And I also want to show not only that there are possible worlds where what are moral requirements in *that* world conflict without being overridden, but also that there are possible worlds where what are moral requirements in *this* world conflict without being overridden.

This strong kind of possibility will indirectly give reasons to believe that moral dilemmas actually occur. Since it is not plausible to claim that moral dilemmas are possible but never actual, my arguments for the possibility of moral dilemmas can be extended to arguments for the actuality of moral dilemmas. We might not know which situations are moral dilemmas, until we know which substantive moral theory is true, but we can still have strong reasons to believe that some situations are moral dilemmas. Even if this is denied, the possibility of moral dilemmas is still important, because it is the possibility rather than the actuality of moral dilemmas that has important implications.

Consequently, I will follow this plan. I will begin with my arguments for the possibility of moral dilemmas. I will then respond to the arguments against the possibility of moral dilemmas. And I will close by discussing the implications of the possibility of moral dilemmas. This will show that moral dilemmas are possible, actual and important.

2

Arguments for Moral Dilemmas

Now that I have defined moral dilemmas, I can present my
arguments for the possibility of moral dilemmas. My overall
argument has two stages. First, I argue that moral requirements can conflict. Then I argue that some moral requirement
conflicts are not resolvable, because neither moral requirement
is overriden. Both parts together will show that these situations
are moral dilemmas, so moral dilemmas are possible.

It is important to remember that the two stages of this
argument reinforce each other. The cases where neither moral
requirement seems to override the other are also the ones that
make it most obvious that both moral requirements are real.
Consequently, the full force of the arguments will not come out
until both parts are completed.

2.1 SOME INADEQUATE ARGUMENTS

Before giving my own arguments, I want to criticize some
common but inadequate arguments for moral dilemmas. Even
the most sympathetic defender of moral dilemmas must admit
that many common arguments for moral dilemmas are too
simple. It is important to locate the flaws in these arguments in
order to avoid them.

The simplest argument for the possibility of moral dilemmas
is that so many moral dilemmas seem to occur. Of course, the
fact that something appears to be the case does not prove that it
is the case. Nonetheless, if there is no reason to deny that things
are as they appear, appearances do give some reason to believe
that moral dilemmas are possible.

The main problem with this argument is that there are so

many ways for apparent moral dilemmas to fail to be real moral dilemmas. A situation that appears to be a moral dilemma is not really a moral dilemma if it turns out either that the agent really can fulfil both moral requirements, or that there really is no moral requirement to adopt one of the alternatives, or that one of the moral requirements really does override the other. Because appearances can mislead in so many ways, and because actual situations are so complex, the fact that so many situations appear to be moral dilemmas cannot prove that any situations really are or even can be moral dilemmas.

A second common argument for moral dilemmas uses the fact that individuals often occupy many roles. The same person can be a friend, a spouse, a mother, a citizen, etc. If each of these roles creates moral requirements, conflicts among these requirements seem inevitable.[1]

Many apparent moral dilemmas do arise from conflicts between the various roles of a single person. Nonetheless, the mere fact that roles can and do conflict does not prove that moral dilemmas are possible or actual. Even if roles sometimes create moral requirements, they need not always do so, and roles might not create any moral requirements when they conflict with other roles. Even if roles always created moral requirements, some roles are more important than others, and the moral requirements of more important roles might override the others. But if one role always overrode the other, no role conflicts would be moral dilemmas.

A similar argument for moral dilemmas uses the common view that there are many moral rules that imply moral requirements. This argument faces similar problems. Pluralist opponents can admit many moral rules but construct these rules so that they can never conflict. Some of these moral codes are implausible, but the possibility of many moral rules without any conflicts at least shows that the mere multiplicity of moral rules does not guarantee moral conflicts. And even if moral rules and requirements do conflict, one moral rule or requirement still might override the other, and then the situation would not be a real moral dilemma.

The argument from the multiplicity of rules is often supported by an analogy with law.[2] The claim is that law and morality develop in similar ways, so moral conflicts must resemble legal conflicts. Legal conflicts cannot be resolved without proper institutions, such as judges, legislatures or elections. Since there is no institution to resolve moral conflicts, some (or all?) moral conflicts must be unresolvable.

It is true that no institution can resolve moral conflicts. Nobody has the authority to declare which moral requirement is stronger. However, the lack of any institution for resolving moral conflicts does not show that moral conflicts cannot ever be resolved at all. This conclusion would follow only if there were no way to resolve moral conflicts except by institutions. But this assumption would be denied by many opponents (and defenders) of the possibility of moral dilemmas. And it is not established by any similarity between the development of law and morality, since there are also many relevant differences between law and morality. Moral rules and principles are not passed in legislatures, as many laws are. Consequently, no analogy with law can show that moral dilemmas are possible.

Although these common arguments are not conclusive, they do have some effect. Analogies to law, conflicts between roles, and the variety and multiplicity of apparent moral dilemmas shift the burden of proof on to opponents who deny that moral dilemmas are possible. One way to carry this burden might be to respond one by one to every apparent moral dilemma and to show in each case which apparent moral requirement is not real or which moral requirement overrides which and why. The problem with this approach is that the examples seem limitless, so this task seems hopeless. A better response would give a general argument against the possibility of any moral dilemmas. A general argument might show that each apparent moral dilemma is not a real moral dilemma even though it would not resolve each one separately. I will criticize the main general arguments in chapters 3 to 6. The point for now is that, even though the possibility of moral dilemmas is not proven by the fact that so many situations appear to be moral dilemmas, this fact does affect the kind of argument that opponents would need in order to show that moral dilemmas are not possible.

2.2 ARGUMENTS FOR MORAL REQUIREMENT CONFLICTS

Although the previous arguments fail, other arguments do show that moral dilemmas are possible. As I said, my argument will have two stages. I will argue, first, that moral requirements can conflict. Then I will argue that sometimes neither moral requirement is overridden.

In order to show that moral requirements can conflict, I need some test of when there is a moral requirement. First, I will use my definition of moral requirements in terms of counterfactuals. Then I will use justified moral residue. Neither of these arguments is a conclusive proof, but they do give strong reasons to believe that moral requirements can conflict.

2.2.1 Counterfactuals

The first argument for the possibility of moral requirement conflicts applies my definition of moral requirements. My definition says that there is a moral requirement to adopt an alternative in the actual situation if and only if it would be morally wrong not to adopt that alternative in a situation that is similar in all relevant respects to the actual one except that the agent has no justification for not adopting that alternative. For example, if I promise to cook you dinner tonight, there is a moral requirement for me to cook you dinner tonight, because it would be morally wrong for me not to cook you dinner tonight in a situation just like the actual one except that I had no justification for not cooking you dinner tonight. This counterfactual is true even if in the actual situation I do have a justification for not cooking you dinner tonight, such as that I must visit my dying mother.

The definition of negative moral requirements is parallel. There is a moral requirement not to adopt an alternative if and only if it would be morally wrong for the agent to adopt that alternative in a situation just like the actual one except that the agent has no justification for adopting it. For example, there is a moral requirement for me not to kill you, because it would be morally wrong for me to kill you in a situation just like the actual one except that I have no justification for killing you. This counterfactual is true even if I do have some justification for killing you in the actual situation, such as that you will kill me if I do not kill you.

This definition of moral requirements makes it easy to establish the possibility of conflicts between moral requirements. The argument can be based on any situation where each alternative would be morally wrong if the agent had no justification. For example, it would be morally wrong for Agamemnon to kill his daughter if he had no justification for killing her, and it would also be morally wrong for him to refuse to lead his troops to Troy if he had no justification for refusing to lead them. Similarly, if someone makes conflicting promises, it would be morally wrong to break either promise without any justification. If these examples are not convincing, many others could be substituted. The examples need not be actual as long as they are possible, and a single example is enough to show that conflicts between moral requirements are possible.

An opponent might respond that my definition of moral requirements is not adequate. However, my definition does give what I mean by moral requirements, and I think it also captures what many others mean by moral requirements and moral dilemmas. My definition is also useful theoretically. This will be shown if my discussion of moral dilemmas captures interesting and important issues. Other definitions might also be acceptable, but this would not show that anything is wrong with my definition.

Another problem is that my argument depends on intuitions about what is morally wrong. It might seem more precise or convincing to specify a general procedure for determining what is morally wrong. However, any general procedure would apply to many irrelevant cases, so it would raise many more doubts than the kind of intuition that I use. The only intuitions in my arguments are about what is morally wrong when there is no justification at all for adopting (or not adopting) the relevant alternative. Almost everyone agrees that it would be morally wrong to kill or harm or break a promise in situations where such acts gain no benefit and prevent no harm. Thus, the intuitions in my argument are widely shared by moral theorists of many kinds. I will limit my discussion to such cases where it is clear what would be morally wrong. If a critic questions my intuitions, I can always give other examples to fit the critic's own intuitions.

A more complex problem is that it is hard to specify exactly which counterfactual situation determines whether there is a moral requirement. One reason is that some things other than justifications can prevent an alternative from being wrong. For example, suppose I promise to cook you dinner tonight, but you die this afternoon. It is still true that it would be morally wrong for me not to have cooked you dinner tonight if you had not died. Thus, if the fact that you died were a justification for not cooking you dinner, my definition would imply that there is still a moral requirement for me to cook you dinner tonight. But there cannot be a moral requirement to cook dinner for someone who died.

The solution is to distinguish justifying conditions or justifications from cancelling conditions or cancellations. The difference is that a justifying condition provides a reason for an incompatible alternative, but a cancelling condition removes a requirement without providing a reason for any incompatible alternative. In the above example, your death removes the moral requirement for me to cook dinner, but it need not give me any reason for an incompatible alternative, so it is a cancelling rather than a justifying condition. In contrast, if I promise to cook you dinner tonight, but I run over someone who will die without my help, this gives me a reason to save that person's life, even if this alternative is incompatible with my cooking you dinner. This makes the need to save the person a justifying condition rather than a cancelling condition. And this distinction shows why the above example does not refute my definition. The situation where you die is not similar to the one where you do not die in all relevant respects except for justifications, since they also differ in cancellations. Consequently, my definition does not imply that there is a moral requirement to cook dinner for a person who died. And the same applies to other cancelling conditions, such as when a promisee releases a promiser from a promise.

A similar problem arises with excuses. Suppose someone promises to cook you dinner tonight, and he has no reason not to do so, but then his oven breaks through no fault of his own, so he cannot cook you dinner tonight. If the fact that his oven broke were a justification not to cook dinner tonight, my definition would imply that he has a moral requirement to cook dinner, since it would be morally wrong for him not to cook dinner in a situation just like the actual one except that his oven does not break. However, many would claim that he cannot have a moral requirement to cook dinner when he cannot cook dinner.

The solution is to distinguish excuses from justifications. To justify something is to show that it is right, but to excuse something is to admit that it is not right but deny that the agent is responsible or blameworthy.[3] In the above example, the fact that the cook's oven broke through no fault of his own shows that he is not responsible for not cooking dinner, but it does not show that his failure to cook dinner is morally right. Thus, his inability is an excuse rather than a justification. This distinction shows why the above example does not refute my definition. The situation where his oven breaks and the one where his oven works are not similar in all relevant respects except justification, since they also differ in excuses. Thus, my definition does not imply that the agent has a moral requirement to cook dinner when he cannot cook it. Whether he does have this requirement depends on whether it is wrong for him not to cook dinner when his oven is broken. Some opponents deny that anything can be wrong when the agent cannot avoid doing it, but I will argue below against this claim. In any case, the present argument is independent of that issue.

These distinctions between justifications, cancellations, and excuses are not always clear, but my argument does not really depend on them, since most situations where moral requirements seem to conflict do not include any cancellations or excuses. Agamemnon's daughter does not consent to being killed, and his troops do not die or release him from his promise to lead them to Troy, so no cancelling conditions are relevant. Agamemnon also has no excuse, because he can kill his daughter, and he also can refuse to kill her. At least when cancellations and excuses are absent, there is a moral requirement to do whatever it would be wrong not to do without any justification. This shows that there are conflicting moral requirements in Agamemnon's situation. And the same argument applies to other examples where no cancellations or excuses are relevant.

Although the argument so far refers to a particular counterfactual situation, another variation uses more general counterfactuals. If excuses, cancellations and justifications are the only conditions that can keep some kinds of thing from being wrong, then there is a moral requirement to adopt an alternative if it would be morally wrong not to adopt any alternative of the same kind in any situation where the agent has no justification or excuse or cancellation. This claim still implies that there are moral requirements to keep promises and not to kill, since it is always wrong to kill and not to keep promises when there is no justification or excuse or cancellation. This shows that moral requirements can conflict, because there can be situations where each alternative is of some kind such that it would always be wrong to do something of that kind without any justification or excuse or cancellation. Some other moral requirements do not pass this test, so the converse of this claim does not hold (because of closure, as I will show). But this test still gives a sufficient condition for moral requirements and that is all the argument needs.

The point of the various counterfactuals is to show how situations that appear to be moral requirement conflicts differ from other situations. Even if the specific counterfactuals are rejected, the differences should still be obvious. It should be clear that there are important differences between a situation where someone must kill one person in order to save others and a situation where the others can be saved simply by spending some money or refusing to work for a charity. These differences are what justify classifying some situations as moral requirement conflicts.

2.2.2 Moral residue

The second, and probably the most common, argument that moral requirement conflicts are possible is the argument from moral residue.[4] Moral residue includes such things as remorse, apologies and compensation, which are justified after a moral requirement is violated. The general argument is that there are some situations where such moral residue is justified after every choice, but there is no justification for this residue except that a moral requirement was violated, and this is evidence that each alternative does violate a moral requirement.

The argument is usually given in terms of remorse, so I will focus on remorse, but I will return to other kinds of moral residue below. I will also use an example where each moral requirement is strong and neither overrides the other by much, if at all. I will argue below that neither might override the other, but that claim is not necessary for my argument here. All I need is an example where remorse is justified after each alternative.

Suppose some terrorists poison the water supply of a large city. Liz is an official who can prevent anyone from being killed, but only by torturing the child of a terrorist in order to get the terrorist to tell her what and where the poison is. Suppose also that hundreds or even thousands of people would die, but, whatever the number, it is high enough that to torture the child is not worse and possibly is better than to let the people be killed.

Even if Liz knows this, if she tortures the child, it would not be inappropriate for her to feel remorse. Remorse is inappropriate when it is based on ignorance or mistake, even if the mistake is justified subjectively. Feelings like remorse can also be a hangover from earlier beliefs that are now rejected, as when a former Mormon feels bad about drinking alcohol even though he no longer believes drinking alcohol is wrong.[5] In contrast, Liz's remorse does not depend on any ignorance or mistake or any belief that she now rejects, so her remorse is not inappropriate in any of these ways. Furthermore, it even seems inappropriate for her not to feel remorse. She should not torture the child and walk away with a smile on her face or even with businesslike indifference. She should not feel too much remorse, and it is not clear how much remorse is justified, but at least some remorse is appropriate.

Similar remarks apply if she chooses not to torture the child and to let the people die from poison. It would not be inappropriate for her to feel remorse for allowing or failing to prevent these murders. And it might even be inappropriate for her not to feel remorse, especially since she was the official in charge and could have prevented these murders.

However, there does not seem to be any adequate reason for Liz to feel remorse except that she violated a moral requirement. It is not her fault that she is in this situation, and she is as certain as possible that torturing the child will work and that there is no other way to prevent the deaths. Even if Liz were not certain, this could justify reluctance now but not remorse later, if the torture works and other plans would have failed. A critic might claim that Liz's remorse is justified by the principle that one should feel remorse when one commits torture, but we still need a reason for this principle, so a moral requirement must be admitted at some point.[6]

The argument from moral residue uses these claims to show that there are conflicting moral requirements:

(1) It is not inappropriate for Liz to feel remorse after torturing the child.

(2) It is not inappropriate for Liz to feel remorse after allowing so many people to be killed by poison.

(3) There is no adequate reason for her to feel remorse after either choice unless she violated some moral requirement.

(4) If it is not inappropriate to feel remorse, but there is no adequate reason for remorse except that a moral requirement was violated, then a moral requirement was violated.

(5) Therefore, Liz has a moral requirement not to torture the child and a moral requirement to prevent the deaths.

(6) Liz cannot prevent the deaths without torturing the child.

(7) Therefore, Liz is in a moral requirement conflict.

(1), (2) and (3) are substantive premises that are supposed to be plausible in this situation. (4) applies the claim that remorse is inappropriate unless there is an adequate reason for it. (5) follows from (1) to (4), (6) is true in this situation, and (7) follows by definition of a moral requirement conflict. It might strengthen the argument to add a premise that it would be inappropriate for Liz not to feel remorse after either alternative, but this stronger claim is not needed to reach the conclusion, so I will not depend on it.

This argument is often misunderstood. The first premises are not that people *do* feel remorse in such situations. That non-moral fact could not show any moral requirement, because remorse can be inappropriate, and inappropriate remorse cannot show that a moral requirement was violated. However, my premises claim that remorse is not inappropriate in Liz's case. This is controversial, but at least the argument does not try to go from psychology to morality.

The argument also does not claim that remorse is appropriate in *all* cases where a moral requirement is violated. If I break a trivial promise in order to avoid killing someone, remorse might not be appropriate, even if a moral requirement is violated.[7] However, the argument claims only that there are some situations where remorse is not appropriate unless a moral requirement was violated. This is enough to reach the weak conclusion that some moral requirement conflicts are possible.

There are still several possible objections. Some opponents might criticize this example, possibly because the best choice for Liz is not to torture the child, or because there is no moral requirement for her to save the poison victims. Such objections depend on peculiarities of this example. No example can fit everyone's intuitions. But the details of this example could be adjusted, or other examples could be substituted. Almost everyone admits the essential judgements in some example. If you find this example unconvincing, just modify some details or substitute your own.

The most common and difficult objection is that this argument confuses remorse with regret.[8] It is not clear how to distinguish remorse from regret, but one common method brings out the force of this objection. Each emotion can be identified as a bad feeling that results from a certain belief.[9] On this approach, someone feels remorse only if he feels bad because he believes that he has violated some moral requirement. In contrast, someone feels regret whenever he feels bad because he believes that something bad happened, regardless of whether he also believes that he violated a moral requirement. For example, I can regret someone's death, even if I know that I was not at all responsible for the death. Such regret is simply a feeling of loss. In contrast, I cannot feel remorse for someone's death if I know I was not responsible at all. Thus, remorse implies a belief that a moral requirement was violated, but regret does not.

The objection is, then, that what is appropriate after each choice in Liz's situation is regret rather than remorse. Regret is appropriate because something is lost by either choice, but someone can be justified in feeling regret without believing that she violated any moral requirement. Thus, even justified regret is not evidence that a moral requirement was violated. And even if what Liz feels is remorse, it begs the question to claim that her remorse is not inappropriate. On the above analysis, this implies that it would not be inappropriate for Liz to feel bad because she believes that she violated a moral requirement. However, if she did not really violate a moral requirement, her remorse would be based on a false belief, so it would be inappropriate. Thus, the first two premises assume that there are moral requirements to adopt the alternatives in question. Since the argument from remorse is supposed to show that there are conflicting moral requirements, the argument begs the question.

This objection is forceful, but it can be met by giving an independent argument that Liz's remorse is not inappropriate. A first attempt to show this uses the claim that the people who do feel remorse are good and would not be as good if they did not feel remorse. However, it is not clear that good people would feel remorse in such cases. They might feel only regret, and then they need not believe that they violated any moral requirement. Even if what they feel is remorse, it is not clear that the moral beliefs of good people are usually true. Mother Teresa might do more good acts than most people, but this does not ensure that she is more acute in difficult moral situations. Finally, the value of remorse can be explained without admitting that the belief component of the remorse is true. The reason why a person would not be as good if he did not feel remorse after torturing a child might be only that such bad feelings induce people to torture less and to avoid situations where torture is needed. If so, it is the effect of the feeling component of remorse that makes people who feel remorse better than those who don't. But then the fact that good people feel remorse in cases like Liz's cannot show that the belief required for remorse is true.

Despite these problems, there is still something to the argument that good people would feel remorse in Liz's situation. Suppose Liz's remorse is not needed to bring about any good effects, because she is already very strongly motivated to avoid torture and moral requirement conflicts. There still seems to be something missing if she tortures the child without feeling any remorse. She does not seem to take the child's rights seriously. This suggests that it is not only the good effects that make her remorse appropriate.

In any case, a better argument that Liz's remorse is not inappropriate can be given by contrasting Liz's situation with similar situations. The point of such contrasts is that different reactions seem appropriate in the different situations, and the best explanation of why they seem appropriate is that the relevant act violates a moral requirement in one situation but not in the others. We can then use inference to the best explanation to conclude that Liz's act does violate a moral requirement in the original situation. I will focus on what seems appropriate if Liz tortures the child, but similar points apply if she allows the people to be poisoned.

The most revealing contrast is with the emotions of a bystander who opposes the torture but cannot stop it. There is a great loss when the child is tortured, and this might make the bystander feel regret. However, it would not be inappropriate for Liz to feel more than a mere bystander, because Liz is the agent who chooses and carries out the torture. She is the one who harms an innocent child. Even though her act was justified, the fact that she caused the harm justifies her in feeling more than just the regret that even an opposing bystander should feel.

The same point comes out if Liz's situation is compared to one where the torture victim is the terrorist's wife, and she consents to be tortured, because she wants to prevent the murders. If Liz tortures in this situation, she should feel very differently from when she tortures the child without its consent, because the consenting wife is an accomplice. Torture with consent is more like a case where a doctor causes pain and disability in an operation with the patient's consent. However, if Liz did not violate any moral requirement when she tortured the child without its consent, it would be inappropriate for her to feel any more when she tortures the child than when she tortures the wife with consent. But consent does seem to change what is appropriate.

The point of these comparisons is that more than mere regret or any feeling of loss is appropriate when Liz tortures the child. Admittedly, this still does not imply that what is appropriate is remorse. There is a whole spectrum of emotions between regret and remorse as I analysed them above. What is appropriate when the wife gives consent to be tortured is not quite what is appropriate when the terrorist himself is tortured. Nonetheless, the various comparisons show that it is appropriate for Liz to feel more when she tortures the child than in the other situations. Her feelings are the kind that are appropriate only when someone intentionally causes harm to an innocent person without consent. This difference in which feelings are appropriate is evidence that different moral judgements are true in these situations, and the best way to register these differences is to admit that she violated a moral requirement and was in a moral requirement conflict.

It is important to realize what this argument does not claim. When Liz tortures the child to save lives, she should not feel the same as if she tortured the child without any justification, and she need not think that she would or should act differently if a similar situation were to arise again. However, this does not show that what she feels is not remorse. On the above analysis, remorse implies a belief that a moral requirement was violated, but not that the violated moral requirement was overriding. The term 'repudiation' can be used for the kind of bad feeling that results from a belief that one made a mistake, violated an overriding moral requirement, and should choose differently in similar cases. So remorse does not imply repudiation.[10] Similarly, remorse does not imply shame if shame is what results from a belief that one is or was a bad or vicious person. And Liz's remorse also does not imply that she feels as if she deserves punishment, since she believes the conflict was not her fault.[11] Some opponents might claim that the fact that Liz does not repudiate her choice or feel shame or feel as if she deserves punishment shows that Liz's feelings should not be called 'remorse'. But it does not matter what her feelings are called. The differences between what is appropriate in Liz's original situation and what is appropriate in the other situations are still evidence that Liz violated a moral requirement even if it was not overriding.

Another argument for this conclusion is suggested by Walzer. When opponents claim that what justifies residue is its good effects, this seems utilitarian. Walzer then argues, 'It is worth stressing that to feel guilty is to suffer, and that the men whose guilt feelings are here called useful are themselves innocent according to the utilitarian account. So we seem to have come upon another case where the suffering of the innocent is permitted and even encouraged by utilitarian calculation.'[12] Walzer's point is that remorse is a kind of punishment for violating a moral requirement, so, just as utilitarianism fails because it justifies punishment of innocent people, similar objections apply to those who deny the possibility of moral requirement conflicts but admit that remorse is justified.

This argument depends on the premise that it is wrong to encourage someone to feel bad if she did not violate any moral requirement. This is questionable. Regret feels bad, but we still think someone is less good if he does not feel regret for a friend's death, even if he is not at all responsible for that death. However, this situation is different from Liz's situation. If a bystander did not care at all about the tortured child, we would criticize him. But we would criticize Liz more strongly and in a different way if she herself did not show any remorse after she tortured the child. Walzer's point is that this extra criticism would be unfair if the only reasons for it were utilitarian and Liz did not violate any moral requirement.

None of these arguments proves conclusively that it is not inappropriate for Liz to feel remorse after torturing a child. But they still provide strong reasons to believe that a moral requirement was violated. And similar arguments apply if Liz feels remorse after allowing the people to be poisoned. These arguments together provide strong reasons to believe that this situation is a moral requirement conflict.

Other forms of moral residue provide more reasons. When someone breaks a promise or harms someone, it might be appropriate for the agent not only to feel remorse but also to apologize or to compensate his victim, or even for a third party to punish the violater. Moral residue includes all such things that are appropriate because a moral requirement was violated. The argument from remorse can, then, be repeated for the other kinds of moral residue.

For example, Thomson uses compensation as evidence of a moral requirement. She argues that 'If you are an "innocent threat" to my life (you threaten it through no fault of your own), and I can save my life only by killing you, and therefore do kill you, I think I owe compensation, for I take your life to save mine. If so, I infringe a right of yours but do not violate it', where the difference between infringing and violating is that 'we *violate* [someone's] right if and only if we do not merely infringe his right, but more, are acting wrongly, unjustly in doing so.'[13] Since there is a moral requirement in my sense not to infringe rights in her sense, her claim is that debts of compensation are evidence for moral requirements.

Thomson's argument implies that moral requirements

conflict in situations where some compensation is owed if either alternative is chosen. For example, suppose Juan promises two farmers to deliver two loads of vegetables to a market today, but he waits too late, so he cannot deliver both loads on time. Unfortunately, no other transportation is available, and the vegetables will be spoiled or less valuable tomorrow, so each alternative causes a loss to one of the farmers. The farmers might have legal recourse, but, even if not, Juan still morally owes some compensation. Someone else might be able to provide the compensation sooner, more easily, or at less cost, but the person who broke the promise still seems to be the one who owes the compensation. This debt shows that the promise still has moral force, since Juan would not owe compensation if the farmer had cancelled the promise because he found another driver. Thus, the best explanation of why Juan owes compensation is that Juan violated a moral requirement. Opponents can still raise objections like those to the argument from remorse, but similar responses are also available, so such arguments from compensation provide more evidence that some situations are moral requirement conflicts. And other forms of moral residue provide even more support for the possibility of moral requirement conflicts.[14]

It is important to realize that these various arguments support each other. In order to determine whether a situation is a moral requirement conflict, we need to consider various kinds of moral residue and various counterfactuals. Each case uses inference to the best explanation, and the various explanations support each other by showing how well our various intuitions cohere. As the evidence accumulates, it becomes clearer that the simplest and most plausible overall approach is to admit that moral requirements conflict in at least some of these situations.

Opponents might respond that these arguments beg the question, because they assume that moral residue is appropriate. However, this objection misses the point of inference to the best explanation. A scientist does not beg the question when she infers that two liquids have different atomic structures because this is the best explanation of why the liquids give different results in crucial experiments. Similarly, my argument begins with intuitions that different emotions, compensation, etc. are appropriate in different situations, and then I infer the moral judgements that give the best explanation of these differences. The intuitions that I assume do not beg the question, because they are not directly about moral requirements but only about differences in what residue is appropriate, and these residues can be distinguished without assuming any moral requirement. I admit that the intuitions that I explain are not as reliable as scientific observations, and inferences to the best explanation are never conclusive proofs, but this argument still provides strong evidence that Liz and others do violate moral requirements and are in moral conflicts.

Nonetheless, these arguments do not show that moral dilemmas are possible. Moral residue is sometimes appropriate even when the moral requirement that was violated is overridden, so moral residue cannot show that the moral requirement that was violated is not overriden. The same goes for counterfactuals. But if one moral requirement overrides the other, the moral requirement conflict is not a dilemma. Thus, the arguments from moral residue and counterfactuals alone do not show that moral dilemmas are possible but only that moral requirement conflicts are possible.

2.3 ARGUMENTS FOR UNRESOLVABILITY

In order to complete my argument that moral dilemmas are possible, I still need to show that, when moral requirements conflict, it is possible that neither overrides the other. On my account of overriding, this means I need to show that there can be conflicts where neither moral requirement can be ranked above the other in any morally relevant way. I will give two arguments that moral requirement conflicts can be unresolvable in this way.

2.3.1 Symmetry

My first argument refers to a special kind of example where there is no morally relevant difference between the conflicting alternatives or moral requirements. I will call such cases 'symmetrical', and I will argue that, when symmetrical examples are inspected closely, there is no escape from the claim that they are moral dilemmas.

Many symmetrical cases could be discussed, but I will concentrate on a variation of a situation in the recent book and film, *Sophie's Choice*. Sophie arrives with her two children at a Nazi concentration camp. A guard asks her to choose one child, and he tells her that the child she chooses will be killed, and the other child will live in the children's barracks.[15]

Sophie does not want to choose at all, but the guard also tells her that, if she refuses to choose, both children will be killed. She and we know he will carry out his threats. She still physically and psychologically can refuse to choose either child, but she morally cannot refuse to choose, since the price is too high. This kind of disability is enough for a moral dilemma.

Sophie has a moral reason not to choose each child. She can prevent the death of her first child, and a mother has some moral reason to prevent her child's death at least when she can. To choose the first child would be to cooperate in a very evil scheme and, more particularly, in her own child's murder. These facts provide strong moral reasons for her not to choose the first child. Similar facts give her a moral reason not to choose the second child either. Thus, she does have a moral reason not to choose each child.

Furthermore, her moral reasons are requirements. This can be shown both by counterfactuals and by moral residue. It would be wrong for her to cooperate in her own child's murder if she had no justification. If she chose one child to be killed when this was not necessary to save the other child or for any other reason, her act would be morally wrong and she would deserve punishment. Sophie does have a justification, but moral requirements were defined by what would be wrong if she had no justification. Thus, even if what Sophie does is not actually wrong, there is still a moral requirement for Sophie not to choose each child.

The appropriateness of moral residue also shows that she violates a moral requirement. If Sophie sent her own child to his death without any remorse, she would not seem as good as if she felt remorse. And when she does feel remorse, it does not seem inappropriate. The story suggests that Sophie went too far in her remorse, but some remorse still seems justified. This shows that there is a moral requirement not to cooperate in the murder of the child that she chooses. And the same factors show that there is a moral requirement for her not to choose the other child.

Her moral conflict is then a moral dilemma if neither requirement overrides the other. But if the conflict is symmetrical, neither moral requirement can override the other, because there is no morally relevant difference between the children or between the moral requirements not to choose each. The book suggests that there is some difference. The younger child is more dependent and thus less likely to survive in the children's barracks. However, I will modify the example so that there is no morally relevant difference between the children. Such symmetry is extreme, but it is possible. A critic might respond that there must be some difference between the children, even if only in their spatio-temporal locations or times of birth. However, such differences are not morally relevant, so they cannot show that one moral requirement overrides the other. Thus, neither moral requirement overrides the other.

The point is not merely that Sophie does not *know* which moral requirement is stronger. She cannot know that either moral requirement is stronger, since knowledge implies truth, and neither requirement is stronger. However, it is not her lack of knowledge that makes her situation a moral dilemma. If there is in fact no morally relevant difference between the alternatives, neither moral requirement in fact overrides the other. That is what makes her situation a moral dilemma.

One possible response is that Sophie can *create* a difference between the alternatives by flipping a coin and promising to abide by the result. However, this makes it too easy to escape

moral problems. Such tricks cannot make one moral requirement morally stronger any more than if she promised to choose
the tallest child or her favourite child. And even if she did flip a
coin, it would not show that one moral requirement was
stronger before the flip, so she was in a moral dilemma at least
before the flip.

A stronger response is that there is a *disjunctive* moral
requirement for Sophie to choose either one child or the other,
since, if she chooses neither, both will be killed. This is
supposed to show that there is no moral requirement for her
not to choose either child separately, so she is not even in a
moral requirement conflict. However, defenders of moral
dilemmas can grant that there is such a disjunctive moral
requirement. This does not imply that there are not also non-
disjunctive moral requirements not to choose each child.
There can be three distinct requirements: a disjunctive moral
requirement to choose either one child or the other, a non-
disjunctive moral requirement not to choose the first child, and
a non-disjunctive moral requirement not to choose the second
child.

One way to defend the disjunctive response might be to claim
that, even if there are conflicting non-disjunctive moral requirements, they are overridden by the stronger disjunctive
moral requirement to choose one child or the other. However,
the disjunctive requirement cannot override the non-disjunctive requirements, because it does not conflict with them.
Sophie can both not choose the first child and also choose
either one child or the other simply by choosing the second
child. This shows that her moral requirement not to choose the
first child does not conflict with her disjunctive requirement to
choose either one child or the other. The same goes for her
moral requirement not to choose the second child. The point is
that a disjunctive moral requirement to choose one child or the
other does not solve the dilemma, because it does not tell which
child to choose.[16]

A final response is that there is no moral requirement not to
choose the first child, because the same kind and degree of
value is lost whether or not the first child is chosen, so there is

no loss in total value when the first child is chosen. The same goes for choosing the second child. But only the total value determines when there is a moral requirement, according to utilitarianism and similar views.

The problem with this utilitarian approach is that it treats individual people merely as part of the whole, so it denies that the distinctness of persons is morally important.[17] Sophie's choice is then supposed to be like a choice between two practically identical pound coins, when all that matters is the total number of pounds. However, Sophie's choice is very different from any choice between pound coins. Individual children are not interchangeable in the way that pound coins are, even if the children are very similar in kind. Sophie's choice does make a difference, because different individual children are lost. Even though the same degree and kind of value is lost on each alternative, different individuals are harmed on different alternatives. Because different individuals are harmed, each alternative violates a moral requirement. This can be shown both by counterfactuals and by moral residue. It is morally wrong to harm any individual without any justification or excuse or cancellation, so it would be morally wrong for Sophie to participate in either child's murder if she had no justification. And some moral residue is justified, whichever child Sophie chooses. This shows that there are conflicting moral requirements, despite what some utilitarians might claim. And this leaves no escape from the conclusion that Sophie's situation is a symmetrical moral dilemma.

Similar arguments apply to many other conflicts between moral requirements. Symmetrical promises can conflict so that each alternative breaks one promise, but each promise was to a different person. Marcus mentions a situation where 'the lives of identical twins are in jeopardy, and, through force of circumstances, I am in a position to choose only one.'[18] A recent American TV advertisement depicts a mother in Ethiopia who is too weak to carry both children to the only food supply, so she must leave one behind. Any one of many such examples is sufficient to show that symmetrical moral dilemmas are possible.

Similar arguments also apply to conflicts that are not between moral requirements. Moral ideals can be symmetrical. For example, I might be able to help only one of two equally worthy charities. Non-moral reasons can also be symmetrical. I might have to choose which of two identical twins to marry when no moral reason but only self-interest is at stake. In any such symmetrical conflict, neither reason overrides the other, because there is no relevant difference between them. This shows that many kinds of symmetrical dilemma are possible.

2.3.2 Incomparability

Once symmetrical examples have shown that moral dilemmas are possible, there is no reason to deny that some non-symmetrical examples can also be moral dilemmas. Nonetheless, non-symmetrical moral dilemmas have an interesting structure and raise interesting questions of their own. They also give additional support to the possibility of moral dilemmas. So they deserve a separate discussion.

Some non-symmetrical conflicts between moral requirements might be moral dilemmas because the moral requirements are equal in strength. However, I want to consider the more radical possibility that some moral requirements are incomparable. Moral requirements are comparable only when some comparative judgement of their strengths is true. The only comparative judgements are that the strength of one moral requirement is greater than, less than, or equal to the strength of the other. Thus, moral requirements are incomparable if and only if neither is stronger than, weaker than, or equal in strength to the other. Conflicts between incomparable moral requirements are then moral dilemmas, because neither moral requirement overrides the other.

Incomparable moral dilemmas differ from symmetrical ones, because symmetrical moral requirements involve equal amounts of the same kinds of value and harm. This makes symmetrical moral requirements seem to be equal in strength, whereas incomparable moral requirements are not equal in strength. Some defenders of moral dilemmas might claim that even symmetrical moral requirements are not equal or, alternatively, that even non-symmetrical moral requirements must be equal if neither is stronger. I will discuss various reasons for denying equality, but this denial is not essential to my main thesis. Even if non-symmetrical moral requirements had to be equal when neither is stronger, a conflict between them would still be a moral dilemma. That is more important for my purposes than the claim that the moral requirements are incomparable rather than equal.

Extreme incomparability

Many arguments for incomparability are too simple and extreme. The implausibility of these extreme arguments explains much of the opposition to more limited claims of incomparability. I will begin by criticizing some of the extreme arguments in order to clear the way for the more limited view that I will defend.

A first argument infers incomparability from mutual irreducibility.[19] Mutual irreducibility is the claim that some moral requirements that conflict cannot be reduced to a single standard of strength. This premise is contrary not only to the strong claim that there is a single standard to which all conflicting moral requirements can be reduced ($\exists\forall$) but also to the weaker claim that, for every pair of conflicting moral requirements, there is some standard to which they are reducible ($\forall\exists$). I will argue for this premise below. The next premise claims that, if two moral requirements are not reducible to any common standard, they cannot be measured or compared. As Aristotle claims, 'The measure is always homogeneous with the thing measured.'[20] This premise is often supported by analogies. Just as the aesthetic values of paintings cannot be measured by their monetary costs, because the former are not reducible to the latter, so the strengths of moral requirements supposedly cannot be measured by any independent factor to which they are not reducible. A choice among moral requirements can still be based on utility or on a flip of a coin, but the fact that there can be some basis for choice does not show that one of the moral requirements is morally stronger. Moral requirements are still not comparable if the only bases for choice are too foreign to the moral requirements to count as a way of comparing them. The crucial claim is, then, that any basis for choice is too foreign to count as a comparison if the conflicting moral requirements are not mutually reducible.

This argument is too simple. If mere mutual irreducibility implied incomparability, then *no* mutually irreducible moral requirements would ever be comparable. However, *some* moral requirements are comparable even though they are not mutually reducible. Even if the moral requirement to keep a trivial promise cannot be reduced to the same standard as the moral requirement not to kill, the latter is still stronger than the former. Those who use this argument often admit that such comparisons can be made, but they do not see that these comparisons show that mutual irreducibility does not imply incomparability.

A second argument for incomparability is given by Thomas Nagel. Nagel distinguishes 'personal' or 'agent-centered values' from 'impersonal' or 'outcome-centered' values. The former include specific obligations, commitments to one's own projects and general rights. The latter include utility and perfectionist ends. Nagel claims that these five fundamentally different kinds of value reflect fundamentally different viewpoints on the world, specifically 'the point of view of one's relations to others . . . the point of view of one's life extended through time . . . the point of view of everyone at once . . . and finally . . . the detached point of view often described as the view *sub specie aeternitatis*'.[21] Nagel then suggests at least two reasons why this variety of viewpoints is supposed to exclude comparability. First, he writes that when values reflect, and thus can be appreciated only from, different points of view, 'one is . . . unable to bring them together in a single evaluative judgement, even to the extent of finding them evenly balanced.'[22] In short, overall comparability requires a shared viewpoint, but there might be none. His second reason is that 'when two choices are very evenly balanced, it does not matter which choice one makes, and arbitrariness is no problem.'[23] He argues that it does matter which choice one makes in some cases, so these conflicting requirements or values cannot be equal.

We have already seen why this second argument cannot exclude equality. In symmetrical moral dilemmas like Sophie's, the choice matters, because different people will die, and people are not interchangeable. But symmetrical moral requirements do seem to be equal in strength, since each alternative produces equal amounts of the same kinds of value and harm. Thus, equality in strength does not imply that the choice does not matter, so the fact that a choice matters cannot show that moral requirements are not equal.

Nagel's first argument also fails. If the variety of viewpoints alone implied incomparability, and if fundamentally different kinds of value could be seen only from different viewpoints, *no* values of fundamentally different kinds would ever be comparable. However, *some* fundamentally different values are comparable. If one alternative produces a little more pleasure but violates many rights, then the latter, personal value overrides the former, impersonal value. On the other hand, if an astronomer can gain much important knowledge about an unexpected comet only by breaking a trivial promise, the former, impersonal value overrides the latter, personal value. Nagel admits the possibility of such comparisons,[24] but he overlooks their implication that mere difference in kind and viewpoint, even if fundamental, cannot alone explain incomparability.

A third common argument for extreme incomparability claims that conflicting moral requirements are incomparable because they belong to fundamentally different kinds and neither kind generally overrides the other. For example, moral requirements not to kill are generally stronger than moral requirements not to lie, so particular requirements of these kinds seem comparable. In contrast, neither moral duties to family nor moral duties to country are generally stronger than the other, since some duties to family override some duties to country, but other duties to country override the same or other duties to family. This is supposed to show that particular requirements of those kinds are incomparable.

However, lack of ranking among kinds of moral requirement does not imply lack of ranking among particular moral requirements.[25] A particular woman can be smarter than a particular man, even if neither women nor men are generally smarter. Similarly, a particular moral duty to one's family can be stronger than some moral duties to one's country and weaker than others, even if these kinds of requirements overlap in strength, so neither kind is generally stronger. Thus, this argument, like the previous two, fails to explain how moral requirements can be incomparable.

Limited incomparability
Such extreme arguments fail, because they are too simple and thus too general. They imply that *no* moral requirement of one kind is comparable with *any* moral requirement of some other kind. However, at least for the mentioned kinds of moral requirement, a very strong requirement of one kind is stronger than and thus comparable with a very weak requirement of the other kind. This suggests that the only plausible view of incomparability admits that *some* particular requirements of one kind are comparable with *some* particular requirements of another kind, but still claims that *some* moral requirements of the first kind are incomparable with *some* moral requirements of the other kind. This relation between kinds of moral requirement can be called 'limited incomparability'.

Intuitionists can claim that such limited incomparability is simply a fact of morality which has and needs no explanation or justification. They claim it is simply true that a moral requirement of one kind can be comparable with some but not all moral requirements of another kind. However, many philosophers are not satisfied by such brute appeals to intuition, especially in particular conflicts. They want an explanation of how incomparability can be limited.

Any such explanation must specify the conditions under which one moral requirement overrides another. If these conditions are met in some conflicts but not others of the same kinds, this might explain limited incomparability. Various explanations of limited incomparability then depend on various ways to give conditions of overriding.

The simplest way is to give priority principles which specify the properties of moral requirements that make them overriding. Common examples of priority principles range from very general principles, such as that a negative or perfect moral requirement always overrides a positive or imperfect moral requirement, to more specific principles, such as that a moral requirement to keep one promise overrides a moral requirement to keep another promise when the former promise was made earlier. These examples are not very plausible (as I will argue below), but more plausible and complex priority principles can be formulated, and many principles can be combined in a system. The point for now is that, however complex such principles and systems are, there is no reason to insist that they must rank all conflicting moral requirements. There is nothing wrong with a system of priority principles that ranks some conflicting moral requirements but does not apply to other conflicts. And such a system implies that a moral requirement of one kind can override a moral requirement of another kind, when some priority principle applies, even though other moral requirements of the same kinds are incomparable when no priority principle applies. The problem with this approach is to discover and justify a set of priority principles, but, if this can be done, this could explain how incomparability can be limited.

A second approach refers not to properties of moral requirements but to the people who rank them. People sometimes can rank conflicting moral requirements even when they cannot cite any principles to justify their rankings. However, such rankings can also suffer from various defects, such as when the ranker is ignorant of relevant facts or is partial and would rank differently if his own interests were not at stake. The present approach tries to exclude any defects that might distort our rankings, so theories of this kind will be called non-defective ranker theories, although they are usually called ideal observer theories. The first step is to list any defects that might distort our reactions or choices or rankings. This list is supposed to reflect the nature of morality, and it usually includes kinds of ignorance, partiality, irrationality, etc. Different theories give different lists, but there is much overlap. In any case, a non-defective ranker has no defect on the list.

Such non-defective rankers are then used to specify when moral judgements are true. In the case of overriding, one moral requirement is said to morally override another only if all ideal or non-defective rankers judge that the former is stronger (or react favourably to it or choose to follow it in this conflict). Universal agreement is necessary for one moral requirement to override another, so, if non-defective rankers do not all agree, neither moral requirement overrides the other. Any non-defective disagreement in a moral requirement conflict then implies that the conflict is a moral dilemma. Furthermore, the moral requirements are not equal in strength if no (or not all) rankers agree that they are equal in strength. Thus, the moral requirements are incomparable. Other moral requirements of the same kinds can still be comparable, if all non-defective rankers agree about them. Therefore, the incomparability between these kinds is limited.

The crucial question is whether non-defective rankers ever disagree. In some moral conflicts, all non-defective rankers seem to agree that one moral requirement is morally stronger than the other. It seems that only defective rankers would rank a moral requirement not to cause a tiny pain above a moral requirement to keep a solemn promise or not to cause a major disability or a great pain. Such situations are not moral dilemmas.

In other moral conflicts, rankers do seem to disagree, even though there seems to be nothing defective about them or their rankings. Many people report examples where keeping a promise or refusing to lie would cause a fair amount of pain to a friend, but rankers disagree about which moral requirement is stronger.[26] On a cultural level, Snare argues that many people in Homeric Greece ranked heroic ideals over justice, but many modern people would rank these values in the reverse order in most cases.[27] Such examples are common. Admittedly, it is always possible that one of the rankers is either ignorant or partial in some relevant way. However, there is often no evidence of any relevant defect, because the rankers do not know the people who will be affected (so they cannot be partial), but they do know the probable effects of each alternative (so they are not ignorant). Even if the rankers' non-moral beliefs are false, some people still seem to disagree in ranking even when they agree in all of their non-moral beliefs. If so, they would still disagree in ranking even if their non-moral beliefs were not false but true, and then they and their judgements would lack the defect of ignorance. This suggests that non-defective disagreement in ranking is at least possible, even if not actual.

Opponents can then respond only that there must be some relevant defect, even though they do not know what it is. Such claims are dubious, because the burden of proof lies on those who claim there is a defect. And such claims must be repeated in every possible conflict in order to exclude the possibility of any non-defective disagreement. The only systematic way to exclude all disagreement is to strengthen the list of defects until any disagreement implies some defect. Such strong lists are often attempted,[28] but they are all either insufficient or implausible in cases like those above.

Anyway, why insist on unanimity in all cases? One reason is to gain a complete moral ranking and exclude moral dilemmas, but that begs the question. Another reason is that, if rankers disagree, one must be wrong, but this forgets that non-defective ranker theories define overriding by the rankers' reactions, so there is no reason to say that one ranker is wrong apart from the rankers' reactions themselves. A third reason is that many moral philosophers follow moral sense theories and see moral rankings as similar to colour perceptions. They then infer that, just as anyone who fails to make correct colour judgements is colour blind, so anyone who fails to make correct moral rankings is morally blind.[29] This view might seem plausible in some examples, but other moral rankings seem more like choices of life style where people can disagree without any mistake or defect. In any case, the claim that non-defective rankers sometimes agree does not show that they must always agree. Thus, it is not only implausible but unnecessary to exclude all disagreement among non-defective rankers.

This argument might seem stronger if I gave a list of defects and then showed that rankers can disagree even when they have no defect on my list. However, any particular list would only raise more doubts, especially since it would have to be complete, and it would apply to many irrelevant cases. My point is that any list of defects must allow some disagreement in order to be plausible in some cases. This explains why moral requirements can be incomparable in a limited way.

Even though priority principles and non-defective rankers do explain how limited incomparability is formally possible, we need to go further. We need an explanation of why non-defective rankers disagree in some conflicts but not in others and why priority principles can resolve some conflicts but not others. This explanation must cite properties of moral requirements and their rankings to explain why limited incomparability is unavoidable.

The best explanation of limited incomparability is probably the *inexactness* of moral rankings. It would be implausible to claim that every moral requirement has an exact strength. One reason is that some kinds of moral requirement come in many increments or degrees, but other kinds come only in large blocks, and moral requirements of the latter kinds cannot be equated with an exact number of units (say 1234) of moral requirements of the former kinds. Consequently, actual rankings are at best rough: one moral requirement may be about as strong as a range of strengths of another moral requirement, but the former is not exactly as strong as any exact amount of the latter.

Although inexactness is usually admitted, it is rarely seen that such inexactness yields limited incomparability. This can be shown by a simple example of a conflict between pain and death. Suppose a doctor must decide whether to operate on an elderly patient who is incompetent to decide for himself and who has no relatives who could decide for him. He will die without the operation, and the operation is very likely to save his life, so the doctor has a strong moral reason to perform it. On the other hand, even a successful operation will leave the patient in intense but intermittent pain for the few remaining years of his life, so the doctor has a strong moral reason not to perform it. Suppose these are the only relevant moral reasons.

They are also moral requirements, since it would be wrong for the doctor not to save the patient or to cause the pain if he had no justification.

Death is clearly worse than a small amount of pain, so some moral requirements of these kinds are comparable. However, some pain can be so intense, long and certain that death is not worse in a morally relevant way. But the pain also might not be worse. If neither is worse, neither moral requirement overrides the other.

But they are also not equal in strength. If death were equal to the exact amount of pain that the patient would suffer after the operation (say 1000 units), then a small increase in the amount of pain would tip the scale. However, if the patient would suffer slightly more pain (say 1001 units), it might still be true that neither moral requirement is stronger. And then any reason to claim that death is equal to the smaller amount of pain would also be a reason to claim that death is equal to the slightly larger amount of pain. But the different amounts of pain are still not equal, since the moral requirement not to cause the greater pain is stronger. Thus, death cannot be equal both to the smaller amount and to the larger amount, because equality must be transitive. Since death cannot equal both amounts, and there is no reason to claim that it equals one amount rather than the other, this is a strong reason to believe that death does not equal either amount of pain. And this implies that the moral requirements in the above case are not equal but incomparable.[30]

An opponent might respond that death is equal to a *range* of amounts of pain (say 800–5000). It seems odd to equate a range of amounts with a specific occurrence like death. But even if equality with a range makes sense in this case, it does not imply equality with any particular value in the range. And if death is not equal to any particular amount of pain within the range, the particular requirements in my example are not equal. It is particular moral requirements rather than ranges that conflict in moral dilemmas, so equality between particular requirements is all that must be denied for the possibility of limited incomparability and moral dilemmas.

Another possible response is that death must equal an exact amount of pain, even though we do not *know* the exact equation.[31] However, if we do not know any exact equation, it is hard to see why any exact equation must be true. I am not arguing that no equation is true because we do not know any equation. My argument against equality is that small differences in the amount of pain do not make one moral requirement override the other, but even small differences would do this if any exact equation held. In the face of this argument, it begs the question to insist without an independent argument that some exact equation must be true even though no exact equation is known to be true.

None of this conclusively proves that death is incomparable with some amounts of pain. However, it is implausible to insist that death must equal an exact amount of pain (say 1234 units). This inexactness implies that the moral requirements in my example are incomparable. And such inexactness also explains why this incomparability is limited enough to fit our intuitions in other cases where death and pain conflict.

Inexactness also explains limited incomparability in many other moral dilemmas where different kinds of moral requirement conflict. For example, freedom also comes in many degrees, but no particular amount of freedom seems to be exactly equal in strength to death or to any particular amount of pleasure or pain. There also seems to be no exact equation between a short but intense pain and a longer but less intense pain. Inexactness produces limited incomparability in countless cases like these.

Limited incomparability can also arise from other sources. Some moral requirements cannot be assigned a *cardinal* number of units of strength, but at most an *ordinal* number of its position on a scale. Ordinal rankings can resolve some moral conflicts, since a ranker can know which moral requirement is stronger without knowing how much stronger it is. However, ordinal rankings run into problems in conflicts where there is more than one moral requirement to adopt one of the alternatives, so we must combine the strengths of both moral requirements. If the first (or forty-first) ranked moral requirement supports one alternative, but both the second and third (or forty-second and forty-third) ranked moral requirements support an incompatible alternative, then no overall ranking can be achieved by adding the ordinal numbers. Some ordinals can be added in some sense, but only within restrictions that are not met by some combinations of moral requirements.[32] Such combinations of moral requirements might have ordinal ranks of their own. However, it begs the question to insist that *all* combinations of moral requirements must be ranked, simply because there must be some complete moral ranking. And if a combination of moral requirements is not ordinally ranked above or below a conflicting moral requirement, neither overrides the other, so the conflict is a moral dilemma. But the alternatives are not equal any more than first is equal to second plus third. So they are incomparable.

A third source of incomparability is the multiplicity of scales. Moral requirements can be ranked on several scales, and moral requirements can conflict when each is ranked higher on a different scale. Such requirements might still be comparable. For example, intensity and duration of pain are two scales, and neither in general is more important. Nonetheless, a moral requirement not to cause a moderately intense pain of long duration (years) is stronger than a moral requirement not to cause a slightly more intense pain of much shorter duration (seconds). In other conflicts between the same kinds of moral requirement, neither overrides the other. For example, the moral requirement not to cause a strong pain for a few minutes neither overrides nor is overridden by the moral requirement not to cause a weaker pain for an hour. However, these moral requirements also might not be equal, because they are not equal on any scale. A critic might respond that the two scales can be combined by taking some kind of weighted average, and the resulting scale would rank the two moral requirements as equal. However, it begs the question to insist that such averaging must always be possible. Even if the separate scales can be combined, the resulting scale might not rank some moral requirements, even as equal. Finally, there are some cases where more than one weighted average seems acceptable, and different weighted averages favour different alternatives, even though there are other cases where every acceptable weighted average favours one alternative.[33] If so, this provides another explanation of limited incomparability.

In sum, incomparability can be produced by inexactness, ordinality, the multiplicity of scales and maybe other factors.[34] It seems implausible to deny that these factors affect some conflicting moral requirements. And the resulting incomparability is limited enough to be plausible. This shows that, and how, limited incomparability among moral requirements is possible, so moral dilemmas are possible.

This argument also suggests that moral dilemmas are actual. My examples are fictional, and I cannot prove conclusively that any actual example includes incomparable moral requirements. Nonetheless, such examples are realistic, and they are both numerous and varied. It might be plausible to deny that any moral conflict can be completely symmetrical, but the prevalence of inexactness makes it implausible to deny that limited incomparability actually occurs. Even if this is denied, my arguments still show that limited incomparability and moral dilemmas are possible. And I will argue later that their possibility has all of the important implications of their actuality.

Similar arguments show that non-moral requirements can also be incomparable. It seems that non-defective rankers can disagree about how to rank conflicting prudential or legal or religious requirements. And such non-moral requirements display the same kind of inexactness that yields limited incomparability in the moral cases that I discussed. Thus, similar arguments show that not only moral but non-moral dilemmas are possible.

This concludes my argument for the possibility of moral dilemmas, but I will close by showing how the various parts support each other. The possibility that neither moral requirement overrides the other supports my arguments for the possibility that moral requirements conflict, because cases where neither moral requirement is stronger are the clearest cases where each moral requirement really exists. And if moral dilemmas can arise through incomparability in non-symmetrical conflicts, there is no reason to deny that symmetrical conflicts of moral requirements can be moral dilemmas as well, and vice versa. And the explanation of limited incomparability in terms of inexactness supports the possibility of non-defective disagreement in ranking, since rankers need not be defective in order to recognize and react according to inexactness. Finally, the fact that my arguments can be extended to non-moral conflicts supports my claims about moral contexts, at least when my points are formal and independent of particular content. All of this together shows that moral dilemmas are possible.

3

Some Opponents

Even though common sense and the preceding arguments suggest that moral dilemmas are possible, the main traditions of moral philosophy deny that moral dilemmas are possible. In this and the next three chapters, I will respond to these opponents' main arguments.

There are two main ways to argue against the possibility of moral dilemmas. The most direct arguments attempt to derive a contradiction from the definition of moral dilemmas. I will consider the main arguments of this kind in chapters 4 and 5. A more constructive approach is to argue for a moral system in which no moral dilemmas can arise. Various attempts of this kind will be criticized in this chapter.

There are several ways to construct a moral theory so as to avoid moral dilemmas, but these attempts fall into two groups. Some opponents try to construct their moral systems so that moral requirements never can conflict. Others admit that moral requirements can conflict but try to give a ranking of moral requirements which is so complete that whenever two moral requirements conflict, one overrides the other.

I will criticize both attempts. I do not deny that opponents can construct a moral system where moral dilemmas cannot arise. A moral system with only one rule, 'Do not kill except to save a life', cannot yield any moral requirement conflicts or dilemmas. However, I will argue that every attempt to construct a moral system without dilemmas fails for at least one of two reasons. Either the moral system does not really succeed in excluding all possible moral dilemmas; or the system is implausible, either because it depends on some arbitrary stipulation or because it does not cover all of morality. If so, no plausible moral system can rule out all moral dilemmas. The cost of excluding moral dilemmas is implausibility.

3.1 MONISM

In most standard moral dilemmas, the conflicting moral requirements seem to arise from distinct sources or principles. For example, Agamemnon and Sartre's student both seem to be caught between family and country. This variety of sources makes many opponents suppose that moral dilemmas can be avoided if (and only if) all of morality is reduced to a single source or principle. Mill claims this explicitly when he writes,

> There must be some standard by which to determine the goodness or badness, absolute and comparative, of ends or objects of desire. And whatever that standard is, there can be but one; for, if there were several ultimate principles of conduct, the same conduct might be approved by one of those principles and condemned by another, and there would be needed some more general principle as umpire between them.[1]

This assumption is shared by utilitarianism's main traditional opponent, Kant. Kant gives at least three formulations of the categorical imperative, but he insists that they are different forms of a single basic principle. He never says why this monism is important, but a plausible speculation is that he is trying to avoid moral dilemmas.

However, even a single basic principle can yield moral dilemmas.[2] For example, a single principle that there are moral requirements to keep promises implies that moral requirements conflict if someone promises to do two things when she cannot do both. And if the conflict is symmetrical, neither moral requirement overrides the other, so this is a moral dilemma. The same point applies to any symmetrical dilemma. Such dilemmas can arise from a single principle, because the same principle can be applied to different aspects of the same situation. A monist might respond that the principles in these examples are not basic, but moral dilemmas still arise within any system where these principles can be derived. Thus, the mere fact that only one principle is basic does not ensure that no moral conflicts or dilemmas can ever arise.

3.2 UTILITARIANISMS

Even though moral dilemmas can arise in some moral systems with a single basic principle, other moral systems with a single basic principle still might not yield any moral dilemmas. The most prominent example is utilitarianism.

Utilitarianism comes in many forms: act and rule utilitarianism, hedonistic and pluralistic (or ideal) utilitarianism, etc. I will discuss hedonistic act utilitarianism first, because it is common and simple, and it is also the version that seems most likely to avoid moral dilemmas.

Act utilitarianism is usually formulated as a claim about what is right or wrong or about what ought or ought not to be done. However, because of the way I defined moral dilemmas, the crucial claims here are about when moral requirements exist and when one moral requirement overrides another. Thus, the relevant versions of act utilitarianism claim that

(UMRq) there is a moral requirement to adopt an alternative if and only if that alternative maximizes utility.

(UOMRq) a moral requirement to adopt one alternative overrides a moral requirement to adopt a conflicting alternative if and only if the first alternative produces more utility.

On either version, the crucial ideas are that the principle applies directly to particular alternatives in particular situations, that what counts is the total consequences of an alternative, and the consequences of an alternative must be compared to those of every available incompatible alternative in order to determine whether there is a moral requirement or an overriding moral requirement. Alternative versions would refer to expected or expectable consequences instead of actual consequences, but such changes would only help my arguments.

Different versions of act utilitarianism can use different theories of goodness, value or utility. Hedonism is the theory of value which claims that pleasure is the only thing that is intrinsically good, and pain is the only thing that is intrinsically bad, so something is good only insofar as and because it either is or causes pleasure or loss of pain, and something is bad only insofar as and because it either is or causes pain or loss of pleasure. In short, hedonists reduce all value, goodness or utility to pleasure and all disvalue, harm or evil to pain. When hedonism is combined with act utilitarianism, the result is hedonistic act utilitarianism. The relevant versions of hedonistic act utilitarianism thus claim that there is a moral requirement or an overriding moral requirement to adopt an alternative if and only if it maximizes the balance of pleasure over pain.

Hedonistic act utilitarianism is supposed to avoid moral dilemmas, because it is not possible for each of two incompatible alternatives to maximize utility. However, one crucial question is whether a situation is a moral dilemma if the conflicting alternatives produce equal total utility, so neither produces more or maximizes utility.

Such ties can be moral dilemmas on (UOMRq). On that version, neither moral requirement overrides the other in a tie, because neither produces more total utility than the other. Consequently, if moral requirements can conflict, each can be non-overridden, so there can be moral dilemmas, even if total utility does determine which moral requirement overrides which. We will see that this version has other problems, but this alone shows that it does not exclude moral dilemmas.

The other version of hedonistic act utilitarianism seems more likely to exclude moral dilemmas. This version (UMRq) implies that there is no moral requirement to adopt an alternative unless the alternative maximizes utility. If each alternative produces the same utility, neither maximizes utility, so there is no moral requirement to adopt either alternative in a tie. There can still be a disjunctive moral requirement to adopt either one alternative or the other, if adopting either one or the other produces more utility than not adopting either. Nonetheless, neither alternative separately maximizes utility, so such ties are still not moral dilemmas or even moral requirement conflicts on this version of hedonistic act utilitarianism. Each alternative is permitted but not required.[3]

This argument is plausible in a few extreme cases. If each alternative produces exactly the same amounts of the same values and disvalues for the same people, then everyone is exactly as well off whichever alternative is adopted. Such exact ties will be very rare. Nonetheless, if they do arise, there is no moral requirement to adopt or not to adopt each alternative, since neither alternative causes any harm or loss of any value to anyone. Such choices are like choices between practically identical pound coins. There is no moral requirement to choose either alternative by itself, even if there is a disjunctive requirement to choose either one or the other. Such situations are not moral dilemmas.

Apart from such rarities, this approach is too simple. In most cases where the best alternatives are supposed to tie, different people are affected differently or different kinds of value or harm are produced. Hedonistic act utilitarians then tell us simply to calculate the total utility or greatest good, but these expressions hide a host of deep problems about how to calculate utility and whether the total is all that counts.

The first problem is that, even if each alternative produces the same amounts of the same basic kinds of value and harm, different people might be affected differently. These utilitarians overlook the fact that different people are affected, because they treat individuals merely as parts of a whole.[4] However, the distinctness of persons does seem to produce moral dilemmas. If one alternative harms one person, and the other alternative harms a different person, then, even if the degrees and kinds of harm are the same, there is still a moral requirement not to adopt either alternative or to harm either person. This can be shown by my definition of moral requirements, since it would be wrong to harm either person without a justification. It can also be shown by cases where moral residue is justified after harming one person instead of the other. I discussed the example of Sophie's choice above. Even if both choices lead to the same total amount of children, pain and pleasure, she still violates a moral requirement when she chooses one individual child to be murdered. The point is that individual interests and claims can create moral requirements, and the resulting moral conflicts cannot be captured by any view that simply totals up everyone's interests or claims. This kind of moral dilemma could arise even if all values and moral requirements could be reduced to a single standard.

Moral dilemmas can arise also because hedonists do not really reduce all values and harms to a single standard. Despite misleading formulations, even hedonists admit that both pleasure and pain are morally relevant. Hedonists some-times present pain simply as the absence of pleasure, but this is clearly wrong. Dreamless sleep and comas cause an absence of pleasure, but they do not cause pain. And pain has a moral relevance that is separate from any loss of pleasure. It is possible that the two best alternatives produce equal amounts of pleasure, but the first produces more pain. If no other value is at stake, the moral requirement not to adopt the first is stronger. The extra strength of this requirement cannot be reduced to or explained by loss of pleasure, since the pleasures are equal. Thus, pain and (loss of) pleasure are not a single standard, so even hedonists must admit that basically different values can conflict.

Hedonists also cannot plausibly resolve all such conflicts. Suppose one alternative produces 100 units of pleasure and 100 units of pain, and the only other alternative produces 10 units of pleasure and 10 units of pain. (I grant such units only for the sake of illustration.) Some utilitarians emphasize pain in that they think it is more important to avoid pain than to gain pleasure. These utilitarians might equate 1 unit of pain with the loss of 2 units of pleasure. On this equation, the total utility is calculated as the number of units of pleasure minus twice the number of units of pain, so the first alternative produces a total utility of -100 units, and the second alternative produces a total utility of -10 units. Thus, the second alternative maximizes utility. In contrast, other utilitarians emphasize pleasure in that they think it is more important to gain pleasure than to avoid pain. These utilitarians might equate 2 units of pain with the loss of 1 unit of pleasure . On this equation, the total is the units of pleasure minus one half the units of pain, so the first alternative produces a total of 50 units of utility, and the second alternative produces a total of 5 units of utility. Thus, the first alternative maximizes utility. This shows that which alternative is favoured by a hedonistic act utilitarian depends on how much pain he happens to equate with how much loss of pleasure.

How can we choose among such equations? All of the utilitarians above consider only pleasure and pain, but they use different equations, so the basic claims of utilitarianism and hedonism provide no justification for either equation. Mill suggests another kind of justification when he asks, 'What is there to decide whether a particular pleasure is worth purchasing at the cost of a particular pain, except the feelings and judgements of the experienced?'.[5] The problem with this suggestion is that the experienced (or non-defective rankers) do not always agree in their feelings and judgements, as I argued above. Utilitarians might simply stipulate a certain equation. However, the equation would have to be exact in order to resolve all moral conflicts, and I argued above that no exact equation is plausible. If this is correct, then hedonistic act utilitarianism cannot exclude moral dilemmas without unjustified and implausible stipulation.

Similar arguments apply to conflicts between certainty and duration of pleasure or pain. If one alternative produces a 10 per cent chance of 2 hours of pain, and the other alternative produces a 90 per cent chance of 10 minutes of pain, which alternative maximizes utility depends on how certainty is weighed against duration. Similar problems arise also for conflicts between extent and certainty, total and average utility, etc. Utilitarians cannot resolve all such conflicts without exact equations which are implausible and unjustifiable.

These problems would arise even if all values and disvalues could be reduced to pleasure and pain, but there are also reasons to deny that all values can be reduced to pleasure and pain. These arguments are well known, so I will not repeat them in detail here. The general idea is to show that, even if two alternatives produce equal balances of pleasure over pain, other factors still might make one alternative better. Similar arguments point out that sometimes it is not worse or wrong to forego a minor gain in total pleasure, when pains are equal, for a substantial gain in one of these other values. Commonly cited non-hedonistic values include life, freedom, abilities, knowledge, fairness of distribution and deontological values such as keeping promises. Some of these values might be reducible to pleasure and pain, but it still seems that at least some things other than pleasure and pain are valuable and morally relevant. This pluralism is even accepted by some utilitarians, such as Moore in his ideal utilitarianism.[6]

Since complete reductions fall, incompatible alternatives can cause basically different harms or losses in basically different values. Suppose one alternative causes a loss of freedom, and the other causes a loss of pleasure, but neither overrides the other. If freedom and pleasure were mutually reducible, opponents could claim that neither alternative causes a loss in the total of the basic value. However, since the values of freedom and pleasure are not mutually reducible, each alternative does produce some loss in some basic value. This shows there is a moral requirement not to adopt each alternative, since it would be wrong to cause a loss of pleasure or freedom without any justification. Such conflicts could be resolved only by an exact equation between freedom and pleasure, but such exact equations would be just as implausible and unjustifiable as those between pleasure and pain. And the same problem arises when each alternative causes a loss in any other basic value and when each causes a basic harm, such as pain, death or disability. Thus, the failure of reductions shows that moral requirements can conflict, even if neither overrides the other.

It is important to realize that these problems do not arise only at some lower level of moral thinking. The implausibility and unjustifiability of precise equations among distinct values do not depend on time limits of practical deliberation, on considerations of simplicity in pedagogy, or on any uncritical use of intuitions. Consequently, utilitarians cannot avoid moral dilemmas simply by distinguishing a critical level from intuitive or practical levels of moral thinking, as Hare suggests.[7]

Some recent utilitarians have responded that values should be reduced not to pleasure and pain but instead to the objects or the satisfaction of desires. Desires can then be ranked by asking people what they would choose when desires conflict. However, there are reasons to deny such reductions, such as that some desires are irrational or morally wrong.[8] Even if such reductions did work, this would not solve the whole problem. Some moral conflicts cannot be resolved without exact equations between conflicting desires, between satisfaction and frustration of desires, between duration and probability of satisfaction, etc. Such exact equations cannot be justified by asking people what they would choose in conflicts, because people are not very confident or consistent about what they would choose in close conflicts.[9] The problems are even greater when the conflicting desires are held by different people, since they might choose differently in close conflicts.[10] Consequently, utilitarians cannot escape all moral dilemmas simply by totalling desires.

Another recent version of utilitarianism is rule utilitarianism. Rule utilitarians count the utility of rules or kinds of act rather than individual acts. The relevant version claims that there is a moral requirement to do something if and only if not doing it would violate a rule such that utility would be maximized if everyone followed (or tried to follow) the rule. This kind of utilitarianism does not even seem to escape moral dilemmas, since rules could each maximize utility and then come into conflict. One common example of a rule that maximizes utility is the rule to keep promises, but we saw how this rule alone can yield moral dilemmas. And other rules that are supposed to maximize utility can also conflict. Some rule utilitarians might try to avoid such conflicts by writing exceptions into the rules. However, if enough exceptions are added to avoid all moral conflicts, then rule utilitarianism collapses into act utilitarianism, so it also cannot avoid moral dilemmas without becoming implausible for the same reasons.

In conclusion, every version of utilitarianism either fails to exclude moral dilemmas or excludes them only by using implausible and unjustified stipulations. Nonetheless, this is not a criticism of utilitarianism or of consequentialism in general. My arguments apply only to those versions that pretend to exclude moral dilemmas. Other versions of consequentialism are not subject to my criticisms, because they do not pretend to exclude moral dilemmas. If consequentialism is the claim that all moral requirements depend only on the consequences of what is required, some consequentialists can admit moral requirement conflicts if they count more than the total of a single value and admit that some moral requirement is violated when an alternative harms one individual at the expense of another or increases one kind of value at the expense of another. Even if they claim that one moral requirement overrides another when the former causes more total value, this still leaves some conflicts unresolved, and they are moral dilemmas. Such versions of consequentialism are more plaus- ible because they allow moral dilemmas, since this shows they are not as simplistic as their critics often assume. Thus, my arguments not only do not refute but might actually help to de- fend some versions of consequentialism.[11]

3.3 NEGATIVE AND POSITIVE

So far I have considered attempts to exclude moral dilemmas by restricting morality to a single basic principle, but this monistic approach is not the only way to construct a moral system without moral dilemmas. Moral dilemmas can also be excluded by pluralists who admit many basic moral principles, if they construct these principles so that they never can conflict. I will discuss such pluralistic attempts in the rest of this chapter.

The first way for pluralists to avoid moral requirement conflicts is to claim that all moral principles and requirements are negative. A moral requirement or principle is negative when it requires someone *not* to adopt an alternative. If a moral system includes only negative requirements, two moral requirements can apply to the same situation, but it seems that the agent always can fulfil both moral requirements simply by doing nothing. For example, if an agent is required not to lie and not to kill, she always can fulfil both requirements by remaining silent and still, since then she does not lie or kill or do anything that she is required not to do. This is supposed to show that negative moral requirements cannot ever conflict.

An advocate of this approach might claim that such negative moral requirements are all there is to morality. However, this would not be very plausible, since much of morality seems to be positive, such as when parents ought to help their children and vice versa. Consequently, this approach is usually supplemented with the claim that positive moral reasons either are not requirements (but only ideals) or cannot conflict or are always overridden by negative moral requirements. In any case, such positive moral reasons are not supposed to create moral dilemmas. This approach is suggested by some versions of the traditional distinction between perfect and imperfect duties, and variations of this approach are suggested by Berkeley, Kant and, more recently, Donagan.[12]

In order to assess this approach, it is necessary to clarify the distinction between negative and positive duties. The problem is that many cases of positive duties seem to be redescribable as negative duties and vice versa. For example, it is not clear whether promises create positive duties to do what was promised or negative duties not to omit what was promised. Similarly, a doctor's duty to release a patient from the hospital can be redescribed as a duty not to keep him in the hospital.

One way to specify this distinction is to identify acts with bodily movements and to claim that to remain still and silent is to do nothing.[13] A moral requirement is then negative if it is fulfilled by anyone who does not move his or her body at all, and a moral requirement is positive if it cannot be fulfilled without some bodily movement. This implies that, whenever negative moral requirements seem to conflict, the agent can always escape simply by not moving his body, doing nothing, and thereby fulfilling both negative moral requirements.

The first problem with this approach is that sitting still is often doing something. Suppose an enemy knocks on a man's door and asks if his wife is home. The husband knows that his wife is home, and the enemy will kill her if he finds her.[14] There is a moral requirement for the husband not to lie, and there is also a moral requirement not to reveal where his wife is and thereby to help the enemy catch his wife. However, he cannot do both, because, if he remains silent, the murderer will know she is at home. Not to move his mouth is to reveal her location and to help his enemy kill her.

An opponent might respond that a husband who remains silent is not killing his wife but only letting her be killed by someone else. Nonetheless, there is still a moral requirement not to remain silent, because he knows that remaining silent will lead to his wife's death when he can prevent it, and that would be wrong if he did not have any justification. Furthermore, if there were no moral requirement not to let his wife be killed, the agent would morally have to remain silent. Kant might accept this, but almost everyone else finds it counterintuitive. If the only way for this approach to avoid this conflict is to claim that the husband must act in a way that he knows will lead to his wife's murder, then this approach cannot avoid moral requirement conflicts without becoming implausible.

The next problem with this approach is that, even if an agent always physically could do nothing, there are cases where the agent morally cannot do nothing. For example, Sophie has negative moral requirements not to pick either child to be killed. She physically can remain still and do nothing, but, if she does not pick either child, both of her children will be killed, so she morally cannot refuse to choose. This is enough to put her in a moral dilemma, even though both of her moral requirements are negative.

Even if negative moral requirements never could conflict, this approach still could not rule out conflicts between negative and positive moral requirements. Some opponents try to avoid such conflicts by denying that there are any positive moral requirements. However, there do seem to be positive moral requirements for parents to take minimal care of their children and vice versa, and the perfect moral requirement to keep a promise is positive when someone promises to do an act of some kind. These are requirements because it would be wrong for the agent not to do an act of the relevant kind if there were no justification for not doing it. And they are positive because they cannot be fulfilled without bodily movement.

Other opponents might respond that positive requirements cannot conflict with negative requirements, because an agent always can fulfil both requirements. The reason is that, on the above analysis of action sentences, a positive requirement requires only that *some* act of a kind be done. But if the agent fails to do any act of that kind in one situation, the agent can still do some act of that kind in some other situation. If an agent does not give to this beggar, she can still give to another beggar. However, there are other cases where an agent does not have any opportunity to do anything that fulfils the positive requirement but does not violate the negative requirement. For example, I might promise to tell the truth when the truth is painful whenever and however it is told, and a parent might not be able to take care of her child in any way except stealing. In such cases, an agent cannot do an act of the required kind without doing an act of the forbidden kind, so a positive moral requirement does conflict with a negative moral requirement.

A final response is that negative moral requirements always override positive ones. However, some negative requirements are trivial, and some positive requirements are very strong. When they conflict, it is implausible to claim that the negative moral requirement is overriding just because it is negative. For example, if the only way to prevent a murder is to lie, the positive moral requirement to prevent the murder overrides any requirement not to lie. Furthermore, the strength of the positive requirement can be varied until it neither overrides nor is overiddden by the negative moral requirement. Such conflicts are then moral dilemmas where one moral requirement is positive and the other is negative.

There can also be conflicts between two positive moral

requirements. Sartre's student has a positive moral requirement to help his mother and a positive moral requirement to help his country. Promises can also create positive moral requirements to go to different places at the same time. In these cases, neither moral requirement can be fulfilled without some bodily movement of the right kind, but the agent cannot both move his body so as to fulfil the first requirement and also move his body so as to fulfil the second requirement. If neither moral requirement overrides the other, then the situation is a moral dilemma. Thus, there can be conflicts between negative moral requirements, between positive and negative moral requirements, and between positive moral requirements.

There are many other ways to distinguish negative and positive moral requirements and many related distinctions. One might define negative requirements so as to include all requirements to keep promises and to care for children (possibly because an agent never violates either requirement if she never moves her body so as to make a promise or have children). One can even include requirements to prevent harm (possibly because cases where an agent is required to prevent harm are cases where preventing is negative because it counts as not allowing). One might also define a perfect requirement as one that can be enforced by external law or 'permits no exceptions in the interest of inclination',[15] or as one that corresponds to a right in someone or leaves no choice as to when and where to fulfil it.[16] However, all such distinctions leave some cases where negative or perfect requirements conflict with each other, and other cases where they do not override positive or imperfect requirements. An opponent might try to rule out all such cases simply by defining negative moral requirements as those that never conflict with each other and always override other requirements, but this leaves no reason to deny that some positive requirements also conflict. Thus, none of these distinctions rules out moral requirement conflicts or moral dilemmas.

Opponents can always come up with other distinctions, but I want to suggest a general reason why no distinction along these lines can rule out all moral requirement conflicts or dilemmas.

There is a tension between the goal of avoiding conflicts and the goal of ensuring that negative or perfect requirements override all others. In order to avoid conflicts, the distinction must be formal, but a formal distinction cannot determine how important a moral requirement is. What determines its importance is how well it fits its basic rationale. The rationale of many negative or perfect moral requirements is to forbid acts that cause harm. But some harms are much greater than others, so some negative moral requirements are much less important than others. This makes it implausible to claim that an agent cannot violate a trivial negative or perfect requirement when this is necessary to fulfil the basic rationale, that is, to prevent or avoid causing a much greater harm. It is implausible to claim that the trivial requirement overrides just because it is negative or perfect. Thus, negative moral requirements can conflict with other requirements (whether one calls the others positive or negative), and the negative requirements do not always override. Since degrees of harm vary continuously, there must also be some conflicts where some negative or perfect moral requirements are also not overridden by the conflicting moral requirements. If so, any plausible way of drawing the distinction between negative and positive moral requirements must leave some conflicts unresolved. These will be moral dilemmas. This argument is not a conclusive proof, since opponents might draw new distinctions. Nonetheless, this does give some reason to doubt that any approach along these lines can rule out all moral dilemmas.

3.4 INTENTIONS

A related attempt to avoid moral requirement conflicts is inspired by the traditional Catholic doctrine of double effect. The basic idea is that an agent does not violate a moral requirement just because he causes harm if he does not cause it *intentionally*. For example, an agent does not violate a moral requirement if he tries to help someone but harms her by accident or mistake. But an agent does violate a moral requirement whenever he causes harm intentionally. This is not the only way to violate a moral requirement, since, even if an agent does not intend to cause any harm, he still violates a moral requirement if he knowingly causes a harm that is disproportionate to or greater than any benefit that he causes. But these are supposed to be the only ways to violate a moral requirement if the notion of harm is extended to include lies, broken promises, etc. Thus, an agent does not violate a moral requirement unless either (1) he causes harm intentionally, or (2) he knowingly causes harm that is greater than (or disproportionate to) any benefit that is gained. Clause (1) is called the principle of intentionality, and clause (2) is called the principle of proportionality. Each principle gives a sufficient condition of a moral requirement, and they are supposed to be jointly necessary for a moral requirement to be violated.

This doctrine seems to rule out moral requirement conflicts, because it always leaves an agent with some way to avoid violating either principle. In any apparent conflict, at least one of the harms is not greater than the other. Either one is greater, and then the other is not; or neither is greater. Thus, there is always at least one alternative that does not cause greater harm or violate the principle of proportionality.

The crucial claim is, then, that the agent always can choose such an alternative without violating the principle of intentionality. Even if an agent cannot avoid causing some harm, the agent does not intend to cause any harm if he causes the harm when his only intention is to avoid an equal or greater harm. In any apparent conflict, the agent always can adopt one alternative with the sole intention of avoiding causing the equal or greater harm of the other alternative. If the agent does so, he does not cause any harm intentionally, so he does not violate the principle of intentionality. Since he can also avoid violating the principle of proportionality, he can avoid violating any moral requirement on either principle. Thus, agents can escape any apparent conflict by choosing a right alternative with a right intention, so moral requirements never really conflict.

Defenders of moral dilemmas must admit that at least one

alternative does not produce greater harm, so moral requirements that depend on the principle of proportionality cannot conflict. But there are still problems with this principle. The principle of proportionality does not cite the right kind of factor to be a test of whether there is a moral requirement. Since this principle refers to comparative harm and degrees of harm, it is more suitable as a test of when a moral requirement is overriding. It is hard to see why the comparative degree of harm could determine whether there is any moral requirement at all, independently of whether it is overridden.

The principle of intentionality creates other problems, even in cases where neither act causes disproportionate harm. The first problem is to clarify when someone causes something intentionally.

When someone causes harm accidentally or unknowingly, he does not cause harm intentionally, and he does not seem to violate any moral requirement. If I trip and fall accidentally, this might cause harm, but it does not violate any moral requirement. And if I turn on the stove without knowing that it will explode and kill someone, I do not seem to violate any moral requirement. However, such accidents and ignorance are not present in at least some moral requirement conflicts. Someone can know that missing a meeting will hurt her colleagues and also know that going to the meeting will hurt her husband, because he needs her at home. Neither choice would be an accident. Thus, the principle that moral requirements cannot be violated accidentally or unknowingly is not enough to rule out all moral requirement conflicts or dilemmas.

Moral requirement conflicts would be ruled out if an act had to have a bad ultimate goal, purpose or end in order to violate a moral requirement. When moral requirements appear to conflict, the agent always can cause one harm with the ultimate goal of avoiding the other harm, and this goal is not bad. However, a moral requirement can be violated without a bad ultimate goal. Reckless driving can violate a moral requirement even if the driver's ultimate goal is only to have fun. And Agamemnon's ultimate goal when he kills his daughter is to lead his troops to Troy, but he still seems to violate a moral requirement. Thus, agents' ultimate goals cannot be used to rule out moral requirement conflicts or dilemmas.

This approach needs what is done intentionally to include less than what is done knowingly and more than an agent's ultimate purpose. The usual account is that an agent intentionally causes a harm if the agent knowingly causes the harm because it is either an end or a means to his end. One common example is that a terror bomber who bombs civilians in order to destroy the morale of the enemy uses their deaths as a means to his ends, so he does intend to kill them. In contrast, a tactical bomber who bombs a munitions factory might know that his bombs will kill civilians who live close by, but he does not intend their deaths because their deaths are not a means of destroying the factory. This strays from the common notion of intention, but the distinction still might be important. The principle of intentionality implies that the terror bomber does violate a moral requirement, but the tactical bomber does not (assuming that the principle of proportionality is met).

This account of intention would rule out moral requirement conflicts if there were always one alternative where the harm is not a means. For example, a commander might seem to be in a moral requirement conflict if terror bombing is his only way to protect his own soldiers. However, if he refuses to terror bomb, the deaths of his soldiers do not seem to be his means of avoiding killing civilians (his end), so he does not cause or even allow their deaths intentionally on this account. If his refusal also does not cause disproportionate harm, it does not violate any moral requirement on this approach. In general, if every apparent conflict includes at least one alternative where the harm is neither a means nor disproportionate, then moral requirements never really conflict.

A first problem with this account is that the idea of a means is not clear in many cases. One way to clarify this idea uses counterfactuals. If a terror bomber dropped some bombs, and they destroyed a factory but did not kill anyone, he would not yet have fulfilled his mission, so he would fly back and drop more bombs. In contrast, if a tactical bomber dropped some bombs, and they destroyed the factory but did not kill anyone, he would have no reason to go back and drop more. This is supposed to show that the terror bomber intends the deaths as his means, and the tactical bomber does not. But this is too quick. The terror bomber need not drop more bombs if his first bombs did not kill anyone but did destroy morale or stop the enemy. Thus, the terror bomber would not kill anyone if he had some other way to destroy morale, just as the tactical bomber would not kill anyone if he had another way to destroy the factory. Both want to stop the enemy with as little killing as possible. Admittedly, the deaths are earlier than and causes of the destruction of morale, whereas the deaths are not earlier than or causes of the destruction of the factory, but there is no reason to think that the direction of time or causation is morally important.[17] Consequently, when the notions of intentions and means are cleared up, they do not seem to determine whether a moral requirement is violated.

Other examples support the same conclusion. The principle of intentionality suggests that an abortion to save the mother is intentional killing and violates a moral requirement when the method is craniotomy (where the fetus' skull is crushed), since the fetus' death is a means, but not when the method is hysterectomy (where a cancerous womb is removed). But the difference between methods does not seem important, since the fetus is killed in either case. Foot adds an example in which we can save five patients by manufacturing a certain gas, but we know that the gas will leak into the next room and kill another patient. If we make the gas anyway, the death is not intended even as a means, and the principle of proportionality is met, so the present approach implies that no moral requirement is violated. But some moral requirement does seem to be violated, because the other patient was killed.[18] All of these examples suggest that intentionality is not necessary to violate a moral requirement, even if the principle of proportionality is met.

Even if intentionality were necessary to violate a moral requirement, this could not rule out all moral requirement conflicts, since sometimes each alternative uses harm as a means. For example, Sophie picks one child as a means to save the other, and vice versa. An opponent might respond that, if Sophie picks one child, but the Nazi guard does not kill the child, her goal will still be met, so her means is not the child's death but only picking the child. However, this distinction seems unimportant in a case where she knows that the guard will kill the child she picks. And in a similar example the guard might tell Sophie that she must kill one child in order to save the other. In this case, each child's death is a means, so she would kill the child intentionally. It is not as clear in this case that Sophie (morally) cannot refuse to kill either, but this does seem true if all she has to do is hit one child in order to prevent a horrible death for this child and many more. In some such case, the amounts of pain and death are more important than whether the pain or death is a means, so the agent morally cannot avoid intentionally causing some harm as a means to prevent much more harm. This makes moral requirements conflict in some such case.

Opponents can always respond that this approach works with a different notion of intentionality. There are many notions of intentionality, and I cannot discuss them all, but I do want to give a general reason to doubt that any such notion can exclude moral dilemmas. To rule out all moral dilemmas, opponents would need a notion of intentionality such that: (1) the agent in any apparent conflict always can choose one alternative without intentionally causing any harm, and (2) there is never any moral requirement not to cause harm when this is not intentional and not disproportionate. To satisfy (1), a notion of intentionality would have to be excluded by the mere presence of a non-overridden justification, since this is all that is common to all apparent conflicts and dilemmas. But such a notion of intentionality would not be necessary to violate a moral requirement, since a moral requirement can be violated even when there is a non-overridden justification. This is shown by counterfactuals and moral residue. Even if there is a non-overridden justification for tactical bombing, it still violates a moral requirement, because it would be wrong if there were no justification, and some compensation is owed to innocent victims (more than if someone else had dropped the bombs).

Thus, no notion of intentionality can avoid all moral requirement conflicts or dilemmas.

Nonetheless, this approach does contain some truth. Intentions can affect judgements of the agent. It seems unfair for
other people to blame or condemn an agent if she is caught in a
moral conflict through no fault of her own and she reluctantly
causes some harm when her only intention is to avoid an equal
or greater harm. This might explain why some opponents have
emphasized intentionality. However, it does not rule out moral
requirement conflicts or dilemmas. The judgements that
define such conflicts are about requirements and alternatives.
They are not about the blameworthiness or condemnability of
the agent. And an alternative can violate a moral requirement
even if the agent should not be blamed or condemned for this
violation. Thus, intentionality is important, but its real importance does not rule out moral requirement conflicts or dilemmas.

3.5 EXCEPTIONS

So far I have discussed pluralists who claim that an agent can escape any apparent conflict by acting or intending in the right
way. A different approach emphasizes that a moral theorist
always has a way out, since he or she always can qualify or
modify moral principles so that they do not really conflict. This
approach is usually ascribed to Hare.[19]

The basic idea is that many moral principles have exceptions,
and, when a situation is an exception to the applicable moral
principle, there is really no moral requirement in that situation.
The way to avoid moral requirement conflicts is, then, to claim
that, whenever moral principles seem to conflict, the situation
is really an exception to one of them. If so, one of the apparent
moral requirements is not real, so the situation is not really a
dilemma or even conflict. For example, if the only principles
that could yield a moral requirement for Agamemnon to lead
his troops to Troy have exception clauses like '. . . unless this
cannot be done without killing one's daughter (or someone)',
then Agamemnon would not really have any moral require-

ment to lead his troops to Troy or to kill his daughter, so he would not be in a moral requirement conflict or dilemma. More generally, all conflicts (or dilemmas) can be avoided by adding to each moral principle a clause '. . . unless this cannot be done without violating a (non-overridden) moral requirement.'[20] If every apparent conflict were an exception in this way, no situation would really be a moral requirement conflict or dilemma.

In order to understand this approach, we need to distinguish two kinds of principles: rules of thumb and absolute principles. Absolute principles are unconditional and exceptionless, and they lack clauses like 'other things being equal'. In contrast, rules of thumb are only supposed to hold usually in normal conditions, so they are admitted to have exceptions. When all of the exceptions are written into rules of thumb, they become absolute, but they are just rules of thumb as long as any exceptions remain.

Some people assume that only absolute moral principles can yield moral dilemmas, and they use moral dilemmas to argue for or against absolutism or the claim that moral principles are absolute. However, moral dilemmas can also arise from mere rules of thumb, since a situation might fall under conflicting rules of thumb without being an exception to either one, and then there are conflicting moral requirements. Thus, both absolute principles and rules of thumb can generate moral dilemmas. For the sake of simplicity, I will focus here on absolute moral principles, but what I say can be extended to rules of thumb.

The next step is to specify what an exception is. If a principle claims there are moral requirements to do something, exceptions to the principle might include only situations where the moral requirement is *cancelled* or also situations where the moral requirement is overridden. For example, one common principle is that promises ought to be kept. One clear exception is if I promise to meet someone but later they tell me they cannot meet me. My obligation is then cancelled, so I have no obligation at all to meet them. In contrast, if I promise to meet them, but a more important requirement overrides my obligation, I still have some obligation to meet them, as is shown by counterfactuals and moral residue. It is not clear whether such situations count as exceptions according to opponents who claim that apparent moral dilemmas are always exceptions to moral principles.

One way to clear up this ambiguity is to distinguish various views of what moral principles are about. Some moral principles are about what ought or ought not to be done, or what is right or wrong. However, since I defined moral dilemmas by moral requirements, the principles that are relevant here are about moral requirements of some kind. There are then three possibilities. Moral principles might have one of the following forms:

(MRP) There is always a moral requirement to do some act (or not to do any act) of kind X.

(NOMRP) There is always a non-overridden moral requirement to do some act (or not to do any act) of kind X.

(OMRP) There is always an overriding moral requirement to do some act (or not to do any act) of kind X.

The crucial question is which of these kinds of principle must have exceptions when they appear to conflict.

Even defenders of moral dilemmas must admit that principles about overriding moral requirements cannot conflict. If they did, there would be overriding moral requirements for incompatible alternatives, but this is impossible. However, this does not show moral dilemmas are impossible, since moral dilemmas are not defined by overriding requirements.

Moral requirement conflicts and dilemmas would be impossible if principles of the form (MRP) must always have exceptions when they appear to conflict, and moral dilemmas would be impossible if principles of the form (NOMRP) must always have exceptions when they appear to conflict (at least if all moral requirements depend on such principles). However, it begs the question to insist without any argument that these kinds of principles must always have exceptions when they seem to conflict. These opponents need independent arguments against the possibility of moral requirement conflicts and dilemmas. They do try to give some arguments, but I will respond to them in later chapters. The point for now is that the mere fact that moral principles of forms (MRP) and (NOMRP) can have exceptions does not show that their exceptions must be arranged so as to avoid all moral requirement conflicts and dilemmas.

There are also strong reasons to deny that some apparent moral dilemmas are exceptions to either kind of principle. The above arguments from counterfactuals and moral residue show that moral requirements really do conflict in some situations, so these situations are not exceptions to principles of the form (MRP). And my arguments from symmetry and incomparability show that neither moral requirement overrides the other in some conflicts, so these situations are not exceptions to principles of the form (NOMRP). These arguments also show that there is often no reason to write an exception into one principle rather than another. Some opponents might respond that non-overridden moral requirements can conflict in my examples, even if these situations are exceptions to the principles, if these moral requirements do not depend on any principles. But then this whole approach breaks down. Consequently, exceptions cannot be used to avoid all moral requirement conflicts and dilemmas. They appear to do so only if one confuses exceptions where moral requirements are cancelled with those where they are overridden or just not overriding.

3.6 RANKINGS

All of the opponents so far deny that moral requirements can conflict. Another way to avoid moral dilemmas is to admit that moral requirements can conflict but to claim that one of the conflicting moral requirements always overrides the other. To show this, opponents must provide a ranking of moral requirements which is both morally relevant and complete in that it ranks one moral requirement above the other in every possible conflict.

Two kinds of moral ranking can be distinguished. General rankings rank general moral principles or kinds of moral requirement. Particular rankings rank moral requirements in particular cases independently of the general kinds of which they are instances.

General rankings cannot exclude moral dilemmas for several reasons. First, many moral principles cannot be ranked generally, because many kinds of moral requirement include some instances that are trivial and others that are important, and the important moral requirements of one kind must be ranked above the trivial moral requirements of another kind, and vice versa. For example, Gewirth gives a very elaborate general ranking, but even he can say only that 'physical assault is *usually* more wrong than lying or promise breaking.'[21] This does not resolve conflicts where a minor physical assault (such as pushing someone gently out of the way) is necessary in order to fulfil an important promise. Such examples invalidate any strict ranking of these and many other kinds of moral requirement. And it does not help here to rank the principles lexically so that an alternative must pass the first principle before the second is even considered, and so on.[22] Finally, even if some general ranking were plausible, it could not resolve conflicts that arise from a single principle alone, since that principle cannot be ranked either above or below itself. For example, even Gewirth has to admit that when 'in order to save R from drowning A has to let S drown, or in order to give starving R enough food to pull him through A has to deny food to starving S . . . there may be no solution other than to urge A to do all he can to save both persons.'[23] This does not resolve the conflict when A cannot do anything to save both persons. And no general ranking of principles can resolve such symmetrical conflicts, since they do not depend on separate principles that could be ranked generally. Consequently, no general ranking can resolve all moral requirement conflicts.

The other approach is to admit that general rankings fail but to claim that particular moral requirements can always be ranked. This approach is suggested by those who claim particular moral requirements are primary, and conflicting moral requirements can be ranked by particular intuitions or judgement in particular cases.[24] This approach does avoid some problems of general rankings, but it also raises many problems of its own.

The main problem is that particular rankings need not be complete. Even if some particular moral requirements can be ranked by intuition, there is no reason to assume that all moral requirements can be ranked in this way. Incomplete rankings are consistent, and there is no reason to demand complete rankings. Furthermore, particular intuition seems inadequate in some conflicts. Intuition cannot resolve symmetrical conflicts and is also unreliable when non-defective rankers disagree, as I argued above. Even particular rankings cannot resolve such conflicts without being unjustified and implausible. Consequently, both general and particular rankings fail to rule out the possibility of moral dilemmas.

3.7 PRIMA FACIE

There are two more positions that are often supposed to be opposed to moral dilemmas. I will argue that the best interpretations of these positions are not really incompatible with moral dilemmas. But they still need to be discussed, because they are so common and influential.

One of the most common responses to moral dilemmas uses some distinction between prima facie and actual or absolute requirements. Earlier writers drew similar distinctions,[25] but W. D. Ross originated the term 'prima facie' and made it the core of his whole moral philosophy. Ross himself did not use this distinction to argue against moral dilemmas as I defined them, but many of his followers seem to.

This distinction would rule out moral requirement conflicts and dilemmas if two claims could be defended. The first claim is that, whenever moral requirements appear to conflict, one of them must be *merely* prima facie (where this will mean that it is both prima facie and not actual or absolute). The second claim is that merely prima facie moral requirements are not really moral requirements at all. If both claims were true, real moral requirements could not ever conflict.

Whether each claim is true depends on what 'prima facie' means. Each claim is true on some interpretation of 'prima facie', and that explains why each seems plausible. However, I will argue that there is no single interpretation on which both claims are true. So the argument seems to rule out moral dilemmas only if the various interpretations are confused.

The basic problem is that, when Ross defines prima facie duties, he fails to distinguish very different kinds of conditions. He defines 'prima facie duty' as 'the characteristic (quite distinct from that of being a duty proper) which an act has, in virtue of being of a certain kind (e.g. the keeping of a promise), of being an act which would be a duty proper if it were not at the same time of another kind which is morally significant.'[26] This is very close to my own definition of a moral requirement. Ross says there is a prima facie duty to do something when it would have been a duty proper if there were no other morally significant facts, whereas I say that there is a requirement to do something when it would have been wrong not to do it if there had been no justification. Ross seems to use 'prima facie duty' much as I use 'requirement', and he seems to use 'duty proper' much as I use 'wrong not to'. This makes the difference look merely terminological.

Although Ross and I are very close, his definition does produce some confusion, because he does not here distinguish the various conditions that can be morally significant.[27] Some of these conditions are justifications, and others are excuses and cancellations, but a prima facie duty in Ross's sense can be violated whether an agent has a justification or an excuse or a cancellation. Excuses are important, but the clearest distinction is between cancellations and justifications. For example, if I promise to paint your house, but later you tell me not to paint it, my obligation to paint it is *cancelled*. It is also cancelled if the house burns down. There is no longer any requirement at all to paint your house, so I do not owe any apology or compensation for not painting your house, and remorse is inappropriate. But these events do not give me any reason to do anything incompatible with painting your house. This situation is very different from one where I have a *justification* for not painting your house, such as that my wife needs me to take her to the hospital at the only time when I can paint your house. This does give me a reason to do something incompatible with painting your house, but I should still tell you that and the reason why I will not paint your house, and I should probably apologize and offer some compensation, such as to paint it later or to get someone else to do it. This residue shows there is still some requirement, so a justification does not have the same effects as a cancellation.

Despite these differences, Ross's definition implies that I have a prima facie duty to paint your house in both cases. Even when you tell me not to paint your house, my act of painting your house still would be a duty if you had not told me not to paint it, so it is still 'an act which would be a duty proper if it were not at the same time of another kind which is morally significant.'[28] Even if the house burns to the ground, so there is no house to paint, I would still have a duty to paint your house if this had not happened, so Ross's definition implies that I violated a prima facie duty. This not only overlooks obvious differences but also makes prima facie duties inadequate to justify moral residue. Since a merely prima facie duty might be totally cancelled, the fact that a merely prima facie duty was violated is not enough to justify moral residue. But this was one of Ross's main reasons to introduce the term 'prima facie'.[29] Thus, Ross's definition of prima facie duties is not only misleading but also fails to serve his own purpose.

Ross's failure to distinguish cancellation from justification also leads him to describe prima facie duties in incompatible ways. One indication of this is that Ross and others contrast 'prima facie' with both 'actual' and 'absolute'.[30] These terms are not synonyms, and their differences suggest at least two ways to interpret the contrasted term 'prima facie'.

The contrast between prima facie and actual suggests that a merely prima facie requirement is not actually or really any moral requirement at all, just like a moral requirement that is cancelled. The term 'merely prima facie' then operates as a spoiler like 'toy', since toy ducks are not real ducks. This interpretation is suggested by the very term 'prima facie', which comes from the Latin for 'at first sight', and thus suggests that there is not really any moral requirement at all when you look again more closely. Some of Ross's followers also refer to actual duties as duties 'all-things-considered', as if anyone who says there really is a duty is not considering something. Sometimes Ross even explicitly says that a prima facie duty 'is in fact not a duty'.[31] He also suggests this when he says that what makes something a prima facie duty is its 'tending to be our duty'.[32] Toyotas tend to start easily, because most Toyotas start easily; and my Toyota tends to start easily, because it usually does; but my Toyota still might not start at all today. Similarly, a certain kind of act might tend to violate a moral requirement, and thus might violate a prima facie moral requirement in this sense, even if that kind of act does not violate any moral requirement at all in a particular situation, such as an apparent conflict.

The second interpretation is that a merely prima facie requirement is a real moral requirement and is not cancelled even though it is either overridden or not overriding. The term 'prima facie' now operates not as a spoiler but as a qualifier, such as 'weak', since a weak force is still a real force. This is suggested by the contrast between 'prima facie' and 'absolute'. If a moral rule is absolute when it can never justifiably be violated, a requirement would seem to be absolute if it is always overriding or never overridden, and a requirement is then merely prima facie if it is not overriding or is overridden. But such requirements must still be real, or there would be nothing to override. Ross suggests this interpretation when he says that to speak of a prima facie duty is to speak of an 'objective fact' and not 'only of an appearance'.[33] He also draws an analogy with forces, and this suggests that, just as a force continues to exist and to affect the actual movement of a body even when it is opposed by a stronger force, so a prima facie duty actually exists and contributes to the agent's total duties even when it is overridden.[34] Finally, one of Ross's main uses of prima facie requirements is to justify moral residue after moral conflicts, but it makes no sense to claim that someone should feel remorse or owes compensation or an apology if the only justification for such residue is that she violated some appearance that really is not a moral requirement at all.[35] All of this suggests that Ross saw even merely prima facie moral requirements as not cancelled but real and forceful, even if they are overridden or not overriding.

Since these interpretations can also be disjoined, this leaves three interpretations of merely prima facie requirements:

(1) as cancelled, so there is really no moral requirement at all
(2) as real and forceful, even though overridden or not overriding
(3) as either cancelled or overridden or not overriding.

The crucial question is whether any of these interpretations rules out moral requirement conflicts or dilemmas.

The most dangerous candidate is the first interpretation on which prima facie requirements are cancelled and are not real requirements at all. This would rule out moral requirement conflicts and dilemmas if it could be shown that, whenever moral requirements appear to conflict, one of them must be merely prima facie in this sense. However, there is no reason to accept this claim on this interpretation. Even if one moral requirement is overridden, it need not be cancelled, and it can retain some force, since it can justify moral residue. This shows that moral requirements can conflict without either being merely prima facie in this sense.

The second interpretation is that merely prima facie requirements are not cancelled and are real, but this still leaves two possibilities: they might be overridden or just not overriding. If a requirement is merely prima facie only when it is overridden, then moral dilemmas would be ruled out if opponents could show that one moral requirement in every apparent conflict must be merely prima facie. However, this claim is not justified on this interpretation. Neither Ross nor any of his followers shows that one moral requirement must be overridden in every conflict. And I argued above that some conflicting moral requirements are equal or incomparable, so neither is overridden. So this interpretation does not rule out moral dilemmas.

On the other hand, if a requirement is merely prima facie whenever it is not overriding, then one moral requirement in every conflict must be merely prima facie, since they cannot both be overriding. However, this does not exclude the possibility that neither conflicting moral requirement is overridden, and this is all that is necessary for moral dilemmas on my definition.

The same point applies to the final, disjunctive interpretation. If even some moral requirements are merely prima facie simply because they are not overriding, then moral dilemmas on my definition are possible even if one moral requirement in every conflict must be merely prima facie. Thus, none of these interpretations of 'prima facie' rules out the possibility of all moral requirement conflicts or dilemmas.[36]

3.8 *SIMPLICITER* AND *SECUNDUM QUID*

A final approach is associated with such prominent philosophers as Aquinas, von Wright, Geach and Donagan.[37] These philosophers emphasize a distinction between two kinds of perplexities: *simpliciter* and *secundum quid*. This distinction by itself cannot rule out moral dilemmas, but some opponents go on to try to use this distinction to refute or at least defuse the possibility of moral dilemmas.

A situation is a perplexity *secundum quid* if and only if the situation arises or is a moral dilemma only because the agent did something wrong or was at fault. In contrast, a situation would be a perplexity *simpliciter* if it were a moral dilemma that neither arose nor was a moral dilemma because of any wrong or fault of the agent. Opponents who adopt this approach deny that any perplexity *simpliciter* is possible. These opponents do admit that perplexities *secundum quid* are possible, but they claim that this possibility either does not show that moral dilemmas are possible or does show that the possibility of moral dilemmas is not important.

Aquinas adopted this approach in response to three examples given by St Gregory.[38] In one example, a priest wrongfully bought a cure of souls, and there is a moral requirement for him not to exercise this wrongful authority. But there is also a moral requirement for him not to desert his flock. And he cannot help but violate one of these requirements. This situation is supposed to be a perplexity *secundum quid*, because the conflict arose from his prior wrongdoing. Aquinas admits that situations like this are possible, but he claims that they do not show any inconsistency in the moral code that implies the conflicting moral requirements.

The strange thing is that this already admits that moral dilemmas are possible. Defenders of moral dilemmas can admit that many moral dilemmas are the fault of the agent, but this does not make them any less moral dilemmas. An agent in a perplexity *secundum quid* still has to choose between conflicting moral requirements, and it does not make the choice any easier to point out that the agent is at fault. Furthermore, the difference between perplexities *simpliciter* and *secundum quid* seems irrelevant to consistency. If the judgements that define a moral dilemma are consistent when the agent is at fault, the same judgements must also be consistent when the agent is not at fault. It still might be inconsistent to put these judgements together with the judgement that the agent did nothing wrong (as von Wright will argue), but this would not show any inconsistency in the defining judgements themselves.

This approach still might be right about its second claim: that perplexities *simpliciter* or faultless moral dilemmas are not possible, because they reveal an inconsistency in the moral code that implies them. Inconsistency can simply be defined so that it is introduced by perplexities *simpliciter* but not *secundum quid*.[39] However, this would not show that perplexities *simpliciter* are not possible unless any moral code with this special kind of consistency must be false or unacceptable. Thus, this approach needs an argument that, whenever an agent is in a moral dilemma, it must be false or unacceptable to deny that the agent did something wrong.

One such argument is given by von Wright. The basic idea is

that it is wrong to do what ensures that you will do something wrong, but you cannot avoid doing something wrong in a moral dilemma, so it is wrong to do anything that gets you into a moral dilemma, and every agent in a moral dilemma did something to get into that dilemma (even if only the negative act of not committing suicide). Von Wright presents this argument more formally when he derives '$[O(A \rightarrow (B_vC))$ & $O - B \& O - C] \rightarrow O - A$' as a theorem in his deontic logic. He paraphrases this formula as 'An act which commits us to a choice between forbidden alternatives is forbidden.'[40]

It is undeniable that this formula is derivable in von Wright's system. However, the derivation depends on the agglomeration principle, and I will argue below that this principle is not valid on any interpretation that rules out moral dilemmas. Even if this formula is accepted, it is not clear how to interpret it. It might imply that every agent in any moral dilemma must have violated a moral requirement or a non-overridden moral requirement or an overriding moral requirement. Von Wright's argument might show that there is always some moral requirement to avoid moral dilemmas,[41] but there might still be overriding reasons to do what brings the dilemma about. For example, doctors, military commanders and parents can avoid many moral dilemmas by not becoming doctors, commanders or parents, but there might be overriding moral reasons to accept such positions even knowing that they can and usually do lead to moral dilemmas. Finally, even if every agent in a moral dilemma did something that violated a moral requirement, because it 'committed' her to in some sense to moral dilemma, this still does not show that the agent was at fault for the dilemma, since she might not have been able to avoid the moral dilemma. For example, Sophie could have avoided her moral dilemma if she could have escaped the Germans, so she did do something (namely, fail to escape) that got her into her moral dilemma. However, she could not escape, because she did not know how. Even if she could escape, she did not know this moral dilemma would arise. Thus, the moral dilemma was not her fault. This shows that von Wright's argument does not rule out all perplexities *simpliciter*.

Another argument against perplexities *simpliciter* comes from Donagan. Donagan gives principles that are supposed to allow perplexities *secundum quid* but not perplexities *simpliciter* in the case of promising. He writes, 'The fundamental principle is that *it is morally wrong to make a promise unless you can keep it and it is morally permissible for you to keep it.*' Donagan admits that, even if a promisor believes that he can and may keep a promise, this belief often turns out to be false, so 'By itself, this principle would be self-defeating.' Donagan tries to solve this problem by substituting a second principle: '*most promises are made and accepted on the twofold condition that the promiser has acceptable reason to believe that he can and may do what he promises, and that if it nevertheless turns out that he either cannot or may not, the promisee will not be entitled to performance.*' Another problem then arises because the promisee might not accept the promisor's reason for believing he can and may keep his promise, but 'this difficulty is resolved by a third principle: that *it is wrong for a promiser to make a promise on any condition on which he does not believe the promisee to understand him to make it.*'[42] These principles are supposed to imply that, when promises conflict, either it was wrong for the promisor to make one of the promises or one of the promisees is not entitled to performance. If the promisee is not entitled to performance, there is no moral requirement to keep the promise. Thus, Donagan's principles seem to show that moral requirements conflict only when it is the agent's own fault, because he made a wrongful promise.

There are several problems with this attempt, but the most important is that it is not clear exactly when a promise *may* be kept in the sense of the principles. Suppose I promise to speak to each of two groups at different times. I have very good reasons to believe that the two groups never meet at the same time and that they also believe this and believe that I believe it. Unfortunately, each speech is later rescheduled for the same time. Neither speech or promise is more important than the other. If I may do whatever violates no *overriding* moral requirement, I both can and may speak to each group and keep each promise. But then even Donagan's principles do not show that it was wrong of me to make the promises or that either group is not entitled to my performance.

Donagan would probably respond that neither group is entitled to my performance. To get this result, Donagan would have to rewrite his second principle so that the promisee is not entitled to performance when this would violate a *non-over-ridden* moral requirement. However, this modified principle is much less plausible. It implies that neither promisee is entitled to performance, but then it is not clear why it would be wrong to break *both* promises. Furthermore, each promisee does seem entitled to performance when no stronger moral reason requires me to break my promise. This can again be shown either by counterfactuals in my definition of moral requirements or by justified moral residue. Finally, Donagan needs to give some independent reason to accept his principles. His only argument is that his principles are needed to avoid perplexities *simpliciter*, and such perplexities introduce inconsistency, because a contradiction can be derived from the definition of moral dilemmas. I will criticize his derivations in later chapters, but, even if they did work, they would rule out not only perplexities *simpliciter* but also perplexities *secundum quid*, since the judgements that are supposed to imply the contradiction would be true in both kinds of perplexity. This takes the whole point out of his principles.

A final problem with this attempt is that promising is a special case. Promissory obligations arise through mutual agreement and depend on previous actions and conventions. There seems to be no way to extend Donagan's principles to other kinds of moral requirements, such as requirements not to cause death or pain or to help your parents. But these other kinds of moral requirements create many moral dilemmas that are not the agent's fault. I discussed Sophie above, and Sartre's student was not at fault for the war with Germany or his mother's needs. Such cases make it implausible to deny the possibility of perplexities *simpliciter*.

Even though both parts of this approach fail, the main distinction is still important. Blame is appropriate in some perplexities *secundum quid*, but it is unfair to blame the agent in a perplexity *simpliciter*. Remorse is sometimes appropriate for the act in a perplexity *simpliciter*, but it is not appropriate for other people to blame or condemn an agent for violating a moral requirement when her act was justified and it was not her fault that she fell into the moral dilemma. The fact that the agent is not blameworthy or condemnable does not show that moral requirements do not conflict, or that the situation is not a moral dilemma, or that any kind of inconsistency is involved. Nonetheless, whether the agent is at fault or blameworthy does affect the way the agent should be judged and treated after the moral dilemma, and maybe even the kind of sacrifice that can be required of the agent in the dilemma. Thus, as with the intentions of the agent, it is important whether the agent was at fault for the dilemma. This might explain why some philosophers have emphasized the distinction between perplexities *simpliciter* and *secundum quid*, even though this distinction does not refute the possibility of moral dilemmas.

Similar points apply to any argument that moral dilemmas cannot occur because of anything about the virtues. Some philosophers have argued that an act that is virtuous cannot also be vicious. For example, an act of injustice cannot also count as an act of charity. However, even if this is so, each alternative can still violate a non-overridden moral requirement. Some theorists have gone so far as to claim that all moral theory should be based on virtues and vices, but their theories are incomplete if they do not refer to moral requirements at some point, so they cannot avoid all moral requirement conflicts and dilemmas. Nonetheless, this doctrine about virtue is still important because it shows that the agent in a moral dilemma need not have any vice in order to act as he does. This affects the way the agent should be judged and treated after the moral dilemma. It also makes it easier to defend the possibility of moral dilemmas when their possibility does not imply that the agent is vicious or has a vice. Thus, questions of virtue and vice, like questions of blame, intention and fault are important, but they must be distinguished from the question of what violates a moral requirement in order to understand moral conflicts and dilemmas.

4

The Argument from ' "Ought" Implies "Can" '

Even though opponents cannot plausibly avoid all moral dilemmas, other arguments still might show that moral dilemmas are impossible. The two main arguments attempt to derive a contradiction from the definition of a moral dilemma. If a contradiction could be derived, no situation could fit the definition or be a moral dilemma. And since every plausible moral theory yields some moral dilemma, every plausible moral theory would imply some contradiction. This would make moral theory impossible and would lead to extreme moral scepticism or even nihilism.

In order to avoid this result, I need to refute every argument that moral dilemmas are impossible. I cannot discuss every argument, but I will respond to the two main arguments in this chapter and the next.

The two main arguments against the possibility of moral dilemmas will be called the argument from ' "ought" implies "can" ' and the argument from 'ought and ought not'. My response to each argument is complex, but my main points are that each argument depends on two confusions. The first confusion is between a semantic and a conversational implication. The first argument succeeds only if 'ought' semantically implies 'can', and the second argument succeeds only if 'ought' semantically implies 'permitted'. However, I will argue that 'ought' only conversationally implies 'can' and 'permitted', and only in certain contexts. The second confusion is between overriding moral requirements and non-overridden moral requirements. Each argument uses a premise that is true for overriding moral reasons but not for non-overridden moral reasons. When these confusions are removed, these arguments fail to refute the possibility of moral dilemmas.

4.1 FORMULATIONS

Because the argument from ' "ought" implies "can" ' attempts to derive a contradiction from the definition of moral dilemmas, its exact formulation depends on how moral dilemmas are defined. The standard definition defines moral dilemmas by what an agent ought to do, so opponents usually present the argument in terms of what an agent ought to do.[1] The argument then runs as follows. A moral dilemma would be a situation where an agent ought to adopt each of two alternatives separately and cannot adopt both together. If an agent ought to adopt each of two alternatives, the agent also ought to adopt both alternatives. But 'ought' implies 'can', so, if the agent cannot adopt both alternatives, it is not true that the agent ought to adopt both alternatives. The basic point is that an agent in a moral dilemma would not be able to satisfy all of his or her moral requirements, but this is supposed to be unfair.

This argument can be formalized if we let 'O' stand for 'morally ought' and let '$\Diamond$' stand for 'can' (as analysed in chapter 1), and view these terms as operators on action sentences represented by 'A' and 'B'. The argument then runs as follows:

(1) OA	the standard definition of
(2) OB	moral dilemmas
(3) $-\Diamond$ (A&B)	
(4) (OA&OB) $\rightarrow$ O(A&B)	the agglomeration principle
(5) O(A&B)	from (1), (2) and (4)
(6) O(A&B) $\rightarrow \Diamond$ A&B	'ought' implies 'can'
(7) $-$O(A&B)	from (3) and (6) by *modus tollens*
(8) O(A&B) & $-$O(A&B)	from (5) and (7)

(1), (2) and (3) formalize the standard definition of moral dilemmas. (4) is an instance of the agglomeration principle, which claims that, if an agent ought to do each of two things separately, the agent ought to do both of those things together. (6) formalizes an instance of the principle that 'ought' implies 'can' where what the agent ought to do and can do is adopt both alternatives. The argument is valid, and (8) is a contradiction.

Thus, the standard definition of moral dilemmas does imply a contradiction if the agglomeration principle holds and if 'ought' implies 'can'.

The argument is not changed much if my definition of moral dilemmas is substituted for the standard definition. Just replace 'ought' with 'there is a moral requirement' or 'O' with 'R' throughout the above argument. The result shows that my definitions of moral dilemmas and even of moral requirement conflicts imply contradictions, if agglomeration holds for moral requirements, and if moral requirements imply 'can'.

Some opponents of moral dilemmas admit that moral requirement conflicts are possible, so they have to deny either agglomeration for moral requirements or that moral requirements imply 'can'. However, they can still substitute weaker principles about non-overridden moral requirements. Simply replace 'ought' with 'there is a non-overridden moral requirement' throughout the above argument. The resulting argument applies to moral requirement conflicts only if they are unresolvable and thus moral dilemmas.

Whichever formulation is considered, there are two main responses. Defenders of moral conflicts and dilemmas can deny the agglomeration principles that 'ought to do each' implies 'ought to do both' and that 'there is a (non-overridden) moral requirement to do each' implies 'there is a (non-overridden) moral requirement to do both.'[2] Another response is to deny that 'ought' and 'there is a (non-overridden) moral requirement' imply 'can' in any way that is strong enough for the argument.[3] I will consider both of these responses, beginning with the latter.

4.2 'Ought' Implies 'Can'

The argument against moral dilemmas has usually been aimed at the standard definition in terms of 'ought', so the crucial claim in the argument has been that 'ought' implies 'can'. However, if moral dilemmas are defined by moral requirements, the crucial claims are that 'there is a moral requirement' and 'there is a non-overridden moral requirement' imply 'can'. Most of those who claim that 'ought' implies 'can' also accept these parallel claims about moral requirements, as well as similar claims about duties and obligations. However, some could claim that 'ought' implies 'can' but deny that moral requirements, duties, and obligations imply 'can', even if they are not overridden.[4] If this approach is defensible, then, even if the argument from ' "ought" implies "can" ' did refute the possibility of moral dilemmas on the standard definition, no similar argument could refute the possibility of moral dilemmas on my definition. Thus, in order to defend the possibility of moral dilemmas on my definition, all I need to show is that 'there is a moral requirement' and 'there is a non-overriden moral requirement' do not imply 'can'.

Nonetheless, the principle that 'ought' implies 'can' is more common, and I do want to defend the possibility of moral dilemmas even on some interpretations of the standard definition. For these reasons, I will focus on the claim that 'ought' implies 'can' and argue that 'ought' does not imply 'can' in any way that is strong enough to refute moral dilemmas. I will later show that my main points apply even more clearly to moral requirements.

It is crucial to distinguish different possible relations between 'ought' and 'can'. The relation is supposed to be an implication, but there are many kinds of implication. I will discuss four kinds of implication, although even finer distinctions could be drawn. The kind of implication that holds between 'ought' and 'can' determines the truth value of a judgement that an agent ought to do something when the agent cannot do it.[5]

The most common interpretations of the claim that 'ought' implies 'can' are semantic. An implication is semantic if it holds by virtue of the meanings of the terms or the truth conditions of judgements with the terms. There are many semantic relations but the two main ones are entailment and presupposition. The difference lies in whether it is false that an agent ought to do what he cannot do. If 'ought' entails 'can', then, for any agent and any alternative,

(OEC) If an agent cannot adopt an alternative, then it is *false* that the agent ought to adopt the alternative.

In contrast, if 'ought' presupposes 'can', then

(OPC) If an agent cannot adopt an alternative, then it is *neither true nor false* that the agent ought to adopt the alternative.[6]

The third possibility is that the principle that 'ought' implies 'can' is not semantic but is instead a universal substantive moral principle. The relation can then be called a moral implication. On this interpretation,

(OMC) If an agent cannot adopt an alternative, then it is *false* that the agent ought to adopt the alternative.

This principle must be universal in order to yield the usual conclusions, and it might even be necessary. But what distinguishes moral implication from entailment is that, if 'ought' morally implies 'can', it is not contradictory but only false to judge that an agent ought to do something but cannot do it. Despite such differences, what unites the first three relations is that, if 'ought' entails, presupposes or morally implies 'can', it can never be true that an agent ought to do what he or she cannot do.

The fourth relation is conversational implication. This relation is not semantic but pragmatic, because it concerns the intended or actual effect of saying what is said. If 'ought' conversationally implies 'can', then

(OCIC) If the agent cannot adopt an alternative, then it is *pointless* to say that the agent ought to adopt the alternative.

The crucial difference between this relation and the first three is that, even if 'ought' conversationally implies 'can', it still might be *true* that the agent ought to do something when the agent cannot do it. This judgement can be true even if it is pointless for a given purpose to say so.

I will argue that the relation between 'ought' and 'can' is neither a semantic entailment nor a presupposition nor a moral implication, because it is sometimes true that an agent ought to do what he cannot do. I will then argue that 'ought' does sometimes conversationally imply 'can'. This weak relation will explain the tendency to believe that 'ought' implies 'can' in some stronger way, since it is easy to confuse the various relations. However, if 'ought' only conversationally implies 'can', it can be true that an agent ought to adopt both alternatives in a moral dilemma even though the agent cannot adopt both. This will show that the argument from ' "ought" implies "can" ' does not refute the possibility of moral dilemmas.

4.2.1 Fallacious arguments that 'ought' implies 'can'

I will begin by criticizing four arguments which often lead people to claim that 'ought' implies 'can'. Not everyone who claims that 'ought' implies 'can' states these arguments explicitly, but these mistakes seem to be at the back of many opponents' minds.

First, 'ought' is supposed to entail or presuppose 'can', because, when agents know that they cannot do what they ought to do, they often ask what they ought to do instead. For example, if a bride cannot get to her wedding, then she ought at least to let someone know and to excuse her absence. However, the fact that she ought to do such *other* things does not change the fact that she ought to go to her wedding. On the contrary, if it were not first true that she ought to go to her wedding, she would have nothing to excuse when she failed to go to her wedding. Excuses are distinguished from justifications in that to justify an act is to show that it is right, whereas to excuse an act is to admit that it is wrong but to deny responsibility.[7] Excuses are, then, appropriate only for what ought not to have been done. However, if someone confuses excuses with justifications, he or she might deny that one ought not to do what one has an excuse for doing. Some such confusion might explain why some people think that 'ought' implies 'can'.

Another common argument that 'ought' implies 'can' is that we do not blame agents for failing to do acts which they could not do, so it is not true that the acts ought to have been done. No such conclusion follows. The premise is about *agents*, but the conclusion is about *acts*. And there are many cases where something ought to be done even though the agent would not be blameworthy for failing to do it, because it is not the agent's fault that she fails to do what she ought to do. For example, suppose a doctor is scheduled to perform an operation tonight, but a terrorist will take her hostage as soon as she leaves her home. She will not be blameworthy for failing to do the operation, but the only reason to deny that she ought to do the operation is that 'ought' implies 'can', and that begs the question, since this is supposed to be an argument for 'ought' implies 'can'. Furthermore, even if the conclusion did follow, the premise is false. We do blame agents for failing to do what they could not do if it is their own fault that they could not do it. For example, we blame drunk drivers for not avoiding crashes which they could not avoid because they got themselves drunk. Similar mistakes occur in arguments concerning the question of when an agent is condemnable, punishable, etc. An opponent might respond that we blame, condemn and punish these drunk drivers for getting drunk, but not for not avoiding the accident.[8] I admit that we blame them for getting drunk, but that is not all we blame them for. When we blame them, we say things like 'You should not have run that old man down' and not just 'You should not have got drunk.' And if two drivers are equally drunk, but one has an accident, we punish the one who has the accident more than the one who does not. And we punish the drunk driver at least as much as a sober driver who has a similar accident. The best explanation of these practices is that, even though there is some blame for getting drunk, there is additional blame for having an accident while you are drunk. Thus, we do blame people for failing to do what they could not do, so the present argument fails to show that 'ought' implies 'can'.

Third, it is sometimes argued that 'ought' must imply 'can' because saying that agents ought to do what they cannot do is pointless and therefore not true. This argument is not valid. The premise concerns the *point* or *purpose* of saying something, but the conclusion concerns the *truth* of what is said. What is said might be true even when saying so could not serve any purpose. Furthermore, the premise is false, since it is not always pointless to say that agents ought to do what they cannot do. Saying this might be pointless as advice, and it might seem that the purpose of saying what the agents ought to do is always to advise them to do it, at least in contexts where 'ought' is followed by a present infinitive and the agents are addressed.[9] However, 'ought' can be used for different purposes in different contexts. For example, the purpose of saying that agents ought to have done what they did not do is not to advise them to do it, since they have already missed the chance. Nonetheless, such uses of 'ought' with a past tense infinitive might serve *another* purpose, such as to blame the agents. And it might be justifiable to blame agents for not doing what they could not do if it is their own fault that they could not do it. Even if not, such judgements can at least be used to express justified attitudes towards what was done. Thus, this argument also fails to show that 'ought' implies 'can'.

Finally, some opponents argue that 'ought' implies 'can' simply by giving an example where the fact that an agent cannot do something seems to be a reason to deny that the agent ought to do it. For example, the fact that Jones has no money is a reason to deny that Jones ought to give money to charities. The simplest response is that such examples beg the question. However, it must be admitted that 'cannot' does seem to be a reason to deny 'ought' in some cases. Nonetheless, it is a hasty generalization to conclude that 'ought' implies 'can'. No single case or type of case can show that 'ought' implies 'can', because ' "ought" implies "can" ' is a universal claim. Those who deny that 'ought' implies 'can' can admit that 'cannot' is sometimes a reason to deny 'ought'. They need to explain why this is a reason in some cases but not others, but they can explain this by citing substantive moral truths that some limited kinds of judgements with 'ought' are not true when the agent cannot do what ought to be done. For example, it might be true that moral ideals lose their force when the agent cannot do what they recommend, even if this is not true of all moral requirements. Some such limited principles can hold even if 'ought' does not universally imply 'can'. Thus, arguments from individual examples also fail to show that 'ought' implies 'can' in the relevant way.

4.2.2 Against entailment

So far I have only criticized arguments for the claim that 'ought' implies 'can'. I will now argue directly against that claim by showing that it is sometimes true that an agent ought to do what he cannot do. If so, 'ought' neither entails nor presupposes nor morally implies 'can'. For simplicity, I will discuss entailment first and then extend my argument to presupposition and moral implication.

Many arguments could be given against the claim that 'ought' entails 'can'. I ought to stop myself from laughing at my friend's new haircut, since it will hurt him deeply, but I just can't stop myself. If I visit a foreign country but fail to learn the customs, I might not know how to avoid insulting my host, but I ought not to insult him. I ought to have finished mowing the grass before Monday, since I promised, but it is already Tuesday, so I cannot now have finished mowing the grass before Monday.[10] Instead of multiplying such examples, I will discuss one in detail.

My example shows that, if 'ought' entailed 'can', an agent could escape having to do something simply by making himself unable to do it.[11] Suppose Adams solemnly promises at noon to meet Brown at 6.00 p.m. but then goes to a film which starts at 5.00 p.m. Adams knows that, if he goes to the film, he will not be able to meet Brown on time. But he goes anyway, simply because he wants to see the film. The cinema is 65 minutes away from the meeting place, so after 4.55 it is too late for Adams to keep his promise. Consequently, if 'ought' entailed 'can', it would not be true at 5.00 that Adams ought to meet Brown at 6.00. Similarly, if Adams is still at the cinema at 6.00, he cannot then meet Brown at 6.00. Consequently, if 'ought' entailed 'can', it would not be true at 6.00 that Adams ought to meet Brown at 6.00.

However, these consequences are counterintuitive. If Adams calls Brown from the cinema at 6.00, it would be natural for Brown to say, 'Where are you? You *ought* to be here (by now)', even though Brown knows Adams *cannot* be there now. Brown's statement seems true, because Adams did promise, the appointment was never cancelled, and the obligation is not overridden. Thus, there is no reason to deny Brown's statement except to save the dogma that 'ought' entails 'can', and that would beg the question. Furthermore, if Adams calls at 5.00 and tells Brown that he is at the cinema, Brown might respond, 'Why haven't you left yet? You ought to meet me in an hour, and it takes more than an hour to get here from the cinema.' Again, Brown's statement seems natural and true, and there is no reason to deny it except to save the claim that 'ought' entails 'can'. Therefore, we must give up the claim that 'ought' entails 'can'.

A common response to such temporal examples is to index 'ought' to times and then to claim that judgements that an agent ought to do something are true only at times when the agent can do it.[12] My example would not refute 'ought' entails 'can' if the judgement that Adams ought to meet Brown at 6.00 were true until but not after the time (4.55) when Adams no longer can meet Brown at 6.00. I agree that such temporal indexing is useful elsewhere and does avoid some other counter-examples to 'ought' implies 'can'. Nonetheless, temporal indexing is not enough to save ' "ought" entails "can" ' from my arguments. I argued that it is still true at 5.00 and even at 6.00 that Adams ought to meet Brown at 6.00, and these are times when Adams cannot meet Brown at 6.00. This shows that 'ought' does not entail 'can' even if 'ought' is indexed to times.

Another response is to admit that Adams ought until 6.00 p.m. to meet Brown but still claim that 'ought' entails 'could have'.[13] However, this claim is too weak to satisfy traditional defenders of ' "ought" implies "can" '. ' "Ought" entails "could have" ' allows that, if Adams plans to meet Brown, but his car is stolen, so he cannot meet Brown, he still ought to meet Brown, since Adams could have parked where the car would not have been stolen. But it is not Adams' fault that he cannot meet Brown, so most defenders of ' "ought" entails "can" ' would deny that after his car is stolen Adams ought to meet Brown. The principle might be qualified so that the agent must also *know* what is necessary and sufficient to do what ought to be done. Adams does not know that parking elsewhere is necessary for him to meet Brown. However, this still will not satisfy many traditional defenders of ' "ought" entails "can" '. In any case, this principle cannot rule out all moral dilemmas, since the agent often did not know what was necessary to avoid the moral dilemma or to be able to adopt both alternatives in it.

The most important point is that a variation of the previous example refutes ' "ought" entails "could have" ' and also provides a still stronger argument against ' "ought" entails "can" ', even with temporal indexing. Suppose Adams knows at noon that his car will not be available, so he will not be able to meet Brown at 6.00. Nonetheless, in order to lead Brown astray, Adams promises at noon to meet Brown at 6.00. In this new example, there is no time at all when Adams can meet Brown as promised. Thus, if 'ought' did entail 'can' or even 'could have', Adams *never* ought to meet Brown.

This is counterintuitive, because it suggests that whether Adams promises to meet Brown makes no difference at all to whether he ought to meet Brown. However, his promise *does* make such a difference. If Adams makes no promise, he has nothing to excuse. But if he does make a promise, an excuse is owed or at least not inappropriate. Similar remarks apply to some apologies, compensation and other moral residue. This is not merely because he has an *obligation* to keep his promise but because he *ought* to keep it. Adams's obligation is not cancelled or overridden, so there is no reason to deny that he ought to fulfil his obligation except that he cannot fulfil it, but that begs the question. Also, Adams owes an excuse not merely for *making* the promise. He has no excuse for that. The excuse is owed for not *keeping* the promise. Indeed, if it were not first true that Adams ought to keep the promise, then there would be no reason why Adams ought not to make the promise.

Furthermore, if Adams unexpectedly becomes able to meet Brown on time, because a helicopter arrives, then Adams ought to meet Brown. But it would be at least odd for this to become true if Adams never ought to meet Brown before the helicopter arrived. Obligations can come into existence as circumstances change, but it would be odd for someone else to make it true that Adams ought to meet Brown simply by arriving in a helicopter and making Adams able to meet Brown, if it were never true before then that Adams ought to meet Brown.[14] In order to escape such difficulties, I conclude that 'ought' does not entail 'can'.

One final response would be to grant that my counter-examples show that *one* sense of 'ought' does *not* entail 'can' but still to claim that *another* sense of 'ought' *does* entail 'can'. A similar move can be made to escape any argument against any entailment. Even if I argue for the obvious claim that 'father' does not entail 'married', an opponent can claim that one sense of 'father' does not entail 'married' but another sense of 'father' still entails 'married'. However, such moves are not plausible unless there is enough independent reason to distinguish the supposedly different senses. In the case of 'ought', it begs the question to claim that 'ought' must have two such senses, because it sometimes entails 'can' and sometimes does not. 'Ought' is used for different speech acts in situations where the agent cannot do what he ought to do, but this difference in speech acts does not prove any difference between senses of 'ought'. Terms do not change their meanings every time they are used for different speech acts. In the absence of any better reason to distinguish such senses of 'ought', it is simpler and better not to multiply the senses of 'ought' but to hold instead that 'ought' has a single sense which never really entails 'can', but only seems to entail 'can' in contexts where it conversationally implies 'can'. I will develop that view below, and this will leave no escape from the conclusion that 'ought' does not entail 'can'.

It is easy to extend these arguments to moral requirements. It is still true at 5.00 and even at 6.00 that Adams has an obligation to meet Brown. Since obligations are a kind of moral requirement, it is still true at 5.00 and 6.00 that there is a moral requirement for Adams to meet Brown. If this were not true, it would be hard to see why Adams ought to meet Brown, why he owes an excuse for not keeping his promise, etc. And the moral obligation and requirement are not overridden. Thus, such examples also show that 'there is a moral requirement' and 'there is a non-overridden moral requirement' do not entail 'can'.[15]

4.2.3 Against presupposition and moral implication

Even though 'ought' does not entail 'can', opponents might retreat to the weaker claims that 'ought' presupposes 'can' or morally implies 'can'.[16] However, my arguments refute these weaker claims as well. If 'ought' either presupposed or morally implied 'can', it could never be true that an agent ought to do what he cannot do. But the above arguments show that it is sometimes true that an agent ought to do something that he cannot do.

Furthermore, there are special problems with the claim that 'ought' presupposes 'can'. If 'ought' presupposed 'can', not only could it not be true, but it also could not be *false* that an agent ought to do what cannot be done. But it can be false. If there is no reason at all for Smith to jump over the moon, then it is false that Smith ought to do so, since it would not be true even if Smith could jump that high. An opponent might respond by denying that Smith ought not to jump over the moon. However, this denial does not imply that it is not false that Smith ought to jump over the moon, since it might be false both that he ought and that he ought not to jump over the moon. Some such confusion of 'ought not' with 'false that ought' probably explains the mistake of claiming that 'ought' presupposes 'can'.

Similar points apply to moral requirements. If there is no relevant fact about jumping over the moon that could provide a moral reason to jump over the moon, then it is false that there is a moral requirement to jump over the moon even though the agent cannot do so. And then it is also false that there is a non-overridden moral requirement. But if these judgements are false in this situation, they cannot presuppose 'can'. Thus, 'there is a moral requirement' and 'there is a non-overridden moral requirement', like 'ought', neither entail nor morally imply nor presuppose 'can'.

4.2.4 For conversational implication

Although the relation between 'ought' and 'can' is neither entailment nor presupposition nor moral implication, there still seems to be some relation, so I need to explain what it is. I will now argue more positively that the relation between 'ought' and 'can' is a conversational implication.

The notion of a conversational implication was developed by H.P. Grice. Grice first introduces what he calls 'the cooperative principle': 'Make your conversational contribution such as is required, at the stage at which it occurs, by the accepted purpose or direction of the talk exchange in which you are engaged'.[17] The conditions of following the cooperative principle are specified further by conversational maxims. The relevant maxim here is that of relation, which says simply 'Be relevant'.[18] Grice defines conversational implication in terms of the cooperative principle and conversational maxims:

> A man who, by (in when) saying (or making as if to say) that *p* has implicated that *q*, may be said to have conversationally implicated that *q*, *provided that*: (1) he is to be presumed to be observing the conversational maxims, or at least the cooperative principle; (2) the supposition that he is aware that, or thinks that *q*, is required in order to make his saying or making as if to say *p* (or doing so in *those terms*) consistent with this presumption; and (3) that the speaker thinks (and would expect the hearer to think that the speaker thinks) that it is within the competence of the hearer to work out, or grasp intuitively, that the supposition mentioned in (2) *is* required.[19]

In short, saying p conversationally implies q when (roughly) saying p for a certain purpose cannot be explained except by supposing that the speaker thinks that q and thinks that the hearer will think that the speaker thinks that q, etc. For example, if someone asks where a petrol station is and gets the response, 'Around the corner', then, assuming its purpose is to help the questioner find petrol, the response cannot be explained except by supposing that the respondent thinks that the station around the corner might be open and thinks that the questioner can work out that he thinks this, etc.

Grice provides several tests of whether such a relation holds. First, 'the presence of a conversational implicature must be capable of being worked out.'[20] It can be worked out if the hearer can give an argument from the fact that the speaker said that p to the fact that the speaker thinks that q, etc. Such arguments must use the cooperative principle and its maxims, the conventional meaning of the words used to say that p, and certain supposedly shared background knowledge. Second, 'a generalized conversational implicature can be cancelled in a particular case'.[21] A conversational implication can be cancelled if a speaker does not contradict himself when he says that p and implies that he does not believe that q. Grice provides other tests, but they need not detain us here.[22]

Before we can apply these tests to a particular type of utterance, we must determine its accepted purpose or purposes. Sometimes a single type of utterance is used for different purposes in different contexts, and the conversational implications of such utterances might vary along with their purposes. For example, an utterance of 'My husband is either in the kitchen or in the bedroom' for the purpose of helping the listener find the speaker's husband conversationally implies that the speaker does not know which room her husband is in. In contrast, an utterance of the same disjunction for the purpose of playing a guessing game does not imply such ignorance.

In order to test whether 'ought' conversationally implies 'can', we must determine the purposes of utterances using 'ought'. This task is complicated, since 'ought' can be used for many purposes. 'Ought' can be used to advise present action or to blame an agent for past acts or to plan for the future. This list of purposes is neither exhaustive nor exclusive nor precise, but I need to discuss only these three purposes. I will argue that 'ought' implies 'can' relative to some of these purposes but not others.

First, consider advising. Suppose Adams goes to the film knowing that, if he goes, he won't be able to keep his appointment with Brown at 6.00 p.m. At 5.55 he repents, but it is too late to meet Brown on time. Adams then asks Chang for advice. Adam asks, 'What ought I to do?'. Chang replies, 'You ought to meet Brown at 6.00 p.m. just as you promised.' This reply is odd because Adams cannot follow Chang's advice, so Chang's utterance cannot serve the purpose of advising. The purpose of advising is not merely to do an illocutionary or speech act of advising. Instead, the purpose of advising is the intended effect or perlocutionary force of an act of advising. Such intended effects can vary, but in some standard contexts, the intended effect cannot occur unless the advisee follows the advice. Hence, assuming Chang has such a purpose and is following the cooperative principle, we cannot explain Chang's advice except by supposing that Chang thinks somehow that Adams can meet Brown at 6.00 p.m. and that Chang thinks that Adams can figure out that she thinks this, etc. Thus, according to Grice's first test, Chang's use of 'ought' conversationally implies 'can'.

An opponent might object that, if Adams responds to Chang by saying, 'I can't do that', Chang will *withdraw* her previous judgement. However, she will *not deny* it. She will not say, 'Then it is not true that you ought to meet Brown.' Nor will Adams deny Chang's judgement. This suggests that Chang withdraws her judgement not because it is false but only because it cannot serve the purpose of advising.

Furthermore, the implication passes Grice's test of cancellability. Suppose Chang says, 'You still ought to meet Brown, but, since you can't, you at least ought to call him'. If 'ought' entailed 'can', this would be self-contradictory, but it is not. Chang is clearly invoking a secondary obligation without denying the primary one, so the implication can be explicitly cancelled. Since this case has no relevant peculiarities, I conclude that 'ought' generally conversationally implies 'can' when 'ought' is used for the purpose of advising.

Next, consider blaming. Suppose Adams goes to the film but plans to leave early and meet Brown as he promised. Unfortunately, Adams's car is stolen. Adams calls Brown at 6.00 p.m. and says, 'I can't meet you on time.' Before Adams can say that his car was stolen, Brown blames him by saying 'You really ought to be here. I missed a great opportunity in order to meet you, and it's your fault.' Brown's utterance with 'ought' does not imply that Adams can be there or keep his promise. Brown does not think that Adams can do either, since Adams has just told him otherwise. Hence, we cannot explain Brown's blaming Adams except by supposing that Brown thinks that it is Adams's own fault that he cannot be there. Otherwise, Adams would not be blameworthy, and some standard purposes or intended effects of blaming will not occur unless the agent is blameworthy. Thus, according to Grice's first test, 'ought' conversationally implies 'can or culpably cannot' when 'ought' is used to blame an agent.

Suppose Adams responds to Brown's blame by saying 'I planned to meet you, but my car was stolen.' Brown might withdraw his judgement that Adams ought to be there. However, this withdrawal is not due to falsity but to the inability of the judgement to serve the purpose of blaming.

Furthermore, this implication passes Grice's test of cancellability. Brown does not contradict himself if he says 'You still ought to be here, but it's not your fault that you can't, so I don't blame you.' Since this case has no relevant peculiarities, I conclude that 'ought' generally conversationally implies 'can or culpably cannot' when 'ought' is used to blame an agent.

Finally, if 'ought' only conversationally implies 'can', some purpose might provide a context in which the implication is absent in general. This is precisely the case with planning. Suppose Adams tells Davis that he is going to promise to meet Brown even though he will not be able to meet him. Davis then argues, 'You ought not to promise to meet Brown, since, if you (now) promise to meet him, then (it will be the case that) you ought to meet him, but you will not be able to meet him.' Davis's second use of 'ought' does not conversationally imply even 'can or culpably cannot'. Davis does not think that it will be the case that Adams can or culpably cannot meet Brown. Such thoughts need not be supposed in order to explain why Davis says what she says for the purpose of planning, which here is to minimize future failures to do what ought to be done. Also, if Adams responds that it will not be his fault that he cannot meet Brown, then Davis will not withdraw, much less deny, what she said. Such uses of 'ought' are admittedly imbedded within both a conditional and the future tense, and such contexts are not expected to preserve conversational implications. Nonetheless, the point is that 'ought' can be used in contexts where it does not conversationally imply even 'can or culpably cannot'.

In sum, 'ought' has different conversational implications when it is used for different purposes. Some of the main purposes and implications can be tabulated as follows:

	purposes	*implications*
1	advising	'can'
2	blaming	'can or culpably cannot'
3	planning	neither of the above

This variety of conversational implications does not imply that 'ought' has various senses, but the cases where 'ought' does conversationally imply 'can' do explain why 'ought' sometimes seems to entail or presuppose 'can' when it really does not.

The same points apply to moral requirements. If I tell someone that he has an obligation or a duty to do something, and I am advising him, then my utterance conversationally implies that he can do it, because otherwise it would be pointless to say so. However, if I utter the same judgement when I am blaming him or planning for the future, then my utterance need not conversationally imply that he can do it. These conversational implications still hold when I say that the obligations and duties are not overridden. Since duties and obligations are kinds of moral requirements, 'there is a moral requirement' and 'there is a non-overridden moral requirement' also conversationally imply 'can' in some contexts but not others.

4.2.5 Application to moral dilemmas

What does this show about moral dilemmas? The original argument against moral dilemmas on the standard definition used the principle that 'ought' implies 'can' to argue that, since the agent in a moral dilemma cannot adopt both alternatives, it cannot be true that the agent ought to adopt both. This would follow if 'ought' entailed or presupposed or morally implied 'can'. However, I have shown that none of these relations holds. I have argued instead that 'ought' conversationally implies 'can'. This implies that it is often pointless to say that an agent in a moral dilemma ought to adopt both alternatives, and it might also be unfair to say this in order to blame the agent (unless it was her own fault that she got into the dilemma or she made her choice with a bad motive or intention). However, it can still be true that the agent ought to adopt both alternatives. Thus, it is not valid to argue from the premise that the agent cannot adopt both alternatives to the conclusion that it is not true that the agent ought to adopt both alternatives. Without this step, the argument from 'ought' implies 'can' fails to prove that moral dilemmas on the standard definition are not possible.

The argument against moral dilemmas on my definition suffers the same defect. Since 'there is a moral requirement' and 'there is a non-overridden moral requirement' neither entail nor presuppose nor morally imply 'can', the fact that the agent cannot adopt both alternatives does not show that there is not a (non-overridden) moral requirement to adopt both alternatives. 'There is a (non-overridden) moral requirement' does still conversationally imply 'can', so it is often pointless to tell the agent that there is a (non-overridden) moral requirement to adopt both alternatives, but this judgement can still be true. Thus, no argument along these lines can refute the possibility of moral dilemmas on either definition.

4.3 THE AGGLOMERATION PRINCIPLE

Since 'ought' does not semantically or morally imply 'can', the argument from 'ought' implies 'can' would not refute the possibility of moral dilemmas, even if the agglomeration principle were valid. Nonetheless, it is still important to determine whether agglomeration holds. One reason is that there are other arguments against the possibility of moral dilemmas that depend on the agglomeration principle. We will see one in the next chapter. Another reason is that we need to know which moral judgements are true in a moral dilemma, and the agglomeration principle determines whether the agent ought to adopt both alternatives in a moral dilemma. Thus, in order to understand and defend moral dilemmas fully, we need to determine whether the agglomeration principle is valid.

Williams was one of the first to reject the agglomeration principle, and he gave several arguments against it. His main arguments were based on analogies between moral terms and non-moral terms. He claims, first, that agglomeration fails for desires or wants: 'Marrying Susan and marrying Joan may be things each of which Tom wants to do, but he certainly does not want to do both.' He then adds that agglomeration fails for certain terms of non-moral evaluation: 'It may be *desirable*, or *advisable*, or *sensible*, or *prudent* to do *a*, and again desirable, or advisable etc. to do *b*, but not desirable etc. to do both *a* and *b*.'[23] Williams seems to give these analogies as evidence that agglomeration also fails for moral uses of 'ought'.

There are two main problems with this argument. First, it is not clear that agglomeration fails for all of the non-moral terms that Williams lists. In the case of wants or desires, a defender of agglomeration could argue that the most natural reason to deny that Tom desires to marry both Susan and Joan is that Tom has stronger desires not to have two wives (for social, legal, or economic reasons). But this shows only that he desires not to marry both. It does not show that he does not desire at all to marry both. Someone can have some desire for something even when he desires something else more. For example, someone can desire to eat ice cream even if he more strongly desires to lose weight. Similarly, Tom can have some desire to marry both Susan and Joan, even though he more strongly desires not to have two wives. But if Tom has even a weak desire to marry both Susan and Joan, then Williams's example fails to refute agglomeration for desires or wants.

It is clearer that agglomeration fails for some of Williams's other non-moral evaluative terms. However, some of his analogies are misleading. 'Sensible' is more analogous to 'morally permitted' than to 'morally ought' or 'morally required', and nobody claims that agglomeration holds for 'morally permitted'. 'Desirable', 'advisable' and 'prudent' also seem open to interpretations parallel to permission. Thus, until more complete analyses are given, such analogies cannot show that agglomeration fails for the relevant judgements in moral dilemmas.

Even if agglomeration fails when these terms are analysed so as to be more analogous to 'ought', the analogies are still not exact. 'Ought' might differ from desires and evaluations in some respects which make 'ought' obey agglomeration even though the other terms do not. The analogies are forceful because these other terms refer to the kinds of fact that count as reasons why someone ought to do something, so what people want and what is advisable, etc., are often relevant to what someone ought to do. Williams adds that anyone who holds that these terms 'are evaluative because they entail "ought" statements will be under some pressure to reconsider the agglomerative properties of "ought" '.[24] However, even if this did show that 'ought' does not obey agglomeration, there still might be something about moral contexts which makes 'morally ought' obey agglomeration. Thus, no such argument from analogy can prove that the moral judgements in moral dilemmas fail to obey an agglomeration principle. Williams's arguments might give some evidence against agglomeration for 'morally ought', and this might be all that Williams wants to claim, but the only way to be more definitive is to look directly at moral cases.

I will argue that whether agglomeration holds for 'morally ought' depends on how 'ought' is interpreted. The three main interpretations of 'ought' imply that an agent ought to do what there is a moral reason to do or a non-overridden moral reason to do or an overriding moral reason to do. Correspondingly, the agglomeration principle might claim that

> (AMR) If there is a moral reason to do A,
>   and there is a moral reason to do B,
>   then there is a moral reason to do both A and B.
> (ANOMR) If there is a non-overridden moral reason to do A,
>   and there is a non-overridden moral reason to do B,
>   then there is a non-overridden moral reason to do both A and B.
> (AOMR) If there is an overriding moral reason to do A,
>   and there is an overriding moral reason to do B,
>   then there is an overriding moral reason to do both A and B.

These claims must be tested separately, because one might be true even if the others are not.

There are many arguments against (AMR). Some counter-examples arise if we allow the agent who ought to do A to be different from the agent who ought to do B. In such cases, it is not even clear what 'ought to do both' could mean. Who ought to do both? However, this problem can be avoided simply by restricting the principle to a single agent. This restriction does not affect the argument against single agent moral dilemmas, although it does show that no such argument can rule out interpersonal moral dilemmas. Other common counterexamples depend on the claim that 'ought' implies 'can'. 'Can' does not obey agglomeration, since often an agent can adopt each of two alternatives but cannot adopt both. If he then ought to do each, and 'ought' implies 'can', agglomeration fails. However, I have just shown that 'ought' does not imply 'can'. Even if it did, such examples would beg the question against opponents of moral dilemmas.

Other counterexamples are harder to escape. The force of these examples can be brought out by my account of moral reasons (although they are independent). As I said, a moral reason to adopt (or not to adopt) an alternative is or is provided by a fact that the alternative has certain properties or consequences, such as that it fulfils a promise (or is a lie) or that it prevents (or causes) harm. Agglomeration then fails because the consequences of doing each of two acts separately can be different from the consequences of doing both acts together. Even if A has a good consequence (prevents a harm), and B also has a good consequence (prevents the same or another harm), it still does not follow that A and B together have any good consequence. For example, if I talk to Farida in my office at 3.00 p.m., this will prevent her from failing the test tomorrow; and if I talk to Steve in my office at 3.00 p.m., this will prevent him from failing the test tomorrow; but if I talk to both of them together in my office at 3.00, this will confuse them both and will not prevent either from failing the test (or prevent any other harm). If the only time when I can talk to either of them is 3.00, then I have a moral reason to talk to Farida in my office at 3.00 p.m., and a moral reason to talk to Steve in my office at 3.00 p.m. but no moral reason at all to talk to both of them in my office at 3.00 p.m., assuming that I have no other moral reason, such as a promise or a professional duty, to meet them both at 3.00.[25]

Such examples stand alone, but I would like to add some speculations about why they work. Their force becomes clearer if we specify exactly which facts are or provide moral reasons. Part of my moral reason to meet Farida at 3.00 is that meeting her at 3.00 is *necessary* to prevent her failing the test. If Farida and I could also meet at 4.00, and if this would also prevent the harm, then I would have no moral reason to meet her at 3.00, since this would not be necessary, but I would still have a moral reason to meet her at either 3.00 or 4.00, if no other time were possible. Meeting her at 3.00 also might be necessary to prevent some other harm, such as breaking a promise to meet her at 3.00, and then I would have a moral reason to meet her at 3.00. Nonetheless, if the only relevant harm is her failing the test, then I have a moral reason to meet her at 3.00 only if meeting her at 3.00 is necessary to prevent that harm.

But necessity is not enough. I would not have any moral

reason to meet Farida if meeting her would not prevent or at least reduce the danger of her failing or some other harm. Meeting her need not be sufficient in itself, but there is no reason to meet her unless this is *part* of some larger course of action that is *sufficient* in the circumstances to prevent or reduce the chance of some harm. And if meeting her at 3.00 will be useless unless I meet her again at 8.00, but I cannot meet her at 8.00, then I have no reason to meet her at 3.00. So I must be able to do or bring about the other parts of what is sufficient to reduce the chance of harm. For simplicity, I will say something is not part of anything sufficient *in the circumstances* unless the agent can adopt the other parts of what would be sufficient. There is then a moral reason to adopt an alternative (to meet Farida at 3.00) only if adopting it is both necessary and part of something that is sufficient in the circumstances to prevent or reduce the danger of some harm.

This explains why I have no moral reason to meet both Farida and Steve together. Meeting them both might be necessary in order to prevent both failing, since there is no other way to help them both. However, meeting both Farida and Steve together is not part of anything that is sufficient in the circumstances to prevent or even reduce the danger of both or either failing (or of my breaking any promise, professional duty, etc.). Thus, there is no moral reason to meet them both together. I have no more reason to meet both together than I would have to drive to a shop that I know is closed, simply because that is the only place to buy what I want. This explains why agglomeration fails in such examples.

Some opponents might object that this conflicts with my arguments that 'ought' does not imply 'can'. If there is no reason to meet Farida unless this is part of something sufficient to help her, there might seem to be no reason to help her unless something is sufficient to help her, and then I can help her. However, this confuses what would be sufficient with what an agent can do. In my counterexamples to the principle that 'ought' implies 'can', there was something that would be sufficient by itself and in the circumstances for Adams to meet Brown and to keep his promise. It *would* be sufficient if Adams went to the meeting place on time. The problem is that Adams *cannot* do this. In my counterexample to agglomeration, I *can* meet Farida and Steve together, but this is *not* part of anything sufficient in the circumstances to help either. It is part of something (the conjunction of meeting both and helping both) which would be sufficient, but I cannot do the other part (helping both), so meeting Farida and Steve together is not sufficient in the circumstances to help either. Thus, the agent in this case can do something, but it is not sufficient in the circumstances; whereas my counterexamples to the principle that 'ought' implies 'can' were cases where something would be sufficient by itself and in the circumstances, but the agent cannot do it. Thus, my counterexamples to agglomeration work without reviving the principle that 'ought' implies 'can'.

Another response might be that talking to Farida is not sufficient in the circumstances to prevent her failing if I talk to her together with Steve, so what I have a moral reason to do is not just to talk to Farida but to talk to Farida *without Steve* (or even alone). However, it is still true that talking to Farida is part of any course of action that will help her, and that talking to Farida is part of some course of action that will help her, so talking to Farida is both necessary and part of something sufficient in the circumstances to help her. That is what gives me a reason to talk to her. I also have a moral reason to talk to her without Steve, but this does not conflict with or take away my reason to talk to her and to do it at 3.00. Furthermore, even if I had no reason to talk to Farida but only to talk to her without Steve, this would not save agglomeration. If I have a moral reason to talk to Farida without Steve at 3.00, I also have a moral reason to talk to Steve without Farida at 3.00, but there is no moral reason to talk both to Farida without Steve at 3.00 and to Steve without Farida at 3.00, since this is contradictory, so it cannot prevent any harm. Thus, this example would still refute agglomeration for moral reasons.

Similar examples arise from moral reasons apart from consequences. Suppose I promise to talk to Farida alone at 3.00 p.m., but I forget, and I also promise to talk to Steve alone at 3.00 p.m. I have a moral reason to talk to Farida alone at 3.00, because this is necessary and sufficient to fulfil a promise, and I have a similar moral reason to talk to Steve alone at 3.00, but I have no moral reason to talk at 3.00 to both Farida alone and Steve alone (even if this were possible) since this would not fulfil either promise.

Additional counterexamples arise from the closure principle which I will defend in the next chapter. This closure principle claims that I have a moral reason not to do what would prevent me from doing what I have a moral reason to do. Suppose an agent makes conflicting promises, so that keeping one would prevent him from keeping the other. The agent then has a moral reason not to keep the first promise (R – A), because keeping the first promise would prevent him from keeping the second promise. The agent also has a moral reason not to keep the second promise (R – B), because keeping the second promise would prevent him from keeping the first promise. However, the agent does not have any moral reason to keep neither promise (– R – (A$_v$B)), or to break both (– R(– A& – B)), since this alternative would accomplish nothing. Thus, agglomeration for moral reasons fails again.

The second agglomeration principle (ANOMR) is also invalid. This principle claims that, if there are non-overridden moral reasons for each of two alternatives, there are non-overridden moral reasons for both together. However, the moral reasons in all of my previous examples might be non-overridden, but there is still no reason at all to adopt both alternatives together. Furthermore, even if the moral reason for each alternative is not overridden, and even if there is some reason to adopt both alternatives together, this reason for the conjunction still might be overridden. This can happen if the conjunction of the alternatives has harmful consequences or violates a moral rule, even though neither alternative alone has these consequences or violates this moral rule. For example, Sophie has a moral reason not to pick her first child and a moral reason not to pick her second child, and neither of these reasons is overridden. She also might have some moral reason to pick neither child, since this will prevent the pain that each child will feel if either is picked. However, this reason is overridden by the fact that the guard will kill both children if she refuses to pick either child. Thus, she has non-overridden moral reasons for each alternative (for not picking each) but only an overridden moral reason for both alternatives together (for picking neither). A similar example occurs if a man has non-overridden moral reasons to marry each of two women, but moral reasons against bigamy override any moral reason to marry both (even if this is legally possible). Such examples show that the agglomeration principle fails when 'ought' refers to non-overridden moral reasons.

Nonetheless, the third agglomeration principle (AOMR) seems valid. The previous principles failed only in examples where the moral reasons for each alternative conflict. However, the reasons in the antecedent of (AOMR) cannot conflict, because each must be overriding, and conflicting moral reasons cannot each be overriding. This protects (AOMR) against any counterexamples like those to (AMR) and (ANOMR). And when there are overriding moral reasons to adopt each alternative, these reasons do not conflict, so the conjunction of these moral reasons does seem to be an overriding moral reason to adopt both alternatives together.

There is also a general argument that no example could refute (AOMR). The only kind of example that could refute (AOMR) would be one where there is a moral reason to adopt a first alternative because it prevents some harm (or keeps a promise, etc.), and similarly for a second alternative, and these reasons are overriding. There then seem to be only two ways there could fail to be an overriding moral reason to adopt both alternatives together. The first is if adopting both together would not prevent either harm (or keep either promise, etc.). But then adopting the first alternative would prevent the agent from preventing the second harm or fulfilling the second reason, and vice versa, so the two reasons would conflict. The only other way there might fail to be an overriding moral reason to adopt both alternatives is if adopting both alternatives caused a larger harm (or broke a more important promise, etc.). But then the agent morally could not adopt both alternatives. Either way, the alternatives and the reasons for them conflict, so they cannot both be overriding, contrary to our hypothesis. And if the reasons for each alternative are not both overriding, the antecedent of (AOMR) is not true, so the example cannot refute (AOMR). This argument is not conclusive, but I conclude that agglomeration for overriding moral reasons (AOMR) is valid. Even if this is wrong, it will not affect my defence of moral dilemmas.

In sum, the agglomeration principle fails for moral reasons in (AMR) and for non-overridden moral reasons in (ANOMR), but agglomeration is still valid for overriding moral reasons in (AOMR). Parallel claims also apply to moral requirements, since the above examples can use moral requirements.

What about 'ought'? If 'ought' is interpreted in terms of moral reasons or non-overridden moral reasons, agglomeration fails for 'ought'. But if 'ought' is interpreted in terms of overriding moral reasons, agglomeration for 'ought' is valid. This explains why agglomeration for 'ought' seems valid in many contexts but fails in contexts of moral dilemmas, where the essential judgements concern non-overridden moral requirements.

This shows that no agglomeration principle can refute the possibility of moral dilemmas. When moral dilemmas are defined by non-overridden moral requirements, the only applicable agglomeration principles are for moral reasons or requirements and non-overridden moral reasons or requirements. Since these principles fail, no agglomeration principle can show that an agent in a moral dilemma has any moral requirement or even reason to adopt both alternatives together. And if moral dilemmas are defined in terms of 'ought', agglomeration also fails for any interpretation of 'ought' that is applicable to moral dilemmas. This leaves no reason to believe that an agent in a moral dilemma ought on any interpretation to adopt both alternatives together. Consequently, the argument from ' "ought" implies "can" ' could not refute the possibility of moral dilemmas even if 'ought' or non-overridden moral requirements did imply 'can'.

5

The Argument from 'Ought and Ought Not'

Even though the argument from ' "ought" implies "can" ' does not exclude the possibility of moral dilemmas, some other argument still might do so. The second main argument against the possibility of moral dilemmas can be called the argument from 'ought and ought not'. Various versions have been presented by McConnell, Hare and Conee.[1] I will argue that this argument also fails to refute the possibility of moral dilemmas.

5.1 FORMULATIONS

The argument from 'ought and ought not' tries to derive a contradiction from the definition of moral dilemmas, so its exact formulation depends on how moral dilemmas are defined. Moral dilemmas are usually defined by what an agent ought to do, so opponents usually present the argument in terms of 'ought'. The argument then has two basic parts. The first part shows that if an agent were in a moral dilemma, the agent both ought and ought not to adopt the same alternative (either one). The second part then claims that it is not possible that an agent both ought and ought not to adopt the same alternative.

More fully, the argument starts with the standard definition of a moral dilemma as any situation where the agent morally ought to adopt each of two alternatives separately but cannot adopt both together, or where

(1) OA

(2) OB

(3) $- \diamondsuit$(A&B).

The next step applies a principle of closure which claims that an agent morally ought not to do anything which prevents him from doing something that he morally ought to do. This closure principle can be symbolized as

(4) $[OA \ \& \ - \diamondsuit(A\&B)] \rightarrow O-B.$

(1), (3) and (4) imply that the agent morally ought not to adopt the second alternative, or

(5) $O-B.$

(2) and (5) can now be conjoined into the judgement that the agent both ought and ought not to adopt the second alternative, or

(6) OB & $O-B.$

The first part of the argument concludes that some judgement of the form of (6) must be true in any moral dilemma.

(6) strikes many people as nonsense or impossible, and its negation is a theorem of standard deontic logic, so one way to finish the argument would simply be to claim that (6) and thus moral dilemmas are not possible. However, this would beg the question, so the argument from 'ought and ought not' needs a second part to show that no judgement like (6) can be true.

I will discuss several such arguments, but one main argument uses the claim that 'ought' implies 'permitted', that is, if an agent ought to adopt an alternative, then the agent is permitted to adopt the alternative, or

(7) OB $\rightarrow$ PB

where 'PB' stands for 'B is permitted'. (7) is supposed to be obvious, and it is a theorem in standard deontic logic. The problem is that 'permitted' is usually defined as 'not ought not', and this implies that, if an agent is permitted to adopt an alternative, it is not true that the agent ought not to adopt the alternative, or

(8) $PB \rightarrow -O-B$.

(7) and (8) then imply

(9) $OB \rightarrow -O-B$

and, by the propositional calculus, (9) implies

(10) $-(OB \ \& \ O-B)$

which contradicts (6). The argument is valid, so no situation can fit (1) to (3) or be a moral dilemma if (4), (7) and (8) are true for all values of 'A' and 'B'.

The argument is not changed much if the standard definition of moral dilemmas is replaced by my definition. Just replace 'ought' with 'there is a moral requirement', or 'O' with 'R', throughout the above argument. The result shows that my definitions of moral dilemmas and even of moral requirement conflicts imply a contradiction *if* the replacements of (4), (7) and (8) are true for all values of 'A' and 'B'.

Some opponents of moral dilemmas admit that resolvable moral requirement conflicts are possible, so they must deny that the replacement of (4), (7) or (8) is valid for all moral requirements. Nonetheless, they can still defend weaker principles and construct a parallel argument against moral dilemmas on my definition simply by replacing 'ought' with 'there is a non-overridden moral requirement' throughout. Qualifications can be added at various places, and I will discuss some variations below, but the basic form of the argument remains the same.

All of these arguments leave two main ways to escape the conclusion that moral requirement conflicts and dilemmas are impossible. First, defenders of moral dilemmas can deny the principles of closure, such as (4) and its replacements. This escape is rare, even though many have expressed doubts about the relevant principles of closure.[2] The second main response is that 'ought and ought not' and its relatives are possible.[3] Those who adopt this approach must deny (9) and its replacements along with either (7) and its replacements or (8) and its replacements.

The defence that is adopted determines which judgements are true in moral dilemmas. If 'ought' is not closed under 'can', it will not be true in every moral dilemma that the agent both ought and ought not to adopt the same alternative. But this will be true in every moral dilemma if 'ought' is closed under 'can'. Defenders of moral dilemmas will then have to show how this odd judgement can be true. They will also have to determine whether the agent is permitted to adopt each alternative and, as we will see, whether the agent ought both to adopt and not to adopt the same alternative. Thus, in order to understand and defend moral dilemmas fully, we need to consider both main responses. I will begin with the denial of closure.

5.2 CLOSURE

Principles of closure are assumed in many common moral arguments. If I ought to cook and serve you dinner, I ought to cook you dinner. If I ought to cook you dinner, and I cannot cook you dinner without turning on a stove, I ought to turn on a stove. If I ought to cook you dinner (at 5.00), I ought to cook a meal (before 7.00). And so on. Such arguments are very common, but they are rarely discussed. Each of them assumes some principle of closure.

A principle of closure specifies that truth is preserved when one sentence is substituted for another sentence within the scope of an operator if the two sentences are related in the proper way. Such principles can also be called principles of extensionality or substitutability. Different principles of closure apply to different operators and require different relations for sentences to be substitutable.

The closure principle that is relevant to my definition of moral dilemmas warrants substitution within the scope of non-overridden moral requirements. However, the argument from 'ought and ought not' is usually directed against the standard definition of moral dilemmas, and I want to defend the possibility of moral dilemmas on some interpretations of the standard definition. So I will focus on closure for 'ought', but I will show later that my conclusions apply as well to moral requirements.

Different closure principles require different relations between action sentences in order to substitute one for another within the scope of the moral operator. I will consider two possible relations and the two corresponding principles.

The weakest principle is that 'ought' is closed under logical implication. This principle claims that, if one action sentence logically implies another, the latter can be substituted for the former within the scope of '(morally) ought'. This closure principle can be symbolized as

(COL) $\boxed{L}(A \rightarrow B) \rightarrow (OA \rightarrow OB)$

where '$\boxed{L}$' stands for logical necessity. To claim that 'ought' is closed under logical implication is to hold that (COL) is true for all values of 'A' and 'B'.

A stronger principle is that 'ought' is closed under 'can'. This means that, if an agent cannot adopt a first alternative without adopting a second alternative, then, if the agent morally ought to adopt the first alternative, the agent morally ought to adopt the second alternative. Symbolically,

(COC) $- \diamondsuit (A \& -B) \rightarrow (OA \rightarrow OB)$

or, equivalently, the premise of the argument from 'ought and ought not':

(COC*) $[OA \ \& \ - \diamondsuit (A \& B)] \rightarrow O-B.$[4]

To claim that 'ought' is closed under 'can' is to claim that these principles are true for all values of 'A' and 'B'.

The first part of the argument from 'ought and ought not' must use (COC) rather than (COL). In standard moral dilemmas, it is logically possible for the agent to adopt both alternatives, even though the agent cannot adopt both. For example, it is logically possible for Sophie to save both children, since it is logically possible for her to fly them out of the Nazi camp. Although far-fetched, this logical possibility is important, because it shows that the moral dilemma arises only because of contingent circumstances.[5] It also shows that (COL) is not enough to derive 'ought and ought not' in every moral dilemma.

Nonetheless, it is important to discuss (COL). One reason is that we understand (COC) better if we contrast it with (COL). Another reason is that an agent cannot do what is logically impossible, so (COC) is not valid unless (COL) is also. Third, one of the alternative arguments for (10) and against 'ought and ought not' will use (COL). For these reasons, I need to determine not only whether (COC) is valid but also whether (COL) is valid.

I will argue that both (COL) and (COC) are valid. For each principle, I will show that it is useful and plausible, and then I will respond to the main objections. I need not and will not try to determine whether these closure principles are semantic or substantive or necessary, since they are enough for the argument from 'ought and ought not' if they are universally true.

There are also many other closure principles for 'ought'. In particular, closure of 'ought' under act identity would claim that, if two descriptions refer to the same act, then, if the agent morally ought to do an act under the first description, the agent also morally ought to do an act under the second description. I will not discuss this principle here, because the alternatives in moral dilemmas often involve distinct actions, so closure under identity is not enough for any argument against the possibility of all moral dilemmas. Nonetheless, it should be clear how my defences of closure under logical implication and 'can' can be extended to such other principles of closure.

5.2.1 Closure under logical implication

As with other closure principles, the principle of closure under logical implication is assumed in many common moral arguments. Everyone assumes that, if I ought to keep my promise, I ought not to not keep it (or that $OK \rightarrow O--K$). And if I ought not to shoot you, I ought not to both shoot you and hit you ($O-S \rightarrow O-(S\&H)$). The most natural way to justify such arguments is with closure for 'ought' under logical implication (COL).

However, closure under logical implication seems to produce several paradoxes. I will discuss Ross's paradox, a Good Samaritan paradox, and a paradox of converse agglomeration. These three paradoxes display three common mistakes that lead people to deny closure under logical implication.

First, Ross's paradox.[6] Suppose Alf ought to mail a letter (OM). It is logically necessary that, if he mails the letter, he either mails it or burns it ($\boxed{L}(M \rightarrow (M_vB))$). Thus, if 'ought' is closed under logical implication, Alf ought either to mail the letter or burn it ($O(M_vB)$). However, it seems wrong to say that Alf ought either to mail the letter or burn it when what he ought to do is mail it. It also seems wrong to say that Alf fulfils an obligation if he burns the letter, but he would fulfil the disjunctive obligation. Thus, closure under logical implication seems to fail.

A defender of closure under logical implication can respond by using conversational principles to explain why such consequences seem wrong even though they are true. It is misleading in most conversations to make a weaker judgement when one can make a stronger one.[7] Thus, if a speaker believes the stronger judgement that Alf ought to mail the letter, it would be misleading to make only the weaker judgement that Alf ought either to mail the letter or burn it. It is also misleading to say only that Alf fulfils an obligation when he burns the letter, since this leaves out the relevant fact that he would fulfil a similar disjunctive obligation if he did not burn it. Nonetheless, it is still true that Alf ought to mail the letter or burn it, because, if Alf does what he ought to do (namely, mail the letter), then it will be true that he either mails the letter or burns it. Thus, closure under logical implication does not really fail in this case.

A more difficult paradox is the Good Samaritan paradox.

There are many versions, but one strong form was presented recently by Forrester.[8] The point of Forrester's paradox is to derive an absurdity from intuitively plausible assumptions using closure under logical implication. The first assumption is that, even though Smith ought not to murder Jones,

(1) If Smith murders Jones, he ought to murder him gently.

Nonetheless, suppose that (it will be true that)

(2) Smith does murder Jones.

(1) and (2) seem to imply

(3) Smith ought to murder Jones gently.

The problem is that

(4) It is logically necessary that, if Smith murders Jones gently, then Smith murders Jones,

so, if 'ought' is closed under logical implication, we can conclude that

(5) Smith ought to murder Jones.

This seems wrong. The fact that Smith does murder Jones should not make it true that he ought to murder Jones. Forrester concludes that we have to give up closure under logical implication.

However, this paradox can be resolved without giving up closure under logical implication if we distinguish various scopes of the operator 'ought'. These scopes are hidden in the paradox, because the action sentences are not analysed. Davidson argues that action sentences like (2) can be made true by any act that is a murder by Smith of Jones,[9] so (2) should be analysed as

(2a) (∃x) Mxsj

and the antecedent of (4), 'Smith murders Jones gently', then becomes

(4a) (∃x)(Mxsj & Gx).

(3) and the consequent of (1) can then be analysed either as

(3.1) O(∃x)(Mxsj & Gx)

or as

(3.2) (∃x)(Mxsj & OGx).

(3.1) claims that there ought to be some act that is a murder of Smith by Jones and is gentle, whereas (3.2) claims that there is an act that is a murder of Smith by Jones and it ought to be gentle. The crucial difference is that the scope of 'ought' in (3.1) includes the whole sentence that Smith murders Jones gently. This sentence does imply that Smith murders Jones, so (3.1) does yield the paradox. In contrast, the scope of 'ought' in (3.2) includes only the adverb 'gently', and this alone does not logically imply that Smith murders Jones, so (3.2) does not yield the paradox, even if 'ought' is closed under logical implication. And (3.2) is all that follows from (1) and (2) if (1) is analysed with (3.2) as its consequent, which is the only analysis that makes (1) true. We can then explain why (3) seems true: because (3) can be read as (3.2), and (3.2) is true. However, (3) yields the paradox only if (3) is read as (3.1), but (3.1) must be false, because it does yield the paradox. Thus, Forrester's paradox can be avoided without giving up closure under logical implication if we are careful about the scope of 'ought' and the logical form of action sentences. And other Good Samaritan paradoxes depend on similar scope confusions.

A third paradox involves the converse of the agglomeration principle. Suppose you are bedridden, and I promise to bring you a book from the library and then return it, so I ought to do both of these acts (O(B&R)). It is logically necessary that, if I both bring you the book and return it, I bring you the book (☐((B&R)→B)). Closure of 'ought' under logical implication then warrants the conclusion that I ought to bring you the book (OB). But suppose I know that, if I bring you a book, I never will return it. This makes it seem false that I ought to bring you the book (−OB). Thus, the closure of 'ought' under logical implication seems to fail.[10]

This paradox can be resolved by distinguishing various interpretations of 'ought' in terms of various strengths of moral reasons. If an agent morally ought to do whatever he has any moral reason to do, it is true that I ought to bring you the book, even though I know I will not return it, since there is a moral reason to do so, even if this moral reason is overridden by the moral reason not to borrow books without returning them. In contrast, if an agent morally ought to do only what he has overriding or non-overridden moral reasons to do, it is not true that I ought to bring you the book and return it, since my reason to do so is overridden by my moral reason not to borrow books without returning them.[11] There might be some special cases where my moral reason to bring you the book override my moral reasons not to borrow the book without returning it, such as if the book will save your life. But then it *is* true that I ought to bring you the book even though I know that I will not return it. As long as every occurrence of 'ought' is interpreted in the same way, 'ought' remains closed under logical implication in this case. The paradox arises only if various strengths of moral reasons are confused.

There are other paradoxes that might seem to refute closure under logical implication, but I cannot discuss them all. These three paradoxes display the main confusions that lead people to deny that 'ought' is closed under logical implication. If these confusions are removed, there is no reason to deny that 'ought' is closed under logical implication. And we saw that this principle is assumed in many common arguments. This makes it best to admit that 'ought' is closed under logical implication.

Similar arguments support the closure of moral requirements under logical implication. This principle claims that there is a moral requirement to adopt anything that is logically implied by something that there is a moral requirement to adopt, or symbolically.

(CRL) $\boxed{L}(A \rightarrow B) \rightarrow (RA \rightarrow RB)$.

Such inferences also seem true when the moral requirements are overriding and not overridden, since requirements that are derived by such principles seem to be just as strong as the requirements from which they are derived. Thus, similar principles can be defended for overriding and non-overridden moral requirements, so the relevant arguments would remain unaffected if my definition of moral dilemmas in terms of moral requirements were substituted for the standard definition in terms of 'ought'.

5.2.2 Closure under 'can'

Even though 'ought' is closed under logical implication, 'ought' still might not be closed under 'can'. Closure under 'can' is stronger and warrants more arguments than mere closure under logical implication. Consequently, closure under 'can' might seem more questionable.

As with closure under logical implication, some principle of closure under 'can' is assumed in many common moral arguments. For example, if I ought to buy some milk, and I cannot buy some milk without getting in my car and driving to the store, then I ought to get in my car and drive to the store. Similarly, if I ought to save my drowning child, and I cannot do so unless I stop reading my book, then I ought to stop reading my book.

These arguments cannot be justified merely by closure under logical implication, since it is not logically impossible for me to buy some milk without getting in my car or driving to the store or to save my drowning child without stopping reading my book. These arguments also cannot be justified by closure under identity (or parts), since my acts of getting in the car and driving to the store are not identical with (or even part of) any act of buying milk, and stopping reading my book is not identical with (or even part of) saving my drowning child. We need a stronger closure principle to warrant these arguments.

The principle behind such arguments seems to be that, if an agent ought to do something, but cannot do it without doing something else, then the agent ought to do the second thing. Symbolically,

(COC) $- \diamondsuit (A\&-B) \rightarrow (OA \rightarrow OB)$.

In some cases, the conclusion is that the agent ought *not* to do something. For example, if I ought to cook dinner, and I cannot both cook dinner and play golf (so playing golf would prevent me from cooking dinner), then I ought not to play golf. It is natural to symbolize this case as

(COC*) $[OA \& - \diamondsuit (A\&B)] \rightarrow O-B$.

A final case is where the *premise* is about what the agent ought *not* to do. For example, I ought not to cheat on my income tax, but I cannot post this (fraudulent) tax form without cheating on my taxes, so I ought not to post this tax form. The principle behind this argument seems to be that an agent ought not to do what is sufficient for something else that he or she ought not to do. This principle of negative closure can be symbolized as:

(COC**) $[O-A \& - \diamondsuit (-A \& B)] \rightarrow O-B$.

All of these formulations are equivalent, since each is supposed to hold for all values of 'A' and 'B', and they differ only in what counts as 'A' and 'B' and in logical transformations.

Although closure under 'can' is needed to warrant common arguments that seem valid, such principles still seem problematic. One odd feature is that closure under 'can' relates a moral operator to a non-moral operator. Further suspicions are raised because such closure takes us from a moral judgement about one action to a moral judgement about a different action.

Despite these general worries, the principle is still defensible if it holds in all cases. The most serious problem is that closure under 'can' seems to produce paradoxes. I will discuss four supposed counterexamples, and they will lead me to grant some minor restrictions, but I will defend the main thrust of closure under 'can' in moral dilemmas.

The first problem occurs when different agents interfere with each other. Suppose Ivan can save his wife's life only by giving her a certain medicine, and Joe has the same problem. Unfortunately, only one dose is available, and Joe obtains it fairly. Ivan ought to save his wife's life (OI) and he cannot save her unless Joe gives the medicine to Ivan for Ivan's wife ($-$ ◇ (I&$-$G)), so closure under 'can' seems to warrant the conclusion that Joe ought to give the medicine to Ivan for Ivan's wife (OG). However, this seems wrong because Joe got the medicine fairly, needs it, and has no special duties or obligations to Ivan or Ivan's wife. It is even stranger if Joe does not even know about Ivan or his wife.

A defender of closure under 'can' might respond that every agent has some moral reason to respect other agents' moral reasons and requirements, and neither reason might be overridden in this example, even though they cannot both be overriding. This response is necessary for the argument from 'ought and ought not' to rule out interpersonal moral dilemmas, but it is not necessary for the argument against single agent moral dilemmas. Since the latter are my main concern, I will simply assume henceforth that closure under 'can' applies only to judgements about a single agent.

Another problem occurs when a necessary condition of what ought to be done seems morally *neutral*. For example, I ought to pay my taxes (OT), and I cannot do so without opening the drawer that holds my tax records, and I cannot do that without moving some air molecules (or certain muscles in my hand) ($-$ ◇(T&$-$M)). Closure under 'can' then justifies the conclusion that I ought to move some air molecules (OM). However, it seems odd or even wrong to say that I ought to move some air molecules, since such acts do not seem to be the right kind of thing to be what morally ought or ought not to be done. They seem morally neutral.

It must be admitted that such consequences of closure are odd, but they can still be true. Their oddness can be explained by conversational principles. First, it is pointless or misleading to utter a weaker judgement when one can utter a stronger one.[12] The judgement that I ought to pay my taxes is stronger and more specific than the judgement that I ought to move some air molecules, since I can move air molecules in many ways, but only some of these count as paying my taxes (unfortunately). Thus, if a speaker believes the stronger judgement that I ought to pay my taxes, it would be misleading for him to say *only* that I ought to move some air molecules. Furthermore, it is also pointless and misleading to describe acts in ways that are irrelevant to the purpose of the conversation.[13] The purpose of many conversations about what I ought to do is to direct my actions or to help others determine whether I have done all that I ought to do. It is then pointless to say merely that I ought to move some air molecules, because this judgement does not specify *how* I ought to move them, so it cannot direct my actions or help others determine whether I have done *all* that I ought to do. A third reason why this judgement is misleading is that people are usually interested not only in what an agent ought to do but also in *why* he ought to do it. To say that I ought to move air molecules gives no clue about why I ought to do so. These violations of conversational principles explain why the conclusions drawn from the principles of closure seems odd. However, this explanation is purely pragmatic, so it allows the conclusions and the principle of closure to be true. In spite of how misleading it is to say so, it is still true that I ought to move some air molecules, because, if I do what I ought to do (namely, pay my taxes), then my act will move some air molecules. My act is not really neutral, even though the misleading way in which it is described makes it seem neutral. Thus, closure under 'can' does not fail in these cases.

A critic might point out that this principle applies even when the agent does not know that air molecules exist, but it is strange to say that an agent ought to move something that he does not know exists. I think the principle can be defended by distinguishing what there *is* a reason to do from what an agent *has* a reason to do because he knows the reason. What an agent ought to do is often determined by reasons that he does not know. For example, if a shop is about to close, and it is the only place that Joe can buy medicine that his wife needs, then Joe ought to leave soon, even if he does not know that the shop is about to close. If someone tells him that he ought to leave soon, this would not be false.

Although the principle can be defended in this way, it is not necessary for the argument against moral dilemmas. In the primary examples of moral dilemmas, the agent knows that she cannot adopt both alternatives, so she knows enough to reach a conclusion of the form 'ought and ought not' even if closure under 'can' is restricted to what the agent knows she cannot do. Consequently, most moral dilemmas would be subject to closure under 'can' even with this restriction, so I will avoid side issues by assuming this restriction henceforth.[14]

A third kind of counterexample to closure under 'can' is supposed to occur when a necessary condition of what ought to be done is morally *wrong*. Foot gives one example of this kind when she writes,

> Suppose, for instance, that some person has an obligation to support a dependent relative, an aged parent perhaps. Then it may be that he ought to take a job to get some money. . . . But what if the only means of getting money is by killing someone? . . . it is not the case that the son or daughter ought to kill to get the money.[15]

Foot claims it is not true that the child ought to kill someone ($-OK$), even though it is true that the child ought to get the money (OM), and also that the child cannot get the money without killing someone ($- \diamondsuit(M\&-K)$). She does accept that one ought to do what is a necessary means of doing what one ought to do, but she denies that killing someone would count as a means of getting the money, because killing is not a 'moral possibility' here, and means must be possible actions. Thus, her proposal is to reject closure under 'can' in favour of a weaker principle of closure under means.

The force of this example rests on the claim that it is not true that the child ought to kill to get the money. Foot never argues for this claim, but it is not obvious. Whether the child ought to kill depends on how 'ought' is interpreted. The most natural way to interpret 'ought' in this context is that an agent ought to do only that for which there is an overriding moral reason. On this interpretation, Foot is right that it is not true that the child ought to kill, since the reasons to kill are not overriding. However, on this interpretation, it is also not true that the child ought to get the money. The child has some moral reason to get the money, but this reason is overridden, because the moral reason not to kill is stronger, and these two reasons conflict, because the child cannot get the money without killing. Thus, the child does not have an overriding moral reason to get the money, so it is not true that the child ought to get the money on the present interpretation. The same response applies if 'ought' is interpreted in terms of non-overridden moral reasons, since the child's reason to get the money is overridden. Thus, Foot's example fails to refute closure under 'can', if 'ought' is interpreted in terms of either overriding or non-overridden moral reasons.

Another interpretation of 'ought' is that an agent ought to do whatever the agent has some moral reason to do, even if the reason is overridden. On this interpretation, it is true that the child ought to get the money, because the child has some moral reason to do so. However, it also seems true that the child has some moral reason to kill, namely, in order to get the money and help her parents. Consequently, the child ought to kill on this weak interpretation, so closure is again not refuted.

Foot might respond that there is not even an overridden moral reason to kill in this example. However, what plausibility this claim has can be explained away. It is easy to confuse various interpretations of 'ought'. The claim that the child ought to kill on the mere moral reason interpretation might seem false, even though it is true, because this claim is confused with the actually false claim that the child ought to kill on the overriding moral reason interpretation.

Even if this confusion is denied, a defender of closure under 'can' can use conversational principles to explain why it seems odd to say that the child ought to kill. It seems odd to say that the child ought to kill, because this judgement does not tell us why the child ought to kill. The description used in the judgement leaves out relevant information, so the judgement violates conversational rules of quantity and relevance. This violation explains why the judgement seems odd without giving up the claim that it is true. But the judgement must be false in order for the supposed counterexample to refute closure. So closure is not refuted.

The general point is that closure applies only when the alternative in the antecedent is incompatible with the negation of the alternative in the consequent. In such conflicts, there can be moral reasons and even non-overridden moral reasons for the alternative in the antecedent as well as for the negation of the alternative in the consequent, but these reasons cannot both be overriding. Cases like Foot's seem to cause problems because one reason overrides the other. It is then false that there is an overriding reason for the lesser alternative, but closure does not imply this. Closure does imply there is some moral reason for the lesser alternative, but this is true, even if it is odd to say so. Either way, closure holds as long as the level of reasons is kept constant throughout.

A final problem will force me to restrict the principle of closure further. When I argued that 'ought' does not entail 'can', I gave examples in which an agent ought to do something that he cannot do ($OA \ \& \ - \Diamond A$). But if the agent cannot adopt that alternative, the agent cannot both adopt that alternative and not adopt another alternative ($- \Diamond (A \& - B)$), regardless of what that other alternative is. Thus, if an agent ought to do what he cannot do, closure under 'can' warrants the conclusion that the agent ought to adopt another alternative (OB), regardless of what the other alternative is. In my example above, Adams cannot meet Brown at 6.00, so he cannot both meet Brown at 6.00 and not kill his children, and closure then implies that he ought to kill his children. Similar arguments show that he ought to tie his shoes and ought to not kill his children. Since these conclusions are absurd, anyone who denies that 'ought' implies 'can' must also deny closure under 'can' in the form that I have presented.

This problem is an instance of a common paradox of implication. The antecedent of closure depends on the formula '$-\Diamond(A\&-B)$' or some equivalent. '$A\&-B$' is equivalent to '$-(A\rightarrow B)$', so '$-\Diamond(A\&-B)$' is equivalent to '$-\Diamond-(A\rightarrow B)$', and this is equivalent to '$\boxed{C}(A\rightarrow B)$', if '$\boxed{C}$' is defined as '$-\Diamond-$'. This transformation suggests that the problem for closure does not arise because of anything peculiar or essential to moral operators but only because a material conditional '$\rightarrow$' is true whenever its antecedent is false or its consequent is true. It is often appropriate to solve such paradoxes of implication by adding restrictions to the antecedent.

Similarly, the unacceptable consequences of closure can be avoided by adding a requirement that the agent can do and avoid doing what he ought to do. The restricted version of closure then claims

$$(\text{RCOC}) \; [\Diamond A \; \& \; \Diamond-B \; \& \; -\Diamond(A\&-B)] \rightarrow (OA \rightarrow OB)$$

or, equivalently,

$$(\text{RCOC}^*) \; [OA \; \& \; \Diamond A \; \& \; \Diamond B \; \& \; -\Diamond(A\&B)] \rightarrow O-B.^{[16]}$$

This move might seem ad hoc, but it is justified by my arguments above that 'ought' does not imply 'can'. Furthermore, the most natural way to state closure in English is to say that an agent ought not to do what would prevent him from doing what he ought to do. But if he already cannot do what he ought to do, doing something else could not *prevent* him from doing what he ought to do. An act can prevent him from doing what he ought to do only if he could do what he ought to do if he did not do the other act. Finally, this restriction will not affect any of the common arguments that apply closure under 'can'. In all of those examples, the agent can do what he ought to do. Thus, closure is still well motivated even when it is restricted.

The restricted principle of closure is also supported by my previous speculations about moral reasons. I said that there is a moral reason to adopt an alternative only if adopting it is both necessary and part of something sufficient in the circumstances to prevent or reduce the danger of some harm (or of breaking a promise, etc.). Part of the reason to adopt the alternative is that it is necessary to prevent a harm, and whatever is necessary for the alternative is also necessary to prevent the harm, so there is so far a similar reason to do whatever is necessary for the original alternative. This is what closure claims before it is restricted.

The restriction on closure is then justified by the other part of the reason to adopt the alternative, namely, that it is part of a larger course of action that is sufficient in the circumstances to prevent or reduce the danger of some harm (or failure to keep a promise, etc.). For example, even if I promise to mow the lawn, and I cannot mow it without starting the mower, there is still no reason to start the mower if the only gate to the lawn is locked, so I will not be able to use the mower to mow the lawn even if I do start it. Starting the mower is part of a larger conjunction (starting the mower and mowing the lawn) which would fulfil the promise, but the circumstances make me unable to adopt the additional part (mowing the lawn), so starting the mower is not part of anything sufficient in the circumstances to mow the lawn, and this is why there is no reason to start the mower. It still might be true that I ought and have a reason to mow the lawn, since this would be sufficient to keep my promise if I could do it, but this is different from and does not imply any reason to do what I can do but would not be sufficient in the circumstances. The basic idea is that there is a chain from what one has a basic reason to do (to keep the promise) to other alternatives that one has a derived reason to do (to mow the lawn and usually to start the mower), but the chain is broken and the derived reasons cease as soon as one runs into an obstacle that one cannot cross (the locked gate). These speculations explain why closure has to be restricted. There is no reason to do anything that would accomplish nothing even if one could do it. And this restriction would be implicit in closure even if 'ought' did imply 'can'.

In the absence of further counterexamples, I conclude that the restricted principle of closure under 'can' is defensible. I have not proved this principle. It is always possible that other objections might be raised, and the principle might have to be restricted further.[17] However, something like this principle of closure is needed for many common arguments, and any principle of closure that is strong enough to warrant the common arguments that seem valid will probably also be strong enough for the argument from 'ought and ought not'.

Similar versions of closure are defensible for moral requirements. Closure of moral requirements under 'can' claims that, if an agent has a moral requirement to adopt an alternative, and the agent cannot adopt that alternative without also adopting another alternative, then the agent also has a moral requirement to adopt the other alternative. A restriction like that above is needed because moral requirements do not imply 'can'. When restricted, the closure of moral requirements under 'can' can be defended in essentially the same way that I defended closure of 'ought' under 'can'. And the same goes for non-overridden and overriding moral requirements.

Even if such closure is not valid, this will only make it *easier* to defend moral dilemmas. The problem arises if such closure is admitted, since this makes it possible in every moral dilemma to derive judgements that the agent both ought and ought not to adopt each alternative. The restrictions do not block the derivation in any moral dilemmas, because I defined moral dilemmas so that there is always a single agent who knows enough relevant facts and act descriptions and who can adopt each alternative separately. Similarly, closure of (non-overridden) moral requirements under 'can' warrants judgements in every moral dilemma that there is a (non-overridden) moral requirement to adopt and also a (non-overridden) moral requirement not to adopt each alternative. These judgements might describe the alternatives in strange and misleading ways, but the judgements will still be true. Consequently, defenders of the possibility of moral dilemmas cannot escape the first part of the argument from 'ought and ought not'.

5.3 'OUGHT' IMPLIES 'PERMITTED'

Even if the relevant closure principles are granted, the argument from 'ought and ought not' still needs a second part. Closure shows that an agent in a moral dilemma both ought and ought not to adopt the same alternative, but this does not rule out moral dilemmas unless it is not possible that an agent both ought and ought not to adopt the same alternative. Opponents have given several arguments against this possibility. However, I will show that these arguments are faulty, so the argument from 'ought and ought not' cannot rule out moral dilemmas even if closure is granted.

The first argument against the possibility of 'ought and ought not', as given on pp. 137–8, uses the claim that 'ought' implies 'permitted'.[18] It runs as follows. If any agent ought to adopt any alternative, the agent is permitted to adopt it. But, if any agent is permitted to adopt any alternative, it is not true that the agent ought not to adopt it. Therefore, if any agent ought to adopt any alternative, it is not true that the agent ought not to adopt the alternative. Symbolically, the argument is that, for every value of 'B',

(7) $OB \rightarrow PB$
(8) $PB \rightarrow -O-B$
(9) $OB \rightarrow -O-B$
(10) $-(OB \ \& \ O-B)$

(7) claims that 'ought' implies 'permitted' and is a theorem in standard deontic logic. (8) follows from the standard definition of 'permitted' as 'not ought not'. (9) follows from (7) and (8), and (10) follows from (9). The argument seems valid, and the premises appear plausible.

This appearance disappears when the terms 'ought' and 'permitted' are analysed carefully. The argument is not valid unless it sticks to the same interpretations of 'ought' and 'permitted' throughout. However, I will show that there are no plausible interpretations of 'ought' and 'permitted' that make the argument sound. The argument then appears sound only if various interpretations of 'ought' and 'permitted' are confused.

The first term is 'ought'. As I have emphasized, the term 'ought' might be used so that an agent ought to adopt an alternative if and only if there is

(MR) a (possibly overridden) moral reason to adopt it,
(NOMR) a non-overridden moral reason to adopt it, or
(OMR) an overriding moral reason to adopt it.

Since 'permitted' is usually defined as 'not ought not', 'permitted' has three interpretations that correspond to (MR), (NOMR) and (OMR). An agent might be permitted to adopt an alternative if and only if there is

(PMR) no (possibly overridden) moral reason not to adopt
   it,
(PNOMR) no non-overridden moral reason not to adopt
   it, or
(POMR) no overriding moral reason not to adopt it.

Which of these interpretations is used determines what is wrong with the argument from ' "ought" implies "permitted" '.

If 'ought' refers to overriding moral reasons as on (OMR), the argument from ' "ought" implies "permitted" ' is sound if 'permitted' is interpreted by either (POMR) or (PNOMR), since, if there is an overriding moral reason to adopt an alternative, there cannot also be an overriding or even a non-overridden moral reason not to adopt the same alternative. So the conclusion, (10), is true. However, on (OMR), this conclusion claims only that it is not possible that there is an overriding moral reason to adopt the alternative and an overriding moral reason not to adopt the same alternative. Defenders of moral dilemmas can accept this conclusion, since, as I argued, they do not define moral dilemmas in terms of overriding moral reasons. The argument on this interpretation attacks a straw man.

In order to exclude the possibility of moral conflicts or

dilemmas as they are understood by their defenders, the argument must use 'ought' to refer either to (possibly over-ridden) moral reasons as on (MR) or to non-overridden moral reasons as on (NOMR). If the argument is sound on either of these interpretations, then moral dilemmas are not possible.

The weakest interpretation is (MR). On (MR), to claim that an agent both ought and ought not to adopt the same alternative is to claim that there is a moral reason to adopt the alternative and a moral reason not to adopt the same alternative. If this were not possible, not only moral dilemmas but even moral conflicts would be impossible.[19]

However, if 'ought' refers to (possibly overridden) moral reasons as on (MR), 'ought' does not imply 'permitted' on any plausible interpretation of 'permitted'. Even if an agent has a moral reason to do something, so he ought to do it on (MR), the agent can still have an overriding moral reason or requirement not to do it, but then he is not permitted to do it on (PMR), (POMR), or (PNOMR). Thus, the argument from ' "ought" implies "permitted" ' has a false premise and fails to rule out moral conflicts or dilemmas, if 'ought' refers to (possibly overridden) moral reasons as on (MR).

The final possibility is (NOMR). On this interpretation, to claim that an agent both ought and ought not to adopt an alternative is to claim that the agent has a non-overridden moral reason to adopt the alternative and a non-overridden moral reason not to adopt the same alternative. If this were not possible, as the conclusion, (10), claims, then moral conflicts might still be possible, but it would not be possible for any situation to be a moral dilemma on my definition.

However, at least one premise of the argument from ' "ought" implies "permitted" ' is false on this interpretation of 'ought'. Which premise is false depends on how the term 'permitted' is interpreted.

If both 'ought' and 'permitted' refer to non-overridden moral reasons, as in (NOMR) and (PNOMR), then 'PA $\rightarrow$ $-O-A$' is true, but 'OA $\rightarrow$ PA' is false. On this interpretation, 'PA $\rightarrow$ $-O-A$' follows from the standard definition of 'permitted' as 'not ought not', since 'ought' and 'permitted' are both interpreted in terms of non-overridden moral reasons. The other premise 'OA → PA' then claims that, if there is a non-overridden moral reason to adopt any alternative, there is no non-overidden moral reason not to adopt the same alternative. This is false in a moral dilemma, since then there are non-overridden reasons to adopt incompatible alternatives, and a reason to adopt one alternative is a reason not to adopt an incompatible alternative, because of closure. Thus, 'OA → PA' is not always true if moral dilemmas are possible. But it begs the question to assume moral dilemmas are not possible in an argument against the possibility of moral dilemmas. And all of my arguments above that moral dilemmas are possible also show that 'ought' does not imply 'permitted' on this interpretation.

The same problem occurs if 'ought' refers to non-overridden moral reasons as on (NOMR) but 'permitted' refers to moral reasons as on (PMR). 'PA → −O−A' then claims that, if there is no moral reason not to adopt an alternative, then there is no non-overridden moral reason not to adopt the alternative. This is a tautology. However, 'OA → PA' then claims that, if there is a non-overridden moral reason to adopt an alternative, there is not any moral reason not to adopt the same alternative. This is false in any moral conflict, so, in the face of my previous arguments for moral conflicts, it begs the question to assume that 'ought' implies 'permitted' on this interpretation.

The remaining interpretation is that 'ought' refers to non-overridden moral reasons as on (NOMR), but 'permitted' refers to overriding moral reasons as on (POMR). On this interpretation, 'OA → PA' claims that, if there is a non-overridden moral reason to adopt any alternative, then there is no overriding moral reason not to adopt the alternative. This is true, because the overriding moral reason not to adopt the alternative would override the moral reason to adopt the alternative, so the moral reason to adopt the alternative would not be non-overridden. However, 'PA → −O−A' is false on this interpretation. This premise is supposed to follow from a definition of 'permitted' as 'not ought not', but this definition breaks down if 'permitted' refers to overriding moral reasons, but 'ought' refers to non-overridden moral reasons. On this interpretation, 'PA $\rightarrow$ $-$O$-$A' claims that, if there is no overriding moral reason not to adopt an alternative, there is no non-overridden moral reason not to adopt the alternative. This is false, if the moral reason not to adopt an alternative is not overriding, but it is also not overridden. Since I have already argued that this is possible, it begs the question to assume 'PA$\rightarrow$ $-$O$-$A' on this interpretation.

In conclusion, however 'ought' and 'permitted' are interpreted, the argument from ' "ought" implies "permitted" ' either attacks a straw man or contains a premise that is false (or, at least, begs the question). Either way, this argument fails to prove that moral dilemmas are not possible. There are other possible interpretations of 'permitted', but none saves the argument from ' "ought" implies "permitted" '.[20]

Not only does the argument fail, but my refutation makes it easy to explain why it seems plausible. One explanation is that each premise is true on some interpretation. 'Ought' seems to imply 'permitted', because it does imply it if either term refers to overriding moral reasons.[21] 'Permitted' seems to imply 'not ought not', because it does imply it by definition if both terms refer to the same level of moral reasons. The argument then seems sound because the various interpretations are easy to confuse.

Even if these interpretations are not confused, there is another explanation of why the argument seems plausible. 'Ought' might seem semantically to imply 'permitted', because 'ought' does conversationally imply 'permitted'. A conversational maxim of quantity says 'Make your contribution as informative as is required (for the current purposes of exchange).'[22] Since cooperative speakers follow this maxim, when a speaker offers some information, if the audience trusts him or her, the audience infers that the speaker does not have any other relevant information. In our case, if a speaker says only that the agent ought to adopt the alternative and does not say that the agent ought not to adopt the alternative, the audience infers by conversational principles that the speaker does not believe that the agent also ought not to adopt the alternative (or does believe this is not true). Thus, 'ought' conversationally implies 'not ought not'. If 'permitted' is defined as 'not ought not', 'ought' also conversationally implies 'permitted'. Such implications are conversational, because they can be explicitly cancelled.[23] The speaker does not contradict himself if he adds that, even though he did not mention it, he also believes that the agent ought not to adopt the alternative and is not permitted to adopt it. Such conversational implications are often confused with semantic implications, but they are crucially different, because conversational implications do not affect truth. Since 'ought' only conversationally implies 'permitted', it can be true that the agent ought to adopt an alternative which the agent is not permitted to adopt, even if this judgement is misleading. This explains why the argument from ' "ought" implies "permitted" ' seems plausible but really is not.

5.4 DISAGREEMENT

Although the argument from ' "ought" implies "permitted" ' is the most common, there are other arguments against the possibility that an agent both ought and ought not to adopt the same alternative. I will consider two more arguments.

The first argument is that speakers seem to disagree when one says that an agent ought to do something and another says that the agent ought not to do it. Suppose Kate says, 'Jane ought to get an abortion', and Seif says, 'Jane ought not to get an abortion.' They seem to disagree. However, if it is possible that Jane both ought and ought not to get an abortion, then both speakers can be right, so these speakers do not really disagree.

In response, a defender of 'ought and ought not' can explain why these speakers seem to disagree. First, the most natural interpretation in most contexts takes their judgements to be about overriding moral reasons. On this interpretation, the speakers cannot both be correct, so they do disagree. In other contexts, the speakers might refer only to (non-overridden) moral reasons, but it is still easy to confuse their judgements with judgements about overriding moral reasons. This confusion will make it seem that their judgements cannot both be true, when really they can.

Even if their judgements are interpreted so that both can be correct, they still might seem to disagree, because each denies something that is conversationally implied by what the other says. When Kate says only that Jane ought to get an abortion, since she does not add any other judgement, she conversationally implies that no other moral reasons are relevant, and thus that it is true that Jane ought not to get an abortion. If she thought also that Jane ought not to get an abortion, then not to say so would violate a conversational rule of quantity and would be misleading. Seif then denies the judgement that is conversationally implied. Similarly, when Seif says only that Jane ought not to get an abortion, since he adds no other judgement, he conversationally implies that it is not also true that she ought to get an abortion, and Kate denies this conversationally implied judgement. They seem to disagree, because each denies what the other conversationally implies, even though both of their explicit judgements can be true.

These speakers can still explicitly cancel these conversational implications. Kate might respond to Seif by saying, 'You are right. It is true that Jane ought not to get an abortion, even though it is also true that she ought to get an abortion.' Seif can then say, 'That is all I meant to claim. I admit that Jane ought to get an abortion, but I added that Jane ought not to get an abortion in order to bring out the other side of the dilemma.' Admittedly, few discussions about abortion are this calm or balanced, but the original judgements still do not explicitly exclude the possibility that both speakers agree that Jane is in a moral dilemma, so she both ought and ought not to get an abortion. If so, they did not really disagree after all.

Whether a disagreement is real or apparent depends not only on what words each speaker uses but also on how each reacts to others' judgements. Their reactions determine how their words should be interpreted. In this way, a defender of the possibility of 'ought and ought not' can explain when there is real disagreement and when there is not. Thus, nothing about disagreement refutes the possibility of 'ought and ought not' or of moral dilemmas. A similar response applies to a similar argument that people seem to give incompatible advice when one says 'ought' and the other says 'ought not'.

5.5 'OUGHT TO AND NOT TO'

A third argument against the possibility that an agent both ought and ought not to adopt the same alternative can be called the argument from 'ought to and not to'. The basic idea is to show that 'ought and ought not' implies a contradiction within the scope of 'ought' and then to show that this is absurd.

More fully, the argument starts with the agglomeration principle, that is, if an agent ought to adopt each of two alternatives, the agent ought to adopt both alternatives. The relevant instance of agglomeration is that, if an agent both ought and ought not to adopt an alternative, then the agent ought both to adopt and not to adopt the alternative. This is symbolized as:

$$(10.1) \ (OB \ \& \ O-B) \rightarrow O(B\&-B).$$

The consequent has a contradiction within the scope of 'ought'.

The next step is to show that '$O(B\&-B)$' is impossible. One argument is suggested by van Fraassen, when he writes, 'If one is required to do the impossible, one is required to do everything, and *all moral distinctions collapse*. But for the person in a moral quandary it is by no means true that all moral distinctions have collapsed – much as he might like to plead this.'[24] The basic point is that a contradiction logically implies everything. This can be symbolized by letting '$\boxed{L}A$' stand for 'It is logically necessary that A', so that '$\boxed{L}(A \rightarrow B)$' stands for 'A logically implies B'. Then, for any value of 'X',

$$(10.2) \ \boxed{L}((B\&-B) \rightarrow X).$$

Standard deontic logic also includes the principle that 'ought' is closed under logical implication, that is, for any 'A' and any 'B'

(COL) $\boxed{L}$(A→B) → (OA→OB).

The relevant instance of this principle is that, for any value of 'X',

(10.3) $\boxed{L}$((B&−B) → X) → (O(B&−B) → OX).

(10.2) and (10.3) imply that, for any value of 'X',

(10.4) O(B&−B) → OX.

This claims that, if the agent ought both to adopt and not to adopt the same alternative, then the agent ought to do everything. However, it seems that there must be at least some value of 'X' such that

(10.5) −OX.

(10.4) and (10.5) then imply that it is not possible that any agent ought both to adopt and not to adopt the same alternative. Symbolically, for any 'B',

(10.6) −O(B&−B).

Finally, (10.6) and (10.1) imply that it is not possible that any agent both ought and ought not to adopt the same alternative. Symbolically, for any 'B',

(10) −(OB & O−B).

Since the argument is valid, anyone who denies (10) must also either deny agglomeration and its instance (10.1),[25] or deny the closure of 'ought' under logical implication and its instance (10.3), or deny that there is any value of 'X' for which 'OX' is not true, as in (10.5).[26] Which response is adopted determines which judgements are true in moral dilemmas.

The first escape is to deny (10.5). (10.5) claims that there is some alternative of which it is not true that it ought to be adopted. To deny this is to claim that every alternative ought to be adopted and also that the negation of every alternative ought to be adopted, so every alternative ought not to be adopted. This claim is not contradictory, but it is extremely implausible. Even if I make equally strong promises to go to different places at the same time, this does not make it true that I morally ought to touch my toes or that you ought to give me a thousand pounds or that I ought to kill a thousand people. More importantly, it is not true that I ought to break both promises or to keep neither (that 'O($-$A&$-$B)' or 'O$-$(A$_\vee$B)'), since keeping neither would not accomplish anything. All of this makes it implausible to try to escape the above argument by denying premise (10.5).

The other escape from the above argument is to deny premise (10.3). (10.3) is an instance of closure under logical implication, or

(COL) $\boxed{L}$(A→B) → (OA→OB).

Some philosophers deny (COL) because of various paradoxes, but I have argued above that these paradoxes depend on various confusions. Nonetheless, the arguments for 'O(A&$-$A)' itself might seem to refute (COL). McConnell says that anyone who thinks that an agent ought both to adopt and not to adopt the same alternative (O(A&$-$A)) but denies of some alternative that it ought to be adopted (denies 'OB' for some 'B') will have a counterexample to closure under logical implication.[27] This counterexample can be avoided simply by adding a restriction to the antecedent of logical closure to get

(RCOL) [$\Diamond\!\!\!\!L$ A & $\Diamond\!\!\!\!L$ $-$B & $\boxed{L}$(A→B)] → (OA→OB)

or, equivalently,

(RCOL*) [OA & $\Diamond\!\!\!\!L$ A & $\Diamond\!\!\!\!L$ $-$B & $\boxed{L}$(A→B)] → OB, where '$\Diamond_L$' stands for logical possibility and is defined as '$-\boxed{L}-$'.[28] This restriction parallels the restriction that I added to closure under 'can' in (RCOC). (RCOL) might seem *ad hoc*, but similar restrictions are a common way to avoid paradoxes of implication which are not peculiar to moral operators. Furthermore, (COL) might seem plausible without the restriction only because we usually do not think of cases where 'O(A&$-$A)'. And (RCOL) is still strong enough to warrant the common arguments that depend on logical closure. Thus, someone who denies (COL) but accepts (RCOL) loses none of the advantages of logical closure but avoids the absurd consequences of 'O(A&$-$A)'. This leaves no argument against the possibility of 'O(A&$-$A)', so the argument from 'ought to and not to' cannot refute the possibility of 'OA & O$-$A', and then the argument from 'ought and ought not' cannot refute the possibility of moral dilemmas.

There is also another way to defend the possibility of moral dilemmas. If 'O(A&$-$A)' cannot be derived in moral dilemmas, then there is no reason to accept the possibility of this admittedly strange judgement, and then there is no reason to reject (COL) in favour of (RCOL). So we need to determine whether 'O(A&$-$A)' really can be derived in moral dilemmas.

The most direct derivation of 'O(A&$-$A)' depends on the claim that, for every value of 'A',

$$(10.1) \ (OA \& O-A) \rightarrow O(A\&-A).$$

This judgement is an instance of the agglomeration principle, so the agglomeration principle must be denied by any defender of the possibility of moral dilemmas who accepts that 'OA&O$-$A' but denies that 'O(A&$-$A)'.

I argued in the previous chapter that whether the agglomeration principle is valid depends on how the term 'ought' is interpreted, and the same goes for (10.1). If 'ought' refers to overriding moral reasons, the agglomeration principle is valid, so (10.1) is also valid, even if only because its antecedent is always false. However, the agent in a moral dilemma does not have overriding moral reasons to adopt either alternative, so this interpretation of (10.1) and the argument from 'ought and ought not' cannot refute the possibility of moral dilemmas as their defenders define them.

In order to be applicable to moral dilemmas, (10.1) must refer either to moral reasons or to non-overridden moral reasons. However, I argued above that agglomeration fails if 'ought' refers either to moral reasons or to non-overridden moral reasons. Sometimes there is no moral reason at all to adopt both alternatives together, because this would accomplish nothing, and sometimes the moral reason to adopt each alternative is not overridden, but the conjunction of these reasons is overridden, because the conjuction of the alternatives has bad consequences (or violates a moral rule) which neither alternative alone has (or violates). An opponent might respond that, even though such agglomeration fails in general, the particular case (10.1) still might be valid. However, there is no reason to accept the special case (10.1) when such agglomeration fails in general. Furthermore, it seems that there cannot be any moral reason, even an overridden one, to adopt a contradictory alternative like 'A&−A' because 'A&−A' cannot prevent a harm, fulfil a promise, etc. Thus, the nature of moral reasons suggests that (10.1) fails along with general agglomeration of moral reasons and non-overridden moral reasons.

Without (10.1) or any applicable agglomeration, there is no reason to believe that 'OA&O−A' implies 'O(A&−A)' if 'O' refers to non-overridden moral reasons. Thus, even if it is not possible that any agent ought both to adopt and not to adopt the same alternative (that O(A&−A)), the argument from 'ought to and not to' still fails to show that it is not possible that an agent both ought and ought not to adopt the same alternative (that OA&O−A), if 'ought' refers to non-overriden moral reasons.

This leaves two escapes from the argument from 'ought to and not to'. A defender of moral dilemmas can either restrict closure under logical implication or deny the relevant instance of agglomeration. I am inclined to do both, but this much is not necessary to defend moral dilemmas.

There always might be some other argument against the possibility that an agent both ought and ought not to adopt the same alternative. However, in the absence of further arguments, I conclude that the argument from ought and ought not fails to refute the possibility of moral dilemmas on the standard definition.

Similar conclusions apply to my definition of moral dilemmas in terms of non-overridden moral requirements. My arguments for the possibility of 'ought and ought not' depend on distinguishing overriding from non-overridden moral reasons. If it is possible for there to be a non-overridden moral reason to adopt an alternative and a non-overridden moral reason not to adopt the same alternative, then it must also be possible for there to be non-overridden moral requirements to adopt an alternative and also non-overridden moral requirements not to adopt the same alternative. The fact that the reasons in question are requirements should not affect any of my arguments. Consequently, no analogue of the argument from 'ought and ought not' can refute the possibility of moral dilemmas of my definition.

6

Consistency

So far I have discussed arguments against moral dilemmas which focus on particular moral judgements. In this chapter, I will turn to an argument which focuses instead on the moral theories from which moral dilemmas are derived. This argument can be called the argument from inconsistency. The same basic argument has many versions, but they all share two steps. The first step claims that all moral theories that yield moral dilemmas must involve some kind of inconsistency. The second step claims that nothing with any such inconsistency is possible or can be adequate. These steps are rarely distinguished or even stated explicitly, but they do seem to lie behind much of the opposition to moral dilemmas.

One problem with this argument is that it is not clear what counts as inconsistent. Different philosophers define 'inconsistent' in different ways, and there is no way to show that any such definition is the only correct one. Even if one definition of 'inconsistency' were correct, we would still have to see whether the other related notions exclude moral dilemmas.

Instead of arguing about what inconsistency really is, I will distinguish several notions of inconsistency, including truth-inconsistency and strong and weak act-inconsistency for particular judgements and general theories. The argument from inconsistency does not rule out moral dilemmas unless there is a single kind of inconsistency such that all moral dilemmas introduce this kind of inconsistency and also such that nothing with this kind of inconsistency is possible or adequate. I will argue that no single notion of inconsistency has both of these properties, so none suffices for the argument from inconsistency or rules out moral dilemmas. The argument from inconsistency seems to rule out moral dilemmas only if different kinds of inconsistency are confused.

6.1 TRUTH-INCONSISTENCY

The most common notion of (in)consistency is truth-(in)consistency. Two particular moral judgements are truth-inconsistent if and only if they cannot both be true; and they are truth-consistent if and only if they are not truth-inconsistent, that is, they can both be true. For example, 'That lie was wrong' and 'That lie was not wrong' are a formal contradiction, so they cannot both be true, and they are truth-inconsistent.

If the defining judgements of moral dilemmas were truth-inconsistent, they could not all be true in any situation, so no situation could be a moral dilemma. However, there is no reason to believe that the judgements that define moral dilemmas are truth-inconsistent. The most direct way to show that a set of judgements is truth-inconsistent is to derive a contradiction from those judgements plus other principles that are necessarily true. The arguments from ' "ought" implies "can" ' and from 'ought and ought not' try to derive a contradiction from the definition of moral dilemmas, but I have already shown how each argument depends on at least one principle that begs the question and is not necessarily true. And there is no reason to believe that any other argument succeeds where these fail. An opponent might respond that some judgements are intuitively truth-inconsistent even if no argument can show this without begging the question. However, I have also argued that moral intuitions not only do not refute but even support the possibility of moral dilemmas. If an opponent still insists that the defining judgements seem truth-inconsistent, I can only ask why. Except in obvious cases, we should not be persuaded by anyone who claims that something is impossible or truth-inconsistent but gives no argument that does not beg the question.

Even if the defining judgements of moral dilemmas are not truth-inconsistent, the notion of truth-inconsistency can be extended to general moral principles and theories, and there still might be no way to derive the defining judgements of moral dilemmas from any general moral theory which is not itself truth-inconsistent. This would create serious problems. A moral theory or set of general moral principles is truth-inconsistent if and only if not all of the principles in the set or theory can be true, so some must be false. But a false theory does not seem to justify what it implies, and some general moral theory seems to be needed to justify the defining judgements of a moral dilemma in a particular case. Thus, if moral dilemmas could be implied only by moral theories that are truth-inconsistent, it might be impossible to show that any particular situation is a moral dilemma. This might even seem to show that moral dilemmas are impossible.

However, there is no reason to believe that all moral theories that yield moral dilemmas are truth-inconsistent. One reason for truth-inconsistency might be that such theories imply some contradiction, but it is easy to construct moral principles that yield moral dilemmas without any contradiction. For example, a single principle against promise breaking can yield moral dilemmas, but there is no way to derive a contradiction from this moral principle. An opponent might respond that this principle is not a complete moral theory, but there is no reason to believe that complete moral theories must imply a contradiction in order to yield moral dilemmas. Since the defining judgements of moral dilemmas are not contradictory, a moral theory that justifies these defining judgements can always be qualified in some way to remove any contradiction without ceasing to yield the judgements that define the moral dilemmas. Thus, neither the defining judgements of moral dilemmas nor the moral theories that yield them must imply contradictions. This removes one of the main reasons to believe that moral dilemmas introduce any truth-inconsistency.

6.2 ACT-INCONSISTENCY

The next kind of (in)consistency can be called act-(in)consistency, because it depends on relations among the acts that are judged. Sometimes two moral judgements are called inconsistent simply because they cannot both be satisfied or followed or obeyed. For example, the judgements that Paul ought to kiss Jane and that Paul ought not to kiss Jane are not formally contradictory, but they are still often called 'inconsistent', simply because Paul cannot adopt both of the alternatives that he ought to adopt according to the two judgements. This inability is logical, but there are other cases where it is logically possible for the agent to follow both judgements even though he cannot follow both in the actual situation. Either way, such particular judgements are act-inconsistent.

The notion of act-inconsistency becomes more complex when it is extended to general principles and theories. We need to distinguish strong and weak act-inconsistency. A moral theory or a set of general moral principles is *strongly* act-inconsistent if and only if there is *no* possible world in which all of its general principles *can* be followed; and it is strongly act-consistent if and only if there is some possible world where all of its general principles can be followed. For example, 'Everyone ought to steal' and 'Everyone ought not to steal' are, together, strongly act-inconsistent, since there is no possible world where everyone steals and does not steal.

Other general principles are not strongly act-inconsistent but are act-inconsistent in a weaker way. For example, there is a possible world where the general principles 'Everyone ought not to steal' and 'Every parent ought to feed his or her children when they are hungry' are both followed, so these general moral principles are not strongly act-inconsistent. However, there are other possible worlds (including the actual world) where some parents cannot feed their hungry children without stealing, so these moral principles cannot both be followed. This is why some people call these moral principles 'inconsistent' in a weaker way. A set of general moral principles is *weakly* act-inconsistent if and only if there is *some* possible world where they can*not* all be followed. This notion is so weak that a set of moral principles is weakly act-inconsistent whenever they might come into conflict, even if they never do conflict in the actual world.

Some defenders of moral dilemmas might deny that this weak notion even deserves the name 'inconsistency'.[1] There is something to this. When we call a scientific theory inconsistent, we are not saying only that there is some world where it is not true. That applies to all contingent theories even if they are true in this world. Instead, a scientific theory is called 'inconsistent' only if there is no possible world where it is true. This makes the kind of inconsistency that refutes scientific theories seem closer to strong than to weak act-inconsistency. On the other hand, moral and scientific theories differ in ways that might justify using a different notion of inconsistency in morality. In any case, the basic issue is not whether these various notions should be called kinds of inconsistency.

The crucial question is whether any notion of act-inconsistency supports an argument against the possibility of moral dilemmas. Act-inconsistency differs from truth-inconsistency, because the definition of act-inconsistency does not mention truth or falsity. This makes it less clear what is supposed to be wrong with moral judgements or theories that are act-inconsistent. It is clear why truth-inconsistency would rule out moral dilemmas, since whether a situation is a moral dilemma depends on which judgements are true. But it is not at all clear why act-inconsistency is supposed to rule out moral dilemmas.

One possibility is that act-inconsistency implies truth-inconsistency or, in other words, that moral judgements and principles cannot all be true if they cannot all be followed. This implication might hold even though act-inconsistency is distinct from truth-inconsistency. And, since truth-inconsistency would be harmful enough to rule out moral dilemmas, act-inconsistency would also be harmful enough to rule out moral dilemmas, if it implied truth-inconsistency, and if it had to be present in all moral dilemmas. The same holds for moral conflicts, even if they are resolvable. Thus, we need to ask whether any notion of act-inconsistency both implies truth-inconsistency and also must be involved in all moral conflicts or dilemmas.

The first kind of act-inconsistency holds among particular moral judgements when they cannot all be followed. The defining judgements of moral dilemmas must be act-inconsistent in this way, and the same holds for the defining judgements of all moral conflicts even if they are resolvable. Furthermore, this kind of act-inconsistency does imply truth-inconsistency for some kinds of judgements. Judgements about overriding moral reasons cannot both be true if they cannot both be followed.

However, the moral judgements that are essential to moral dilemmas are about non-overridden moral requirements, and there is no reason to believe that these judgements cannot be true simply because they cannot, even logically, be followed. I argued above that act-inconsistent judgements about non-overridden moral requirements neither imply a contradiction nor conflict with moral intuition. It then begs the question to claim without any argument that act-inconsistency among these moral judgements implies truth-inconsistency.

An argument for this implication might seem to be provided by standard formal semantics for deontic logic. Such semantics imply that an agent ought to do something in this actual world only if the agent does do it in all worlds that are ideal with respect to this actual world. This makes it impossible that an agent ought to do each of two things if it is impossible for the agent to do both of them in any world that is ideal relative to this world. This already rules out moral judgements that logically cannot both be followed. And if no world can be ideal relative to this world unless the agent can obtain that world, then standard formal semantics also imply that moral judgements cannot both be true if the agent cannot follow both.

However, this argument begs the question. There is no reason to accept those parts of standard formal semantics which are needed to rule out act-inconsistent judgements. If standard formal semantics rule out moral dilemmas, all of my previous arguments for moral dilemmas suggest that standard formal semantics are not adequate to the complexities of moral judgements and reasoning. Standard formal semantics might capture judgements about overriding moral reasons, but they cannot show that act-inconsistency implies truth-inconsistency among the moral judgements that define moral dilemmas.[2]

The next kinds of act-inconsistency concern general moral theories or principles. First, a moral theory is *weakly* act-inconsistent if there is some possible world where some agent cannot follow all of its principles. A moral theory that yields any moral dilemmas must, then, be weakly act-inconsistent, since not all of its principles can be followed by the agent in the world where the moral dilemma occurs. The same holds for moral theories that yield any moral conflicts, even if they are resolvable.

However, there is again no reason to believe that a moral theory cannot be true simply because not all of its principles can be followed in some possible world. Such moral theories need not imply any contradiction, and I have argued that moral theories that yield moral dilemmas not only do not conflict with but are supported by moral intuition and common sense. General principles about overriding moral reasons cannot be true if they are weakly act-inconsistent, but principles about non-overridden moral reasons can still be true if they are weakly act-inconsistent, and that is all that is necessary for moral dilemmas.

There might seem to be more reason to believe that *strong* act-inconsistency implies that a moral theory is truth-inconsistent. If a moral theory cannot be completely followed in *any* possible world, it might seem hard to see why anyone would claim the whole theory is true. The primary examples of strongly act-inconsistent moral principles are principles like 'Everyone always ought to steal' and 'Everyone always ought not to steal', and it seems clear that principles like this cannot be true.

Even if no strongly act-inconsistent principles can ever be true, this cannot rule out moral dilemmas. The reason is that moral theories that yield moral dilemmas need not be strongly act-inconsistent. A moral theory is strongly act-inconsistent only if there is no possible world where all of its moral principles can be followed. But even if a moral theory or set of moral principles implies that some situation in the actual world is a moral dilemma, there still might be another possible world where the moral theory implies that no situation is a moral dilemma. For example, even if a moral theory implies that I am in a moral dilemma when I cannot tell the truth without hurting my friend in this actual world, the moral theory still might not yield any moral dilemma in another possible world where I can always tell the truth without hurting any friend. The point is that moral dilemmas always arise because of contingent circumstances and inabilities that do not exist in other possible worlds. Whenever an agent cannot do all that he or she ought to do, there is always another possible world in which he or she can do all that he or she ought to do. This shows that the moral rules that yield the moral dilemma can all be followed in some possible world, so the moral theory that yields the moral dilemma is not strongly act-inconsistent.[3]

An opponent might respond that, even if moral theories that yield dilemmas can be true in some possible worlds, they cannot be true in any world like the one where the dilemma arises, because they are inconsistent with the facts of that world. Levi suggests this when he writes,

> A decision problem may be presented to [an agent] in which the requirements of patriotism and pacifism are to apply to him but in which the joint satisfiability of the constraints is inconsistent with what the agent knows. . . . In some respects, recognition of this inconsistency is analogous to recognition that two or more mutually consistent hypotheses entail a result confounded by experiment. The set of hypotheses may be mutually consistent, but this set and the report of the results are inconsistent.[4]

The point is that, just as we must revise scientific theories when they conflict with the results of experiments even if the theories by themselves are not inconsistent, so we must revise moral theories when we find that they imply moral dilemmas even if the theory by itself is neither truth-inconsistent nor strongly act-inconsistent.

It must be admitted that we do often revise a moral theory when we find that it implies that an agent ought to adopt incompatible alternatives. If 'the requirements of patriotism' are supposed to include overriding moral requirements to defend one's country, and if 'the requirements of pacifism' are supposed to include overriding moral requirements against all killing, then a theory which includes the requirements of both patriotism and pacifism must be revised if an agent ever knows that he must kill in order to defend his country against an invader. But this revision is necessary only because the requirements are supposed to be *overriding*, and there cannot be overriding moral requirements to adopt incompatible alternatives. And we also must revise any theory which implies that an agent ought to adopt incompatible alternatives if 'ought' refers to overriding reasons. On the overriding reasons interpretation, such implications are truth-inconsistent, so they are analogous to confounding results in scientific experiments. This explains the force of Levi's point.

Nonetheless, this cannot show that moral dilemmas force us to revise our moral theories. Moral dilemmas are defined by *non-overridden* moral requirements, so a moral theory that implies a moral dilemma need not imply any contradiction or be truth-inconsistent. Levi points out that 'the joint satisfiability of the constraints is inconsistent with what the agent knows.' But non-satisfiability is only act-inconsistency, so it does not show that the facts and the moral theory cannot both be true. If it did, not only moral dilemmas but even resolvable moral conflicts would force revisions. Thus, moral dilemmas are not analogous to confounding experiments in science, and they do not refute or force revisions in moral theories that imply them.

In sum, moral dilemmas do introduce some kinds of act-inconsistency, including act-inconsistency between particular moral judgements, weak act-inconsistency in general moral theories, and some kind of inconsistency between moral theories and the facts of situations that are moral dilemmas on those theories. And these kinds of act-inconsistency would imply truth-inconsistency among judgements about overriding moral reasons. However, none of these kinds of act-inconsistency implies truth-inconsistency in the judgements or theories about non-overridden moral requirements that are essential to moral dilemmas. On the other hand, strong act-inconsistency does seem to imply truth-inconsistency, but moral theories that yield moral dilemmas need not be act-inconsistent in this strong way. Thus, none of these notions of act-inconsistency can rule out the possibility of moral dilemmas. This also explains why the argument from inconsistency seems to rule out moral dilemmas if opponents confuse strong with weak act-inconsistency or overriding with non-overridden moral reasons.

There are other intermediate levels of act-inconsistency. Some opponents might claim that a moral theory is culpably act-inconsistent unless there is some way for every agent to fulfil all moral requirements if he plans ahead and does nothing wrong.[5] If this kind of act-inconsistency implied truth-inconsistency, perplexities *simpliciter* would not be possible but perplexities *secundum quid* would be possible. Similarly, opponents of moral dilemmas but not moral conflicts might claim that a moral theory is irresolvably act-inconsistent if there is any possible world where its principles cannot all be followed and the theory does not rank the principles that conflict. And there are other kinds of act-inconsistency. An opponent can almost always define some kind of inconsistency to capture just those theories, judgements and situations that he wants to claim are impossible.

However, a general argument suggests that none of these notions can rule out moral dilemmas. Some of these kinds of act-inconsistency will not be introduced by all moral dilemmas. If any kind of act-inconsistency is introduced by all moral dilemmas, this itself is a reason to deny that moral judgements or theories with this kind of inconsistency cannot be true or are truth-inconsistent. I have already argued for the possibility of moral dilemmas, and these arguments show that moral dilemmas do not introduce any kind of inconsistency that implies truth-inconsistency. Consequently, no argument from act-inconsistency to truth-inconsistency can rule out moral dilemmas.

6.3 PURPOSES OF MORAL THEORIES

So far, I have discussed the implications of act-inconsistency only for truth. However, some opponents of moral dilemmas might deny that moral judgements can ever be either true or false. Other opponents might claim that act-inconsistency is a defect in a moral theory even if it does not prove that the theory is not true. Such opponents might then try to use act-inconsistency to refute the possibility of moral dilemmas independently of truth or truth-inconsistency.

In order to construct such an argument, opponents need to show that there is something bad about act-inconsistency, so the best moral theory cannot imply moral dilemmas or be act-inconsistent. The basic argument will then take the following form:[6]

(1) Every moral theory that yields any moral dilemmas is act-inconsistent.

(2) For any moral theory that yields any moral dilemmas, there is another moral theory that does not yield those moral dilemmas and is not act-inconsistent but does yield the same moral judgements in all other situations.

(3) Any moral theory that is act-inconsistent is worse than another moral theory that is act-consistent unless there is some other reason to prefer the moral theory that is act-inconsistent.

(4) There is no other reason to prefer a moral theory that yields moral dilemmas to another moral theory that does not yield moral dilemmas and is act-consistent if they yield the same moral judgements in all other situations.

(5) Therefore, for any moral theory that yields moral dilemmas, there is a better theory that does not yield moral dilemmas.

(6) Moral dilemmas are possible only if the best moral theory yields moral dilemmas in some possible situations.

(7) Therefore, moral dilemmas are not possible.

This argument is valid, if there is no equivocation, so a defender of the possibility of moral dilemmas must deny at least one premise.

Premise (1) is supposed to follow from definitions of moral dilemmas and act-inconsistency. However, premise (1) is not true for strong act-inconsistency, since a moral theory need not be strongly act-inconsistent just because it yields moral dilemmas. Nonetheless, premise (1) is true for weak act-inconsistency, since moral principles cannot all be followed if they imply that an agent ought (or has non-overridden moral requirements) to adopt incompatible alternatives. The same holds if a moral theory implies any moral reasons for incompatible alternatives, even if the moral conflict is resolvable.

Since premise (1) is true for weak but not strong act-inconsistency, and the argument must use the same notion of consistency throughout in order to be valid, I will assume for now that the entire argument refers to weak act-inconsistency. I will return later to discuss intermediate levels of inconsistency.

Premise (2) sets up a comparison between moral theories that yield moral dilemmas and ones that do not. Let us call a moral theory dilemmatic if it yields moral dilemmas or implies that any possible situation is a moral dilemma. A theory is then non-dilemmatic if it yields no possible moral dilemmas. A moral theory is a non-dilemmatic counterpart of a dilemmatic theory if the former does not yield any moral dilemmas but does yield the same moral judgements as its counterpart in all other possible situations. Premise (2) then claims that every dilemmatic moral theory has a non-dilemmatic counterpart.

The argument for premise (2) is simple. Whenever a moral theory implies that some situations are moral dilemmas, we can construct another moral theory by adding a principle or a qualification which applies only to the supposed dilemmas and resolves them by implying that one of the conflicting requirements is either overridden or cancelled. The additional principle might be as simple as that, whenever a situation would otherwise be a moral dilemma, the agent must use some random procedure (such as flipping a coin) to determine which moral requirement overrides or cancels the other. This theory might not be very plausible, but it does show that every dilemmatic moral theory has at least one non-dilemmatic counterpart.

Similar claims apply to moral theories that yield moral conflicts. Any theory that yields any moral conflicts can be replaced by an otherwise similar moral theory that does not yield any moral conflicts. Simply add to each principle of the form 'There is a moral reason to do A' an exception clause like '. . . except when this moral reason would conflict with another moral reason'. Thus, every conflictual moral theory has a non-conflictual counterpart, so premise (2) holds for moral conflicts as well as dilemmas.

The next step in the argument is to show that dilemmatic moral theories are worse than their non-dilemmatic counterparts. This is implied by premises (3) and (4). Premise (3) claims that act-inconsistency is a defect. Premise (4) then claims that the non-dilemmatic counterpart has no counterbalancing defect.

In order to support premise (3), opponents need to argue for some standard by which to judge when one moral theory is better or worse than another. Such standards are often based on the purposes for which we construct or adopt moral theories. If we adopt moral theories for certain purposes, one moral theory is better than another when the former more fully achieves our purposes. Premise (3) can, then, be supported by pointing out some purpose of a moral theory such that weak act-inconsistency makes a moral theory unable or less able to achieve its purpose. This would provide some reason to prefer moral theories that are not act-inconsistent and do not yield moral dilemmas. Of course, there might be more important defects in any other moral theory, including its non-dilemmatic counterpart, but that would also have to be shown by reference to some other standard or purpose of moral theories. Thus, the crucial question turns out to be: what are the purposes of moral theories?

One cognitive purpose of some moral theories is to determine which moral judgements are true. Another cognitive purpose is to organize or systematize our moral intuitions and make them cohere with each other and with non-moral facts. Such purposes make one moral theory better than another if the former includes more truth or less falsity or if it organizes more or stronger or deeper intuitions. I have already argued in previous chapters that moral dilemmas not only do not conflict with but are supported by many moral truths and intuitions and much common sense. If my arguments work, the standards of truth, intuition and common sense suggest that dilemmatic moral theories are not only not worse but better than their non-dilemmatic counterparts. These purposes cannot, then, support premise (3).

Other purposes of moral theories do seem to support premise (3). Purposes of moral theories are often derived from purposes of moral judgements, and one common view is that the purpose of uttering a moral judgement is not (just) to state a truth but to advise or prescribe an action.[7] If so, moral judgements that are act-inconsistent might seem to be unable to achieve their purposes. It might seem that it cannot ever be good advice to tell someone that she both ought and ought not to adopt the same alternative or even that she ought to adopt each of two alternatives when she cannot adopt both. This suggests that the moral theory that yields moral dilemmas cannot serve the purpose of advice as well as a non-dilemmatic counterpart.

If a moral theory allows moral conflicts but resolves them all, the theory as a whole does offer advice in all moral conflicts. Nonetheless, the theory still implies particular judgements about conflicting moral reasons and about overridden moral reasons, and it might not seem to be good advice to tell someone that she has an overridden reason to do something. If these judgements are not useful for advice, the theory that implies them might seem defective with respect to the purpose of advice.

But this is too quick. Even if act-inconsistent judgements cannot be used directly to advise an agent to favour one alternative in a moral dilemma, such judgements can still be used to guide the agent indirectly. Judgements about conflicting moral requirements can be used to give the agent reasons to feel remorse and/or to offer apologies, excuses or compensation. Act-inconsistent judgements can also be used to advise the agent to plan so as to avoid similar conflicts in the future.[8] The judgement that neither moral requirement overrides the other also tells the agent not to criticize others who choose differently in relevantly similar situations. The argument from advice overlooks such indirect forms of guidance.

Furthermore, even act-inconsistent judgements do give some direct advice to agents in moral dilemmas. Dilemmatic moral theories put limits on which alternatives are permitted, so they advise the agent not to adopt some alternatives (such as any alternative which violates both conflicting moral require-ments). The judgement that neither moral requirement over-rides the other also tells the agent that he is permitted to choose between the non-overridden alternatives in the sense that there is no overriding moral requirement not to choose either. The argument from advice forgets that to limit an agent's options and to tell him what he is permitted to do is to give direct guidance.

Finally, the argument from advice forgets that moral judge-ments can be uttered for many purposes other than to advise the agent whose acts are judged. Some people make moral judgements simply in order to state truths or to express attitudes that are justified. Others utter moral judgements to blame someone or to justify punishing that person. Such judgements do not guide the judged agent so much as other people who must choose how to react to his actions. And these purposes can be served by the judgements that define moral dilemmas.

In sum, the argument from advice seems to assume that the only purpose of moral judgements is to advise the judged agent, and that the advice must directly favour one alternative over all others. This is too simple a view of the many purposes for which we utter moral judgements. Part of the lesson of moral conflicts and dilemmas is that moral judgements have many purposes other than direct unique advice. Moral theories might not serve such other purposes as well if they did not imply moral conflicts and dilemmas, so moral theories might be not only not worse but better if they imply act-inconsistent moral judge-ments.

When the purpose of particular moral judgements is seen as direct unique advice, the purpose of general moral theories is often seen as giving a complete moral decision procedure. A *decision procedure* is a method of picking out one alternative as uniquely right in such a way that no incompatible alternative is right in the same way. A decision procedure is *complete* if it picks out one such alternative from every set of incompatible alternatives in every possible situation. Since some situations are morally neutral, moral theories should not be expected to provide complete decision procedures, but moral theories are still often expected to provide complete *moral* decision procedures. A moral decision procedure is complete if it picks out one uniquely right alternative from every morally relevant set of incompatible alternatives in every morally relevant situation. However, a theory that yields moral dilemmas does not pick out one of the incompatible alternatives in its moral dilemmas, so it fails to provide a complete moral decision procedure. Such a dilemmatic theory can aid decision in situations that are not moral dilemmas, but there still might be some reason to prefer a theory that is closer to being complete, because it aids decision in a greater number of morally relevant situations. If so, a dilemmatic moral theory might seem inferior to its non-dilemmatic counterpart.

This argument does not apply to moral theories that yield moral conflicts but resolve them all and thus do not leave any moral dilemmas. Such theories do specify only one incompatible alternative in each moral conflict as the one that fulfils the overriding moral requirement. Thus, the present argument would rule out moral dilemmas but not resolvable moral conflicts.

The first step in responding to this argument is to point out how much it needs to claim. A moral decision procedure might be seen as complete in a weaker way even if it left some moral decisions indeterminate in the sense that the agent was permitted to adopt either of two alternatives. However, this weaker kind of completeness would not be enough to exclude dilemmatic moral theories, since even dilemmatic theories can be complete in this weaker way. Thus, the argument against dilemmatic moral theories must claim that the purpose of a moral theory is to provide a moral decision procedure that is complete in the stronger way so that it does not leave any decision indeterminate in any morally relevant situation.

This should make it clear that the purpose of moral theories is not to provide such a complete moral decision procedure. There are several reasons. First, this goal cannot be achieved. Since any moral theory must be formulated in terms that will be vague to some degree, no moral theory alone can completely solve every possible moral problem, even if we know all of the non-moral facts.[9] Furthermore, it does not help but distorts moral theorizing to seek this impossible goal. For the sake of completeness, moral theories are often constructed in ways that are implausible, such as when they pretend to be more exact than they can be or limit themselves to the total of a single value. In such cases, the theory would be more plausible if the goal of completeness were abandoned.[10]

Even if a moral decision procedure could be complete, we would not want a moral theory to require one choice in every moral situation. A moral theory should leave the choice to the agent when the alternatives are equal or incomparable in all moral respects. The main cases are moral dilemmas, but we can compare dilemmas to cases with no moral reason on either side. For example, when I decide whether to part my hair on the right or the left, this is morally neutral (assuming I did not promise to part it either way, etc.). A moral theory that required or even gave any moral reason for either choice would be implausible. We would not want morality to be so intrusive into details of our lives. However, if moral theories should not help us decide in all situations, it is not clear why they should be expected to help us decide in all moral conflicts. The mere fact that there are moral reasons or requirements for each alternative does not imply that we want, much less need, a moral theory to pick out one choice as the only acceptable one.

Another reason to avoid a complete moral decision procedure is that moral theories cannot resolve all moral conflicts without using rankings that are *unjustified*. When moral requirements conflict, the agent must choose, and there might be nothing wrong with choosing without any moral justification. However, it seems wrong to go further and say that one moral requirement is morally stronger when there is no morally relevant justification for this ranking.

One problem with unjustified judgements in morality is that they are *unfair*. Morality differs from games in this way. If one rule in a game takes priority over another, there need not always be a reason for this priority. Even if the ranking is totally unjustified, this is not unfair if the ranking was announced in advance. The reason is that the players chose to enter the game, and they can leave the game. In contrast, people do not choose to be subject to morality, and they are not allowed to take moral holidays in moral dilemmas. This makes unjustified rankings in morality unfair in a way they are not in games. Furthermore, the rules of a game are usually known in advance, so the players can predict reactions to their moves. But morality is not written down in any authoritative text, so, if moral rankings were not justified, there would be no way for agents to predict how others would or should react to their actions. Thus, if moral requirements were ranked without any justification, those whose interests were ranked lower would have legitimate complaints.

In a more practical vein, an unjustified judgement that one moral requirement overrides another can cause *resentment*. For example, suppose I must choose between causing a great loss to one close friend (Mary) and causing a different but equally great loss to another close friend (Robert). Now suppose a moral theory declares without any justification at all that my requirement not to harm Mary is overriding. I see no reason to prefer this moral theory to one that leaves the conflict unresolved and yields a moral dilemma. I would resent being told that I am morally required to prefer Mary to Robert when there is no reason for this preference. Robert might also resent it if I claim that the requirement not to harm him is less important than the requirement not to harm Mary when there is no reason for this preference, since this would suggest that he was given less consideration or standing than Mary. Finally, if I think that my obligation not to harm Mary is morally overriding, I am committed to the judgement that anyone who would choose not to harm Robert in a similar situation is defective in

some morally relevant way.[11] This judgement can cause resentment among people who choose differently in similar situations. Since unjustified judgements create such problems, and
since completeness cannot be achieved without unjustified
rankings, there are many reasons to prefer incompleteness and
moral dilemmas.

Opponents might respond that, whenever a conflict is not
resolved, the agent can flip a coin or use some other random
and fair decision procedure. This is supposed to give the agent
a justification for his choice as well as a complete moral decision
procedure. I admit that a random decision procedure is often
permitted or even required when conflicts cannot be resolved
in any other moral way. However, such random methods do
not resolve the conflict in a way that excludes moral dilemmas.
To say that a coin flip resolves a moral conflict is like saying that
a question of which house is better can be answered by flipping
a coin. The coin flip may be a basis for choice, but it is not a
basis for judging one house to be better. In fact, to resort to a
coin flip is to admit that neither house is better (if one knows all
of the other facts about both houses). Similarly, when it is only
the flip of a coin that decides in a moral conflict, this external
event does not reveal anything about the moral requirements
themselves which makes one more important morally. If a
moral obligation to abide by the result of the coin flip is added
to the moral requirement that originally favoured the winning
alternative, the overall moral requirement to adopt that
alternative might be overriding. Nonetheless, there was no
such imbalance before the coin flip, so neither moral requirement was overriding before the flip, and there was a moral
dilemma then. Consequently, even if random methods were
always permitted or required, this would not show that the
purpose of moral theories is to provide a decision procedure
which is complete in any sense which would rule out moral
dilemmas.

There are also other purposes which moral theories might
serve better if they allowed moral dilemmas and conflicts.
Many philosophers see moral theories as tools for helping
people live together in society. This purpose is served better if

people recognize the worth and rights of others, and this is done when an agent displays regret or offers excuses, apologies or compensation after violating a moral requirement. Theories that exclude moral conflicts cannot serve this purpose as well, because they cannot justify such residue when the moral requirement was overridden. Others argue that moral theories should be teachable, but a moral theory could not be taught if it were complex enough to avoid all possible moral conflicts and dilemmas.[12] All such arguments suggest that moral theories have many purposes other than to give a complete moral decision procedure, and these other purposes can make a moral theory not only not worse but better if it allows moral conflicts and dilemmas.

These arguments do not show that act-inconsistency and incompleteness are not defects in moral theories (or that they are). They show only that *other* purposes of moral theories make act-inconsistent and incomplete moral theories better overall. Completeness might still be better if it could be achieved without unjustified rankings. If so, defenders of moral dilemmas should deny premise (4) rather than premise (3) of the argument on p. 179. Other defenders might deny premise (3) and make the stronger claim that weak act-inconsistency and incompleteness are not defects at all. Either way, weak act-inconsistency and incompleteness cannot force us to reject all moral theories that yield moral dilemmas.

Similar arguments apply to intermediate kinds of act-inconsistency. Each intermediate kind of act-inconsistency is caught between two traps. Some kinds of inconsistency are like strong act-inconsistency in that they are not implied by all moral dilemmas. Others are like weak act-inconsistency in that they do not show that moral theories that yield moral dilemmas must be worse overall than their non-dilemmatic counterparts. My previous arguments suggest that no notion of act-inconsistency can avoid both traps, so no notion of inconsistency can rule out the possibility of all moral dilemmas.

7

Moral Realisms

Now that I have argued that moral dilemmas are possible, I can discuss why their possibility is important. I have already mentioned some important implications in the previous chapter. Moral dilemmas show that moral judgements have many purposes other than direct unique advice, and they also show that it is not legitimate to require moral theories to provide complete decision procedures. In these ways, moral dilemmas force us to rethink the purposes and limits of moral theories and judgements.

Another reason why moral dilemmas are important is that they are supposed to have implications for or against the objectivity or reality of morality. Moral dilemmas are often used to argue against moral realism, but they are also used to argue against moral anti-realism. My arguments in section 6.3 have already shown how moral dilemmas create problems for one kind of moral anti-realism, prescriptivism, which claims that moral judgements are always used to prescribe or command behaviour, even if indirectly.[1] Nonetheless, other versions of moral anti-realism are not incompatible with moral dilemmas, despite some arguments to the contrary.[2]

In this chapter, I will focus on more common arguments from moral dilemmas against moral realism. Although some of these arguments fail, I will give another argument which does show that moral dilemmas do refute one extreme universal version of moral realism. I must begin by defining moral realism.

7.1 What Moral Realism Is

Moral realism has been very popular recently, but its various
defenders and opponents define it in various ways: as the claim
that moral judgements can be true, as the claim that moral
judgements are independent of the mind, as the claim that
moral judgements obey the law of excluded middle,[3] as the
claim that moral facts can enter into causal or explanatory
relations,[4] etc. Some of these definitions can be criticized for
being too vague or for failing to capture paradigm cases.
Nonetheless, since 'moral realism' is a technical term, no
definition is the only correct one. I will offer a definition, and I
hope my definition falls within part of common usage, but I do
not claim that all other definitions are wrong. My aim is simply
to specify the claim that is supposed to conflict with the possibility of moral dilemmas.

The claim that is relevant to moral dilemmas concerns
whether and how moral judgements can be true. Moral realism
is often defined simply as the claim that moral judgements can
be true or false. Others associate moral realism specifically with
the correspondence theory of truth, so they define moral
realism as the claim that some moral judgements are true
because they correspond to a (moral) fact or state of affairs.
However, the notions of truth, correspondence and fact are
flexible enough for moral anti-realists to be able to agree that
moral judgements can be true by virtue of corresponding in
some way to some kind of fact. Correspondence can be seen
simply as the relation that holds between a judgement and a
fact when the judgement is true if and only if the fact obtains,
and even moral anti-realists can agree that the judgement that
an agent morally ought to do an act is true if and only if the
agent morally ought to do the act.[5] And facts can be defined by
truth. Anyone who then denies that moral anti-realists can talk
about truth, facts and correspondence must specify exactly
what is essential to these notions.

In order to distinguish moral realism from anti-realism, one
must specify the kind of fact or truth condition that is supposed
to correspond to moral judgements. Many moral realists

suggest that the crucial test is independence of the mind. For example, Wiggins suggests that moral realism is the claim that moral judgements have regular truth, and one truism implies 'the independence of regular truth both from our will and from our own limited means of recognizing the presence or absence of the property in a statement'.[6] Similarly, Platts defines moral realism by three claims: 'the first is that, if a moral judgement is true, if it hits its target, that is so in virtue of an independently existing moral reality; the second is that the realistic truth conditions of a moral sentence, the conditions that determine its meaning, can transcend the recognitional capacities of those who can use and understand that sentence', and the third is that 'these things are so independently of our desires'.[7] Nagel also requires independence of 'motivation', 'inclination', and 'our beliefs'.[8] Such quotations suggest that moral realism should be defined as the claim that moral judgements are true or false independently of certain mental states. Moral anti-realists must then either deny that moral judgements have truth values or claim that their truth values depend on certain mental states.[9]

This definition contains several terms that need to be explained. The first is 'independent'. To say that the truth values of moral judgements depend on certain mental states is to say that, necessarily, the truth values would change if the mental states changed in relevant ways, but all other factors remained the same. This necessary covariance is implied by the stronger claims that the meaning and truth conditions of moral judgements are constituted by facts about the relevant mental states.[10] In any case, moral realists must deny even that moral judgements are necessarily equivalent to propositions that essentially concern certain mental states.

Even when moral realism is defined by independence, it is crucial to specify exactly what moral judgements are supposed to be independent of. Moral realists and their opponents are rarely clear on such details, but this causes much confusion, so we need to be more precise here.

The truth values of moral judgements might be independent of certain mental states but not others. Moral realists seem to agree that the truth values of moral judgements are independent of choices and moral beliefs. However, some moral realists seem to admit dependence on other mental states, such as feelings of pain or pleasure, human needs, agents' intentions, and/or agents' cognitive abilities and beliefs about non-moral aspects of the situation. It is not clear whether moral realists must claim independence of many such factors. In any case, the arguments below concern only moral beliefs and choices, so I need to specify only that moral realism implies independence of choices and moral beliefs.

Whose choices and moral beliefs? The most common candidates include the people who make the judgements and the agents who are judged or whose actions are judged. The truth values of moral judgements might be independent of the mental states of one but not the other.[11] All moral realists seem to claim that the truth values of moral judgements are independent of the choices and moral beliefs of the person who makes the judgement. Many suggest that they are also independent of the mental states of the person who is judged. Moral realists might add that moral truth is independent of other 'people', such as God or society. In any case, the crucial claim for the arguments below is that the truth values of moral judgements are independent of the choices and moral beliefs of the people who judge and are judged.

Finally, the truth values of moral judgements might be independent of *actual* but not *ideal* moral beliefs and choices. This happens in ideal observer theories where the truth values of moral judgements necessarily depend on what people would believe, choose or feel in ideal circumstances, such as when they are impartial, rational, omniscient (of non-moral facts), etc.[12] According to such views, moral judgements are similar to colour judgements on analyses where a surface is a certain colour if and only if it appears to be that colour to normal perceivers in ideal perceptual conditions. Such truth conditions are sometimes called 'realistic', and they are objective in a way. However, the argument below will not be directed against such theories, so I will not call them 'realistic'.[13]

This variety of factors shows that moral realism is not a single view but has many degrees. If someone asks whether you are a moral realist, you need to ask the questioner exactly how much independence must be claimed to be a moral realist. Moderate moral realists claim that moral judgements are independent of some but not all of the factors listed above, so we can distinguish belief realism from feeling realism, judger realism from judged realism, and actual realism from ideal realism, etc.[14] However, the arguments below will be directed against the extreme view that moral judgements are independent of *all* of these factors, so I need to define moral realism in an extreme way. For the sake of simplicity, I will say that the truth conditions of a moral judgement are realistic only if whether or not they hold is independent of the actual and ideal moral beliefs and choices of the person judged and the person who makes the judgement. A moral judgement is then realistic if and only if its truth conditions are realistic.

It is still difficult to label many moral theories simply as realistic or not. Some theorists claim that some moral judgements are realistic, but others are not.[15] The most precise way to deal with such mixed theories would be to specify which moral judgements have realistic truth conditions on each moral theory. A theory is then realistic only with regard to a class of judgements, so we can distinguish realism about values from realism about requirements, rankings, 'ought', etc. Nonetheless, it will be useful to have some way of talking about moral realism in general. I will call a moral theory a version of moral realism only if the theory claims that *every* moral judgement has realistic truth conditions. Such universal moral realism can then be refuted if the arguments below show that any moral judgement is not realistic.

Finally, moral realism is not only about truth conditions or semantics. A moral theory is not realistic if it agrees that all moral judgements have realistic truth conditions but denies that any moral judgement is true because it denies that there is any independent moral reality.[16] Moral realism is not epistemological, so moral realists need not claim that we do or even can know which moral judgements are true. Nonetheless, moral realists must claim that at least some moral judgements are true, so there is some independent moral reality. This makes moral realism not only semantic but also ontological.

Moral realism can now be defined as the claim that some moral judgements are true and every moral judgement is true if and only if certain conditions obtain that are independent of the actual and ideal moral beliefs and choices of the people who judge and are judged. Moral realism then implies, for example, that, if abortion is morally wrong, it would still be morally wrong even if everyone who gets or judges an abortion would believe that it is not wrong and would choose it (when possible) even if they were fully informed, rational, impartial, etc. Weaker theories can be called 'moral realism', but the arguments below will be aimed at the extreme view. I will return later to weaker views to see which can escape the arguments.

7.2 REALISTIC VERSUS PERSONAL MORAL DILEMMAS

Before turning to the arguments against moral realism, I need to add a few comments about how moral realists see moral dilemmas. I defined moral dilemmas as conflicts between non-overridden moral requirements. This definition might seem to beg the question against moral realism or anti-realism by referring to requirements and overriding. However, both terms are neutral between moral realism and anti-realism.

As I said in chapter 1, a moral reason to adopt (or not to adopt) an alternative is (or is provided by) a fact that the alternative has a morally relevant property or consequence, and a moral reason is a requirement if it would be morally wrong not to act on it without any moral justification. Moral realists then claim that the facts that provide moral reasons and requirements are independent of certain mental states. Moral anti-realists can claim that the relevant facts are about mental states, or that which facts provide moral requirements depends on certain mental states. Thus, moral realists and anti-realists can both agree that there are moral reasons and requirements in my sense.

The notion of overriding is trickier. One moral requirement overrides another only if the former is stronger overall in some morally relevant way. Moral realists and anti-realists disagree about what is essential to morality and thus about which rankings are morally relevant and which situations are moral dilemmas. Moral realists must claim that a ranking is not morally relevant unless it is realistic, that is, unless the higher moral requirement is so strong that anyone who violates it does what is morally wrong, regardless of his or her actual and ideal moral beliefs and choices. If so, I will say that the stronger moral requirement realistically overrides the other. Conflicts between moral requirements that cannot be ranked realistically can then be called 'realistic moral dilemmas'.

In some realistic moral dilemmas, moral anti-realists might claim that there is a justified personal moral ranking, so one and only one of the incompatible moral requirements is such that it would be morally wrong for the individual agent to violate it, even though similar acts would not be wrong for all other agents. If there is such a personal moral ranking, the realistic moral dilemma is not a personal moral dilemma. Moral anti-realists might then refuse to call such a situation a 'moral dilemma' at all, but moral realists would respond that such situations are moral dilemmas, because personal rankings are not morally relevant.

Whether or not they are called 'moral dilemmas', it is conflicts of moral requirements that can be ranked personally but not realistically that cause trouble for moral realism. Such situations are still realistic moral dilemmas, so the issue is whether moral realism can handle realistic moral dilemmas with personal rankings. Even if a moral anti-realist denies that such situations fit my earlier definition of moral dilemmas, my previous arguments still show the possibility of realistic moral dilemmas where the agent does not have any personal moral ranking as well as the possibility of realistic moral dilemmas where the agent does have a personal moral ranking, if such rankings themselves are possible.

7.3 SARTRE'S ARGUMENTS FROM FREEDOM AND IGNORANCE

Perhaps the most famous arguments from moral dilemmas against moral realism are given by Sartre. Sartre describes the moral dilemma of his student during the Second World War who must decide between joining the Free French Forces and staying in France to help his mother. Sartre tells him, 'You are free, therefore choose – that is to say, invent. No rule of general morality can show you what you ought to do: no signs are vouchsafed in this world.'[17] Although much in this passage is unclear, the term 'invent' suggests that there is no morality prior to choice, and choice determines what is moral. Thus, Sartre seems to deny moral realism.

Sartre's first argument seems to be that the student must choose, so he must invent. However, this confuses choosing what one *will* do with choosing what one *ought* to do. Sartre is correct that his student and any agent in a moral dilemma must choose what he will do. However, this does not imply that he must choose what he ought to do or that he must invent morality. Agents can choose which acts to do and which judgements to make, but they cannot choose which moral judgements are true, if moral realism is correct. So it begs the question to assume otherwise.

Sartre's other argument is that his student must invent morality, because he cannot be shown or know what he ought to do. However, even if a moral judgement cannot be *known*, it might still be *true* independently of whether anyone can know it is true. It is not knowledge but truth that is essential for moral realism, since moral realism is semantic and ontological but not epistemological. Admittedly, it might be implausible to postulate a moral reality which can never be known, but such complete ignorance has not been and cannot be shown by moral dilemmas, since not every moral judgement is about a moral dilemma. Thus, no argument from ignorance in moral dilemmas can refute moral realism or show that moral realism is incompatible with the possibility of moral dilemmas.

7.4 WILLIAMS'S ARGUMENTS FROM REGRET AND INCONSISTENCY

More sophisticated arguments are given by Williams. His first argument is based on a supposed disanalogy between belief conflicts and moral conflicts. Williams claims that in a moral conflict 'If I eventually choose for one side of the conflict rather than the other, this is a possible ground for regret, [even if] I am convinced that in the choice I made I acted for the best',[18] but no similar residue is justified after deciding that one belief is the best in a belief conflict. There are problems for this disanalogy,[19] but, even if it does hold, this disanalogy alone does not refute moral realism. Williams also needs to claim that, if moral realism or cognitivism were true, there would not be any ground for regret after the best choice in a moral conflict. His argument for this claim is that

> in purely cognitive accounts of the matter; since it is just a question of which of the conflicting ought statements is true, and they cannot both be true, to decide correctly for one of them must be to be rid of error with respect to the other – an occasion, if for any feelings, then for such feelings as relief (at escaping mistake), self-congratulation (for having got the right answer), or possibly self-criticism (for having so nearly been misled).[20]

Williams concludes that moral realism is inadequate.

I argued above that Williams is right that there are some conflicts where there is some ground for regret and remorse after either alternative, even the best. Williams's crucial claim here is that moral realists cannot explain such grounds for regret. However, moral realists can respond that the ground for such regret is that even the best choice violates a realistic moral requirement. All that moral realists deny is that mental states, such as regret, determine when moral judgements are true. This does not imply that mental states like regret cannot have realistic grounds or be justified by violations of realistic moral requirements. A judgement that regret is morally justified can, then, still be objective, cognitive and realistic.

Williams's only argument that regret cannot have realistic grounds is that moral realists must say that 'to decide correctly for one of them is to be rid of error with respect to the other.' The problem here is that it is not clear which error is at issue.

Williams's point seems to be that to decide that one moral requirement is overriding is to be rid of the error of believing that the conflicting moral requirement is overriding. However, in a moral dilemma, neither moral requirement is overriding or overridden, so it is possible that neither choice either depends on or removes any error, even if moral realism is correct. And each alternative violates a non-overridden moral requirement, so moral realists can cite that non-overridden moral requirement as a ground for regret and remorse. The claim that such moral requirements are realistic and correspond to an independent moral reality does not make them any less able to provide a ground for regret and remorse. Even in resolvable moral requirement conflicts, it is still not an error to believe that the best choice violates some moral requirement, and this can justify remorse in at least some cases, even if the requirement is realistic. Thus, Williams's first argument fails.

In a later article, Williams gives a separate argument from moral dilemmas against moral realism. He writes,

> on a realist view . . . moral judgements being straightfor-wardly assertions, two inconsistent moral judgements cannot both be true, and hence (truth being the aim of assertions) cannot both be acceptable. . . . [The] non-realist approach may well allow for the possibility that one can be forced to two inconsistent moral judgements about the same situation, each of them backed by the best possible reasons, and each of them firmly demanding acceptance. . . . If the picture of moral conflict that I have here ascribed to the non-realist is, as I suppose, nearer to the truth . . . then . . . Ethical Realism is not vacuous, but is false.[21]

This argument has two premises. The first is that, if moral realism is true, inconsistent moral judgements cannot be acceptable. The second premise is that, if moral dilemmas exist, some inconsistent moral judgements must be acceptable. It follows that, if moral dilemmas exist, moral realism is false. Williams argues that moral dilemmas do exist, so he concludes that moral realism is false.

The downfall of this argument is its equivocation between two kinds of inconsistency. Two moral judgements are truth-inconsistent if and only if they cannot both be true. In contrast, two moral judgements are act-inconsistent if and only if the judged agent cannot act on both.[22] Williams's argument seems convincing because each premise is true of one kind of inconsistency, and they are easy to confuse, but the argument fails because there is no kind of inconsistency of which both premises are true.

If Williams's argument refers to truth-inconsistency, the first premise is true, since truth-inconsistent moral judgements cannot both be acceptable to a moral realist who sees truth as the aim of moral judgements. The second premise then claims that, if moral dilemmas exist, some truth-inconsistent moral judgements must be acceptable. I argued against this in the previous chapter. It would be truth-inconsistent to claim that there are overriding moral reasons for incompatible alternatives, but such judgements need not be true in a moral dilemma. The only moral judgements necessary for a moral dilemma are that there are non-overridden moral requirements to adopt incompatible alternatives, but these judgements do not imply any contradiction, as I argued, and Williams seems to agree. Williams might be assuming that all moral realists adopt moral sense theories and assimilate moral judgements to perceptual judgements, so that judgements about reasons for incompatible alternatives are like judgements that an object is blue all over and red all over. However, moral realists need not see moral judgements in this way, so they need not think that the moral judgements necessary for moral dilemmas are truth-inconsistent. Thus, Williams's second premise is false if it refers to truth-consistency.

On the other hand, Williams's second premise is true if it refers to act-inconsistency, because the defining judgements of moral dilemmas are act-inconsistent. The first premise now claims that, if moral realism is true, act-inconsistent moral judgements cannot be acceptable. However, there is no reason why moral realists cannot accept act-inconsistent moral judgements, since act-inconsistency does not imply truth-inconsistency, as I argued in the previous chapter. Thus, act-inconsistent moral judgements can be acceptable even to moral realists, so Williams's first premise is false. Since one premise is false for each kind of inconsistency, Williams's argument fails to prove that moral realism is false or incompatible with moral dilemmas.

7.5 AN ARGUMENT FROM INTERPERSONAL COMPARISON

Even though Sartre's and Williams's arguments fail, there is a better argument from moral dilemmas against moral realism, which I will give.[23] Sartre's and Williams's arguments differ from mine in two main ways. First, they consider judgements of only a single agent, but I compare judgements and choices of different agents in relevantly similar moral dilemmas. Second, they try to argue against moral realism in general, but my argument refutes only one extreme universal version of moral realism and not moderate moral realism. These differences make my argument work when theirs fail.

The basic idea of my argument is that realistic moral facts do not favour either alternative in a moral dilemma, but different agents can still personally favour different alternatives, and then their personal rankings or choices can determine what they morally ought to do. Since moral realists deny that any moral judgements depend on mental factors like moral beliefs or choices, extreme universal moral realism is false.

The force of the argument can be brought out by an example. Suppose Fritz promised a professional colleague to finish a project by a certain date, but, through no fault of his own, he is late and has only one day left. On the other hand, today is his daughter's birthday, and the family usually goes sailing on her birthday. Fritz did not promise to go, but he is expected to come along, and his daughter will be disappointed if he does not. Thus, Fritz cannot keep his professional promise without causing some pain to his daughter. I assume there is a moral requirement to keep the promise and a moral requirement not to cause the pain, because it would be wrong not to keep the promise or to cause the pain without any justification. However, the importance of the promise and the amount of pain are balanced so that neither moral requirement realistically overrides the other. The promise is not so important that it would be morally wrong for anyone to break it in a relevantly similar situation. Also, the pain is not so great that it would be morally wrong for anyone to cause it in a relevantly similar situation. The conflicting moral requirements might be seen as equal or incomparable, but, either way, Fritz's situation is a realistic moral dilemma.

Now suppose that Pedro is in a situation that is similar to Fritz's in all respects that could be morally relevant according to moral realism. Pedro's keeping his promise would cause just as much pain to Pedro's family as Fritz's keeping his promise would cause to Fritz's family. Pedro's promise is just as important professionally as Fritz's. Thus, neither moral requirement realistically overrides the other in Pedro's case, just as in Fritz's case.

Despite such realistic similarities, Fritz and Pedro still *personally* rank the moral requirements differently. Fritz believes that his daughter's pain is more important to him than his professional promise, because he chooses to be a family man committed to a family way of life. In contrast, Pedro personally ranks his professional duty and promise more highly than the moral requirement not to cause pain to his daughter, because he chooses to be a professional man whose priorities are to the professional way of life. Pedro and Fritz consider exactly the same realistic factors, and both consider only factors that both agree are morally relevant. Neither person's choice or personal ranking depends on any error, ignorance, irrationality or partiality. Neither way of life is morally wrong, since neither person is so committed to his way of life that he would violate a realistically overriding moral requirement in order to further his family or profession. And neither has to condemn the other's choice or way of life. Nonetheless, Fritz and Pedro still arrive at different personal rankings of the moral requirements.

The crucial question for moral realism is that of which moral judgements are true in this situation. I will discuss judgements about what each agent ought to do (assuming a moral context throughout), and I will distinguish different interpretations of these judgements. Nonetheless, my conclusions can be extended to other moral judgements.

The argument against extreme moral realism now runs as follows:

(1) Pedro ought to keep his (professional) promise.

(2) Fritz ought not to keep his (professional) promise.

(3) If Fritz ought not to keep his promise, then it is not the case that Fritz ought to keep his promise.

(4) Therefore, it is not the case that Fritz ought to keep his promise.

(5) Therefore, whether or not an agent ought to keep his promise depends on the agent's choice and personal ranking.

(6) If moral realism were true, what an agent ought to do would not depend on the agent's choice or personal ranking.

(7) Therefore, moral realism is false.

(1) and (2) are the judgements that cause trouble for moral realism. (2) is derived by closure from a judgement that Fritz ought not to hurt his daughter. (3) is an assumption that is needed to derive (4). (5) follows from (1), (4) and the supposition that there is no relevant difference between Pedro and Fritz other than their personal rankings and choices. (6) is supposed to follow from the definition of moral realism. (7) follows from (5) and (6).

The crucial premises of the argument are, then, (1), (2) and (3). It might seem easy for a moral realist to escape simply by denying (1) or (2), that is, by denying either that Pedro ought to keep his promise or that Fritz ought not to keep his promise (or both). However, whether this denial is plausible depends on how (1) and (2) are interpreted, so we need to consider various interpretations of the term 'ought'. The argument is sound only if there is a single interpretation of 'ought' on which (1), (2) and (3) are all true.

ment. For example, MacIntyre writes, 'the function of "I ought to do so-and-so" when it is used to express a decision in a case like that of Sartre's pupil . . . is plainly to commit oneself.'[24] It must be admitted that moral judgements are often used to perform *speech acts* such as to express personal commitments and decisions. However, this does not refute moral realism, since moral realists deny only that the *truth values* of moral judgements depend on such personal factors. Anti-realists might respond that moral judgements do not have any truth conditions or that they are used *only* to express commitments or decisions, but neither of these responses is plausible. Thus, the argument against moral realism would confuse speech acts with truth conditions if it depended on any such interpretation of 'ought'.

In order to refute moral realism, judgements with 'ought' must be interpreted so that their truth values depend on some subjective factor. But not just any subjective factor will do. Some agents choose without any reason at all, but then it is not true that they *ought* to do as they choose. Other agents choose on the basis of self-interest, and then they prudentially ought to do as they choose, but it is still not true that they *morally* ought to do as they choose. Such cases cause no trouble for moral realism.

The troubling cases are when an agent's choices or moral beliefs determine what an agent morally ought to do. This might happen even with isolated and temporary choices and beliefs, but the clearest cases are when an agent chooses an alternative because of a long term commitment to what can be called a 'way of life'. This notion is vague, but what is important here is that a way of life includes moral beliefs and choices. A way of life in my sense is not just a pattern of behaviour but also a set of values and rankings that give the agent's reasons for the behaviour. Furthermore, an agent who adopts a way of life not only chooses the way of life but also chooses to choose that way of life, so he is not indifferent to whether he changes his way of life tomorrow. He need not condemn others who choose different ways of life, but he does not want to change his own values or rankings. Such ways of life can be chosen, and they include rankings that are moral beliefs. Since moral realists deny that mental factors such as choices and moral beliefs affect the truth values of moral judgements, moral realists must deny that the truth values of moral judgements depend on the way of life of the judged agent.

However, such ways of life *do* affect what agents ought to do in some moral dilemmas. If Fritz asked me what he ought to do, I would tell him that he ought to break his promise in order to avoid hurting his daughter. Why? Because this choice fits best into his family way of life, and this way of life is both morally and rationally permissible, so to choose otherwise would show a lack of integrity on his part. Fritz's family way of life is rationally permissible, because his choice of it does not depend on any defect, such as error, ignorance or irrationality. Fritz's family way of life is also morally permissible, because he is not so committed that he would help his family if there were a realistically overriding moral requirement not to do so. Still, if he hurt his family when there was no realistically overriding moral reason to do so, he would violate his way of life and his integrity.

Furthermore, the agent's way of life and personal rankings are the proper basis for choices in situations of this kind. Since the situation is a realistic moral dilemma, the choice cannot be based on realistic moral factors or on other people's interests, since these are balanced. The personal rankings of the people affected cannot be used to decide, since several people are affected, and their rankings might conflict. It might seem that the person making the judgement can use her own ranking, but there is no justification for imposing a ranking on an agent when the agent can reject that ranking without any rational or moral defect. The judger might not even be affected by the choice, but the agent is responsible for the decision, so it is the agent's own ranking and way of life that determine what he ought to do. Therefore, even a judger who is committed to the professional way of life must admit that Fritz ought to break his promise.

This does not mean that Fritz *must* break his promise or that it would be morally wrong for him to keep his promise. Such stronger judgements imply that Fritz becomes liable to punishment or condemnation of some kind if he chooses contrary to his way of life. This might be true, but it is not obvious, since Fritz can change his way of life. In any case, such stronger judgements are not necessary for my argument, and they are not implied by the judgement that Fritz ought to break his promise.

Parallel arguments yield a different judgement for Pedro. If Pedro asked me what he ought to do, I would tell him that he ought to keep his professional promise and ought to hurt his daughter. These different judgements are true, because Pedro is committed to a different way of life – a professional way of life – but this way of life is also both morally and rationally permissible. If he violated his professional obligation when he had no realistically overriding moral reason to do so, this would show a lack of integrity in Pedro. Thus, Pedro ought to do what Fritz ought not to do, and vice versa, even though their situations are similar in all respects that can be morally relevant according to moral realism.

In order to interpret such judgements, moral anti-realists need to build ways of life, choices or personal rankings into the truth conditions of moral judgements. There are many ways to do this, but let me suggest one. An agent ought to do something if (and only if) there is a moral reason for the agent to do it, and this reason is either realistically overriding or permissibly personally overriding, where a reason is permissibly personally overriding when it is not overridden realistically, and it fits best into a rationally and morally permissible way of life that the agent chooses without depending on any defect such as error, ignorance, irrationality or partiality. This interpretation does not capture everyone's use of 'ought', but it is coherent, and it does capture the point of the anti-realist argument.

On this interpretation, Pedro ought to keep his promise and to hurt his daughter, but Fritz ought not to keep his promise or to hurt his daughter, so (1) and (2) are true. (3) is also true, since, if breaking a promise fits best into a way of life, keeping the same promise in the same situation cannot also fit best into the same way of life. The argument then shows that judgements with 'ought' on such interpretations do not have realistic truth conditions. Therefore, extreme universal moral realism is false.

7.5.3 Responses

Several objections might be raised against this argument. First, moral realists might respond that the anti-realist interpretation of 'ought' fails to capture common usage, but moral realism is a claim about common usage, so the anti-realist interpretation fails to touch moral realism. However, this response either overestimates what anti-realists need to claim or underestimates the flexibility of common usage. The argument is not supposed to show that no moral judgements are realistic, so moral anti-realists need not claim that their interpretation captures all uses of 'ought'. And the anti-realist interpretation does capture some uses of 'ought' that do not violate any rules of common usage. It is not unintelligible to claim that an agent's way of life affects what an agent ought to do, at least in special cases such as moral dilemmas. Many competent English speakers make or assume such judgements. Moral realists might try to explain such uses in terms of speech acts and pragmatic effects rather than truth conditions. However, no pragmatic explanation seems adequate, because it seems true that Pedro ought to keep his promise but not that Fritz ought to keep his promise, regardless of which speech act is done or which pragmatic effect is intended. This suggests that the agents' ways of life determine the truth values of the judgements, rather than only their speech acts and pragmatic effects. Finally, even if no actual uses of 'ought' could be interpreted in the anti-realistic way, judgements about moral requirements and permissible personal overriding would still not have realistic truth conditions. Thus, the first response fails.

A second response might be to deny that judgements with 'ought' on the anti-realist interpretation are *moral* judgements.[25] If such judgements are not moral judgements, moral realists can admit that such judgements lack realistic truth conditions but still claim that all moral judgements have realistic truth conditions. Premise (6) of the argument on p. 202 is then false, so the argument fails to refute moral realism.

It must be admitted that many judgements with 'ought' are not moral judgements. For example, if someone judges that Pedro ought to break his promise, but only because breaking his promise is in his interest, then this judgement with 'ought' is not a moral judgement. However, I have already said that Pedro and Fritz do not consider any non-moral factors, and I also assume that the person who makes the judgement considers only moral factors and the agents' rankings of them.

If so, there is no good reason to deny that judgements with 'ought' on the anti-realist interpretation are moral judgements. Such judgements have all of the features that are essential to morality on common definitions. Regarding content, they concern harm to others. Regarding force, they can override non-moral judgements. Regarding form, the tricky question is whether judgements with 'ought' on the anti-realist interpretation are universalizable. They are in one way but not in another. These judgements are universalizable in the sense that all agents who choose the same way of life ought to do the same acts in relevantly similar situations. They are not universalizable in the stronger sense that similar judgements are not true of all agents in situations that are relevantly similar apart from subjective factors, since not all agents choose the same way of life. However, it begs the question to assume that moral judgements must be universalizable in this strong sense. This definition of morality assumes that differences in moral beliefs, choices and ways of life are never morally relevant, but that is precisely the issue between moral realists and anti-realists.

Furthermore, if moral realists define moral judgements so that no judgement is moral unless it is realistic, this makes it circular for them to claim that all moral judgements are realistic.[26] This claim does not become completely empty, since moral realists still claim that some judgements are both realistically true and moral, but the universality of moral realism – the claim that not only some but all moral judgements are realistic –rests solely on a definition. And there is still no argument for excluding the anti-realistic judgements from the domain of morality that does not beg the question. In the absence of any such argument, I conclude that these anti-realistic judgements are moral judgements, so the second response fails.

A third response might be that, even though different moral judgements are true of the two agents, there must be some relevant realistic difference between the agents if they are committed to different ways of life. Similar actions by different agents can cause different amounts of harm when the agents are committed to different ways of life. If Fritz the family man hurts his daughter, his self-esteem and his daughter's trust will be damaged. Some similar effects might flow from Pedro's hurting his daughter, but the harm will be less, since Pedro will not have violated his professional way of life, so, if his daughter knows this, she should expect and understand such treatment. Similarly, if Pedro breaks his promise, he will lose more self-esteem and professional trust than if Fritz breaks his promise, since Pedro is committed to the professional way of life, but Fritz is not. A moral realist might cite such differences to explain why Pedro ought to keep his promise, but it is not true that Fritz ought to keep his promise.

However, this response avoids the problem without solving it. Even if the agent's way of life does affect how much harm each alternative would cause, the situations can still be redescribed as realistic moral dilemmas, simply by adding extra harms on to one alternative to balance the harm caused by violating the agent's way of life. For example, suppose Fritz made his promise to more of his professional colleagues, so there will be more professional loss if he breaks it. Fritz's breaking his professional promise can then cause just as much harm as Pedro's breaking his, even though it is not supported as strongly by Fritz's family way of life. Similarly, suppose Pedro has more children who will be hurt along with his daughter if he keeps his professional promise, so that it prevents just as much harm for Pedro to break his promise even though Fritz's family way of life supports that alternative more strongly. In some such way, the details of the example can be described so that neither moral requirement realistically overrides the other, even though the way of life of each agent supports one alternative above the other. The agents will then be in realistic moral dilemmas, and the argument will go through much as before. There will be realistically relevant differences between the situations, but these differences will be balanced, so they will not explain why Pedro ought to do what Fritz ought not to do.

A fourth response is that moral realists do not deny that the truth values of moral judgements can depend on past choices, since they admit that whether an act is morally wrong can depend on whether the agent chose to promise to do it.[27] However, promises are not like commitments to ways of life. Promises are speech acts, so one can choose to make a promise but never make or even be in a position to make that promise, and then no obligation is created. And a promise does create an obligation even if there is no subjective intention to fulfil it. Thus, it is an act of promising itself rather than any choice or other subjective accompaniment that makes such a moral judgement true for a moral realist. In contrast, it is Fritz's and Pedro's subjective commitments that determine what they ought to do on the anti-realist interpretation, even if their commitments are not reflected in any objective actions or speech prior to these conflicts. Furthermore, personal rankings are moral beliefs, but moral realists deny that whether one has a moral obligation to keep a promise depends on one's moral beliefs. Thus, the argument shows that moral judgements depend on more subjective factors in realistic moral dilemmas than in standard cases of promises.

A final, related response is that moral realists can admit that agents ought to have integrity and ought not to violate their ways of life, because these general judgements have realistic truth conditions. However, such a general judgement together with the premise that Pedro acts with integrity only if he keeps his professional promise imply the particular conclusion that Pedro ought to keep his promise. It is this particular moral judgement that does not have realistic truth conditions and that refutes universal moral realism. Even if this judgement is derived from a general premise with realistic truth conditions, this does not show that the conclusion has realistic truth conditions. If it did, moral realism would lose its contrast with even the most relativistic theories, since even a relativistic premise such as 'Everyone ought to do whatever he thinks is right' or 'Everyone ought to follow the conventions of his society' can have realistic truth conditions. In any case, if moral realists admit that the truth values of particular moral judgements depend on such subjective factors as the way of life chosen by the agent, then they grant all that my argument attempts to show.

Moral realists might have other responses, and the argument does rely on some intuitions that might be questioned, so the argument is not a conclusive proof. Nonetheless, in the absence of any adequate response, I conclude that some moral judgements do not have realistic truth conditions, so extreme universal moral realism is false.

7.5.4 Qualifications

It is important to realize what this argument does not claim to show. The argument does not try to prove that every version of moral realism is false. It is aimed at only the most extreme version of moral realism. Less extreme versions of moral realism are not affected by the argument.

First, the argument is directed against only universal moral realism, not partial moral realism. The argument shows only that *some* moral judgements lack realistic truth conditions, but *other* moral judgements still might have realistic truth conditions. The argument does raise the problem of where to draw the line, and it might shift the burden of proof. Still, the argument does not directly attack the claim that some but not all moral judgements have realistic truth conditions. That is all that some moral realists wanted to claim anyway.

Second, even for those moral judgements which the argument shows not to be realistic, the argument refutes only the extreme claim that their truth conditions are independent of even *ideal* mental states of agents. It is not plausible to make judgements with 'ought' depend on the agent's *actual* choice if the agent would choose differently were he or she rational or informed on non-moral matters. Thus, judgements with 'ought' depend at most on ideal, not actual, choices and moral beliefs, so the argument does not refute a moderate moral realist (or objectivist) who claims independence from actual but not ideal mental states.

Third, the argument shows dependence on the choices and beliefs of only the *agent*, not the *judger*. On the anti-realist interpretation, anyone can judge that Fritz ought to break his promise and Pedro ought to keep his promise. The truth of these judgements does not depend on who it is that makes the judgement.[28] Thus, the argument can be accepted by moderate moral realists who claim that the truth values of moral judgements are independent of only the judger's mental states. This is enough to make moral judgements parallel to some scientific judgements, such as psychological ones, so some moderate moral realists might be content with this much independence.

These qualifications should allay the fears of opponents who think that my argument leads to an unacceptable form of subjectivism or relativism. If extreme moral realism were the only alternative to moral relativism, it would be disturbing to find that extreme moral realism is false. However, my argument applies only to some moral judgements and only in moral dilemmas, so it does not lead all the way to wholesale relativism.

This might seem to take the sting out of my conclusion. However, it is important to realize that moral realism has its limits, because these limits make moral realism more plausible. Extreme moral realism underestimates the complexity of moral life when it overlooks the importance of individual choices and moral beliefs in moral dilemmas. More limited moral realism can recognize that such subjective factors are morally relevant in moral dilemmas, and it can still impose realistic limits on choices so as to avoid the problems of wholesale relativism. Thus, limited moral realism can accept the insights and avoid the problems of more extreme theories.

Nonetheless, I have not argued that limited moral realism is true. There are several other arguments against moral realism, and some apply to limited moral realism as well as to extreme moral realism. These other arguments would have to be refuted in order to defend even limited moral realism. I am not sure whether this can be done.

In any case, all I have tried to do here is to show that the only version of moral realism that might be defensible is limited moral realism. Since moral dilemmas also refute some but not all versions of moral anti-realism, moral dilemmas do not completely resolve this age-old debate, but they do set limits to the options on both sides that might be acceptable.

8

Applications

We have seen how moral dilemmas affect debates about moral realism and the purposes of moral judgements and theories. Moral dilemmas are also important because they affect how we should think about individual moral problems and general social policies. I will discuss some of these implications in this chapter.

8.1 INDIVIDUAL MORAL PROBLEMS

The possibilities of moral conflicts and of moral dilemmas have some general effects on how we should think about any concrete moral problem. If moral conflicts were not possible, there would always be one choice that an agent could make without worrying about remorse or compensation afterwards. However, since moral conflicts are possible, it is not enough for an agent *just* to determine which action is the best one. This action still might violate a moral requirement, so the agent must also determine what he or she should do or feel *after* the best choice is made. Such questions about moral residue are often overlooked when the possibility of moral conflicts is denied. And even when such questions are asked, we cannot give the right answer for the right reason without recognizing the possibility of moral conflicts.

Other questions arise when moral requirement conflicts are not resolvable, that is, when they are moral dilemmas. If realistic moral dilemmas were not possible, an agent could not choose one alternative in a moral conflict without implying that anyone who chooses otherwise in a similar situation is defective in some morally relevant way. However, since realistic moral dilemmas are possible, an agent can defend his or her own choice without criticizing different choices by others even in similar situations. Such judgements of others are especially important when peers have to evaluate each others' work, when a subordinate has to decide whether to obey a superior's command, and when a superior has to judge a subordinate who refuses to obey his or her command.

The possibility of realistic moral dilemmas also affects what kinds of argument are adequate to justify judgements of other people and their acts. People often form moral judgements of other people and their acts by asking what they themselves would (or should) do if they were in the others' situations. However, the possibility of realistic moral dilemmas shows that this is not an adequate basis for moral judgements of other people, since what I do (and what I should do) might depend on a ranking that is purely personal, even if it is also purely moral. My personal ranking cannot justify a judgement of another person if his or her personal ranking is different but still permissible both rationally and morally. Thus, the possibility of realistic moral dilemmas affects not only which moral judgements are true but also what kinds of argument are acceptable in moral reasoning.

These various implications can be clarified by using an example of an individual decision in a war. Suppose one country unjustly invades another country. A commander in the defending forces orders some troops to go to a friendly village and promises to provide air protection against enemy attack. The commander later learns that some enemy soldiers have set an ambush in the village and will kill his soldiers if they enter the village unawares. There is no way for the commander to let his soldiers know about their danger, so the only way to save his soldiers is for the commander to bomb the enemy soldiers in the village. Fortunately, many of the villagers are working in the fields, so the bombing will not kill all the villagers. Unfortunately, some villagers will be killed, and all of their homes will be destroyed.

This situation is a moral requirement conflict. There is a moral requirement for the commander not to order the bombing, because it will kill some civilians and will destroy the others' homes, and this would be wrong if there were no justification. It is perhaps more controversial to claim that there is a moral requirement to bomb the village. Nonetheless, I think it would be wrong not to save the soldiers if there were no justification for not doing so (that is, if the bombing would not kill anyone, except possibly enemy soldiers, or destroy any homes). It would be wrong because the commander is required to protect his soldiers when they are following his commands, especially if he promised to provide protection. We can also add that the soldiers were drafted, the war is just, and any other condition that might be necessary to create a moral require-ment in this case. When such details are added, this situation is a moral requirement conflict.

There are many different situations that fit this general pattern, since the numbers of villagers, enemy soldiers and protected soldiers can vary. Some such conflicts are resolvable. If the bombing would kill many villagers but save very few soldiers and accomplish little else, then the moral requirement not to bomb the village is realistically overriding. This is all too often the case in actual bombings in actual wars. However, there can also be cases where the bombing will save very many soldiers and greatly slow an unjust attack even though it kills some villagers. In some such cases, the moral requirement to bomb the village is overriding or at least not overridden.

Suppose, first, that the moral requirement to bomb the village is realistically overriding. Even though the conflict is resolvable, it is still important to realize that moral require-ments conflict in this situation. Although this does not affect whether the commander ought to bomb the village, it does affect what the commander ought to do after he bombs the village. After the bombing, there are villagers who are wounded and who have no homes, and this raises the question of who should help them.

If moral requirements did not conflict, the act of bombing

the village would not violate any moral requirement. The commander who dropped the bombs might still have some obligation to help the people in need, since we might all have some obligation to help the needy when we can and nobody else will. But if he violated no moral requirement, the commander would have no more obligation to help the villagers than a bystander (such as another country or the Red Cross) who opposed the bombing but was just as able as the bomber to help the victims; and no more obligation than he would have if someone else had dropped the bombs and he opposed them, or if it had been his own buildings that he destroyed and that the victims occupied without permission and contrary to warnings.

However, such implications seem wrong. Even if the bombing was justified, the commander who dropped the bombs still seems to have some special obligation to help the wounded and homeless villagers. The reason is that it was his acts that caused their needs, and this puts him into a special relation to those he harmed. If he does not help them, his bombing will have caused more harm than if he does help them. For example, suppose a villager is hurt so badly that he will die without help, but the commander can save his life. If the villager dies, the commander will have killed the villager, so the moral requirement not to kill this villager creates a moral requirement for the commander to save the villager's life. This is not true of anyone who did not cause the villager's wounds in the first place. The enemy also has an obligation to help the villagers, since they attacked the country. Nonetheless, if the commander who bombed the village knows that the enemy will not help the villagers soon enough, this commander has a special moral obligation to provide the villagers with medical care and new housing. There would be no special obligation (or no adequate way to show a special obligation) if moral requirement conflicts were not possible. This would let the commander off too easily.

These implications of moral conflicts are not just theoretical but also practical. If the commander thinks moral conflicts are not possible, he will be less likely to help those whom he harmed. And if a commander refuses to help those whom he harmed, or if he claims someone else should help them, then we need to show that he has a special obligation to help the villagers – more obligation than a mere onlooker – in order to justify our claim that it is the commander rather than someone else who should bear the burden of helping the victims. The special obligation cannot be adequately justified unless we recognize that he violated a moral requirement. The commander still might not listen to our arguments or agree or help the victims. However, military people listen to reason more often than their critics admit, and we cannot give adequate reasons for his compensatory obligations unless we recognize that the situation was a moral requirement conflict.

Thus, moral conflicts do have real implications for action. Too often, military people simply say that they were justified in doing what they did, so they forget to clean up afterwards. This attitude produces more misery and resentment among those who were harmed by their actions. Some of the wretchedness of war might be reduced by recognizing that even just wars create moral conflicts rather than merely questions of which actions are right.

So far I have considered implications of moral requirement conflicts regardless of whether or not they are resolvable. But there are also some cases of the above pattern where neither moral requirement overrides the other. Such cases are moral dilemmas, and they raise other practical questions. The most important ones concern how people should view each other when they choose differently in similar situations.

First, suppose one commander chooses to bomb the village in the above situation, and then he sees that another commander is in a relevantly similar situation, but the other commander chooses not to bomb the village. What should the first commander think or do about the second commander and his choice?

If the first commander thinks every moral conflict can be resolved realistically, and if he also thinks his bombing was adequately justified, he must think that the moral requirement to bomb the village realistically overrides the moral requirement not to bomb it. This implies that the second com-

mander violated a realistically overriding moral requirement
when he refused to bomb the village. His information might
have been insufficient or there might have been too much uncertainty for him to be blameworthy, but at least he made a mistake. It might not be worthwhile to report him to his superiors
or to punish him, since such acts have various costs. However,
his view of the second commander can have other practical
consequences. The first commander would have to think that
the second commander is less capable as a commander, and this
would be relevant when promotions or assignments are considered. Thus, the failure to recognize the situation as a moral
dilemma can have many practical consequences when different
commanders choose differently in similar situations.

On the other hand, if the first commander thinks the
situation is a realistic moral dilemma, he can judge the second
commander very differently. He can think that the second
commander's decision not to bomb the village did not violate
any realistically overriding moral requirement. Furthermore,
there is no reason to think that all military people must share
exactly the same personal rankings or ways of life in my sense.
So the first commander can think the second commander was
not mistaken in any way. He need not criticize the second
commander's decision in order to claim that his own decision to
bomb the village was adequately justified. Both of their choices
can be adequately justified even though they are different.
Their different choices also need not show that either one is
better as a commander or as a person. Since neither choice
might be mistaken, one commander need not criticize the
other at all in order to defend himself.

This also shows that one commander cannot always judge the
other by asking what he would have done if he were in the
other's situation. If the situation is a realistic moral dilemma, it
might be true that one commander would have chosen differently than another and would be right to do so, but this still
does not imply that the other commander was wrong. This
makes it inappropriate to judge the other commander or his
choice by asking what one *would* have done. It is even inappropriate to judge the other commander by asking what one *should*

have done. If no realistic ranking is available, permissible personal rankings can determine what each commander should do. Since different personal rankings can be permissible, the fact that one commander should do one thing does not imply that the other commander should also do the same thing even in an otherwise similar situation. Consequently, to judge the other commander or his acts, one must ask directly what the other commander *should* have done.

Moral dilemmas can also affect the relations between commanders and subordinates. The failure to admit that a situation is a moral dilemma often makes leaders intolerant of those they command. Suppose a leader commands a subordinate pilot to bomb the village in the above situation, but the pilot refuses. If the commander believes the moral requirement to bomb the village is realistically overriding, he must also believe his subordinate's refusal to obey violates a realistically overriding requirement (assuming the subordinate has no special obligations, such as if his own children are in the village, etc.). The commander could not admit that the subordinate was justified in refusing to obey without implying he was wrong to command in the first place. He still might not force or punish the pilot, either because he needs this pilot for other missions or because he thinks another pilot with fewer scruples will do a better job on this mission. Nonetheless, the commander must think that this pilot's refusal to obey is wrong and violates a realistically overriding moral requirement.

In contrast, suppose the commander thinks he was in a moral dilemma when he decided to issue the command, because neither of his moral requirements was overriding. The subordinate still might not be in a moral dilemma when he has to decide whether to obey the command, since there is some cost whenever a subordinate refuses to obey. However, if the moral requirements that conflict are massive enough, they might also be inexact enough so that a little extra weight on either side will not make one override the other. The commander might think that the cost of disobedience in this case is not enough to make the pilot's moral requirement to obey his command override the moral requirement not to kill the villagers. If the leader sees the conflict in this way, he can admit that the subordinate was justified in refusing to obey without admitting that his original command was wrong. The commander also need not criticize another subordinate who does obey the command, since different subordinates can choose differently and rank the moral requirements differently without either being defective either morally or rationally. Thus, commanders can be more tolerant and less authoritarian if they admit the inexactness of moral requirements and the possibility of moral dilemmas.

Military commanders rarely give this much leeway to subordinates, but that is mainly because some will refuse to obey out of fear or self-interest. Nonetheless, if a commander knows his subordinate refuses for justified moral reasons, the commander can allow the subordinate to act on his own personal moral ranking rather than that of his commander. Such cases are similar to missions that involve extreme danger. When death is probable, commanders sometimes ask for volunteers instead of issuing commands. There is no reason why a commander could not show a similar tolerance when the moral stakes are high and different people could weigh them differently without being defective in any way. Such cases might be rare, but the possibility of moral dilemmas still suggests why commanders need not and should not be as authoritarian as they often are.

None of these points is peculiar to war or the military. Similar cases arise in many other fields as well. Business executives often make decisions with moral implications. Moral conflicts show that they should accept more of the burden of compensation than they often admit, and moral dilemmas show that they sometimes can and should recognize that their subordinates can reasonably choose not to obey their commands. Similarly, lawyers should recognize that other lawyers can justifiably refuse to accept a case that they themselves would accept, and doctors should admit that other doctors can be justified in providing (or refusing) treatment that they themselves would not provide (or refuse). Even teachers need to admit others can be justified when they handle discipline and grading differently. When such cases have moral implications, it is theoretically and practically important to recognize the possibility of moral conflicts and dilemmas.

8.2 SOCIAL POLICIES

Moral conflicts and dilemmas also raise many questions about general policies for the government or leadership of societies. What kinds of law or policy should be made in and about situations that are moral dilemmas? The right answer to such questions is a matter of great dispute.

People who emphasize the value of individual freedom often claim that governments should never pass laws which interfere with an individual's choice when that individual is in a moral dilemma. This side argues that, since neither moral requirement overrides the other realistically, the individual must be allowed to choose for himself or herself. This position is supported not only by the value of individual freedom but also by the many costs of governmental interference in such difficult decisions.

On the other hand, a society or government itself is often in a moral dilemma. If a law restricting certain behaviour is passed, some values might be gained, but others will be lost, at least freedom. If the government is in a realistic moral dilemma, there is no realistically overriding moral requirement either to pass the law or not to pass it. In such cases, some people argue that the majority of the society must be allowed to choose as a group what kind of society to construct, even though their choice does restrict the freedom of some individuals. The most common reasons are that people should have the right to choose what kind of society to live in when they do not violate any realistically overriding rights, and that society works better when it has the kind of social cohesion that results when the majority agrees on social policies.

These positions might seem to conflict. One says that the government should not restrict individuals in moral dilemmas, and the other says that the government can restrict individuals when it is in a moral dilemma. However, these positions are not really incompatible, because they apply to different kinds of case. The first argument refers to situations where an individual is in a moral dilemma. The second argument refers to situations where the government itself is in a moral dilemma. If individuals are in moral dilemmas, the first argument implies that the government usually has overriding moral reasons not to pass laws which restrict their freedom, so the government is not in a moral dilemma. One the other hand, if the government really is in a moral dilemma, the loss of freedom if the law is passed must already be counterbalanced by some separate benefit of passing the law, so the reasons not to restrict freedom are not overriding. Thus, the two arguments apply to different kinds of case.

The differences between these kinds of case can be clarified by comparing some examples. First, individuals are often in moral dilemmas when they must decide about euthanasia for others. Let us suppose that a certain kind of euthanasia has been isolated where the individual who must decide is in a realistic moral dilemma. The government must then decide whether or not to pass a law that forbids euthanasia in this class of case. Those who favour the law might argue that we cannot allow someone to die when we have no overriding moral reason or requirement to do so. However, those who oppose the law can respond that we should not cause so much pain and expense unless we have an overriding moral requirement to do so. In such a conflict, it seems reasonable to put the burden on those who would restrict the freedom of the individuals who must choose in such cases. If freedom has the value that many claim, the government should not restrict it when all other factors are equal or incomparable. The government might not then be in a moral dilemma at all. The reasons for the legislation might be realistically overridden by the reasons against it plus the value of individual freedom. This will not solve the dilemma for the individuals who must decide, but it will keep the government out of areas where individuals should have freedom to decide, because morality does not overridingly require any single choice.

A different kind of case occurs when the society or government is in a realistic moral dilemma. For example, some preferential treatment programmes are necessary to compensate individuals or groups for past discrimination and its present effects, but some of these programmes also violate some rights of the excluded individuals. With some such programmes, the moral requirements on one side are clearly stronger. With others, neither moral requirement is realistically stronger or overriding. Suppose we isolate the latter kind of preferential treatment programme. The government or society must then decide whether to allow this kind in its public schools or employment policies. This question cannot be answered in the same way as in the case of euthanasia. It would not help to say that the government should give primacy to individual freedom because such programmes do not restrict anyone's freedom (if freedom is distinguished from opportunity), and, even though they do lessen the opportunities of some, they also increase opportunities for others. If the harms on opposite sides are equal or incomparable, the government is in a realistic moral dilemma. In such cases, an individual can recognize the strength of the conflicting moral requirements but still rank them and choose between them, and different people can choose differently without either being defective. Similarly, one society or government can choose to have such programmes, and other societies can choose not to have such programmes, and neither has to claim that the other violates a realistically overriding moral requirement or is morally defective in any way. There might be disagreements within society which create problems in deciding what to do, but there can also be consensus within each society even though the societies disagree. There is, then, no good reason not to allow different groups to construct their societies as they choose. The advantage of this is that it brings greater social cohesion. Society functions more smoothly when most people agree to its rules, and this cohesion is valuable as long as the rules do not violate realistically overriding moral requirements.

A similar case is that of pornography. Let us assume, as some evidence suggests, that pornography increases violence towards women. There is still a cost in restricting the freedom of those who want to use pornography. Some societies might consider both moral factors and decide that it is more important for them to keep pornography out of their community. Other societies might decide that freedom is more important to them, even if they are impartial between the interests of men and women. If the governments are in moral dilemmas when they choose whether or not to have anti-pornography laws, neither choice violates a realistically overriding moral requirement. Here the laws do restrict individuals' freedom, as in the case of euthanasia. However, this does not prove that the government should not restrict pornography, because the loss in freedom to the pornographer still might be balanced against the reduction in violence against women, so the government still might be in a realistic moral dilemma. If so, one community can ban pornography, and another can allow it, and neither has to claim that the other is wrong in order to defend its own choice.

None of these cases has been proven. Any such social question depends on many detailed facts, so it is never clear whether a government really is in a realistic moral dilemma. Advocates (or opponents) of any legislation might admit that the legislation would be unjustified (or justified) if the government were in a moral dilemma, but they can go on to argue that the government is not in a moral dilemma at all. Thus, no social questions will be answered simply by pointing out that it is possible for goverments to be in moral dilemmas.

Nonetheless, the recognition that governments can be in moral dilemmas has some consequences. First, it opens up the possibility that different societies can choose different laws without either of them being mistaken or defective in any way. This should make us more able to realize and accept some cultural and social differences without giving up all moral restrictions on what societies do.

These considerations are also important because they suggest a general justification of democracy restricted by basic protections.[1] We need basic protections because governments are not always in moral dilemmas. Some laws or policies would violate realistically overriding moral requirements, such as some which restrict individuals' freedom in moral dilemmas. We need some restrictions on which laws the majority can pass in order to ensure that realistically overriding moral requirements are not violated.

What moral dilemmas add is, then, a justification for democracy as a method of decision when no realistically overriding moral requirement would be violated. If there were always one alternative that morality required overridingly, there would be no clear reason to allow the majority to decide which laws to pass. There is no obvious reason why the majority would be more likely to pick the overriding moral requirement. Some elite group might be better at determining which moral requirement overrides which. However, if we admit that governments are sometimes in realistic moral dilemmas, there are reasons to favour democratic decisions in such moral dilemmas. Democratic procedures will be more likely to lead to policies that bring about a coherent and happy society, and groups of people do seem to have a right to decide what kind of society to live in, when no realistically overriding moral requirement is violated. Thus, once adequate protections are in place, the possibility of moral dilemmas provides reasons to favour some democratic form of government.

None of these claims about social theory has been proven. To do so would take much more argument about the values of individual freedom and social cohesion. All that I have tried to do here is to point out some areas where the possibility of moral dilemmas forces us to rethink old issues and suggests a plausible way of handling such problems. Even where moral dilemmas do not have definite or definitive practical implications, one of the main reasons why moral dilemmas are important is that they do force us to look at some of these old issues in new ways.

Notes

CHAPTER 1 WHAT MORAL DILEMMAS ARE

1 Sartre, 'Existentialism is a Humanism' (1957), pp. 295–6.
2 Williams, 'Ethical Consistency' (1965), p. 173.
3 I assume this qualification throughout, so moral dilemmas do not include moral binds in the sense of Zimmerman, 'Remote Obligation' (1987), p. 200.
4 Harman, *The Nature of Morality* (1977), pp. 59 and 118–19.
5 The univocity of 'ought' can be tested by linguistic transformations. Cf. Zwicky and Sadock, 'Ambiguity Tests and How to Fail Them' (1975). The univocity of 'ought' is defended in Wertheimer, *The Significance of Sense* (1972) and White, *Modal Thinking* (1975).
6 There would be an important difference between epistemic and moral dilemmas if epistemic reasons or requirements implied truth, since then epistemic reasons and requirements could not conflict. However, there are looser ways to interpret epistemic reasons and requirements so that they do not imply truth. One real difference between epistemic dilemmas and moral dilemmas is that one can refuse to commit oneself either way in many epistemic dilemmas, but the agent cannot simply refuse to choose in a moral dilemma without effectively choosing one alternative. For more on epistemic dilemmas, see Levi, *Hard Choices* (1986), ch. 3.
7 Legal dilemmas differ from moral dilemmas if a judge or the highest court of appeal settles which legal requirement is overriding. Such differences might suggest that legal dilemmas are not possible even if moral dilemmas are. Cf. Dworkin, 'Is There Really No Right Answer in Hard Cases?' (1985).
8 Cf. Quinn, 'Moral Obligation, Religious Demand, and Practical Conflict' (1986).
9 Cf. Frankena, 'Recent Conceptions of Morality' (1963). These issues arise even if morality is not strictly definable.

10 I am grateful to Bernie Gert and Shelly Kagan for forcing me to realize the importance of this distinction. Cf. Gert, *Morality* (forthcoming), ch. 8: 'Moral Ideals'. This distinction is similar to a traditional distinction between perfect and imperfect duties, but the traditional distinction is more confusing, because it has been made in so many different and inadequate ways.

11 Mill, *Utilitarianism* (1979), ch. 5, pp. 47ff.

12 Lemmon, 'Moral Dilemmas' (1962), p. 148. The example is modified from Plato, *Republic* (1961), 331c.

13 McConnell, 'Moral Dilemmas and Requiring the Impossible' (1976), p. 409; and Conee, 'Against Moral Dilemmas' (1982), p. 87; both quoted below in the text.

14 E.g. Greenspan, 'Moral Dilemmas and Guilt' (1983), p. 117, who criticizes Marcus for counting resolvable moral conflicts as moral dilemmas.

15 Cf. Swank, 'Reasons, Dilemmas, and the Logic of "Ought" ' (1985), pp. 115–16.

16 Gowans, 'Introduction: The Debate on Moral Dilemmas' (1987), p. 24; and Rescher, *Ethical Idealism* (1987), p. 41.

17 McConnell, 'Moral Dilemmas and Requiring the Impossible', p. 409.

18 Conee, 'Against Moral Dilemmas', p. 87.

19 Nagel, 'The Fragmentation of Value' (1977), pp. 128–9.

20 E.g. van Fraassen, 'Values and the Heart's Command' (1973); Williams 'Conflicts of Values' (1979); Swank, 'Reasons, Dilemmas, and the Logic of "Ought" ' and Quinn, 'Moral Obligation, Religious Demand, and Practical Conflict', pp. 198–9.

21 Cf. Marcus, 'Moral Dilemmas and Consistency' (1980), pp. 135–6.

22 Most of what follows is due to Davidson, *Essays on Actions and Events* (1980), pp. 105–22, but I do not commit myself to some of the more controversial aspects of his theory.

23 If not all moral dilemmas could be reduced to two alternatives, I would have to reformulate some of my claims below. Further complications are suggested when Levi argues against 'the binary character of rational valuation of feasible options' (*Hard Choices*, p. 70; see also pp. 33, etc.). However, I believe that my basic arguments are not affected essentially by such complications.

24 Marcus, 'Moral Dilemmas and Consistency', p. 122. See also McConnell, 'Interpersonal Moral Dilemmas' (1986), and Zimmerman, 'Lapses and Dilemmas' (unpublished).

25 The moral requirement not to adopt both alternatives might also be

neither stronger nor weaker than the moral requirements to adopt each alternative, but such cases do not affect my main points. Cf. Greenspan, 'Sophie's Choices: More on Exclusive Requirement' (1986).

26 Cf. Geach, *God and the Soul* (1969), p. 128; discussed in Donagan, *The Theory of Morality* (1977), p. 147.

CHAPTER 2 ARGUMENTS FOR MORAL DILEMMAS

1 E.g. Beardsmore, *Moral Reasoning* (1969), p. 111.

2 E.g. van Fraassen, 'Values and the Heart's Command' (1973), pp. 11–12.

3 For more on the distinction between justifications and excuses, see Austin, 'A Plea for Excuses' (1970); and Woodruff, 'Justification or Excuse: Saving Soldiers at the Expense of Civilians' (1982).

4 E.g. Williams, 'Ethical Consistency' (1973), pp. 172–3; and Marcus, 'Moral Dilemmas and Consistency' (1980), pp. 132–3.

5 A similar example is discussed in Rawls, *A Theory of Justice* (1971), p. 482; and in Marcus, 'Moral Dilemmas and Consistency', p. 132.

6 Levi, *Hard Choices* (1986), p. 27, suggests another explanation of why remorse is appropriate. Most of us start out with a belief that torture with remorse is better than torture without remorse. Levi points out that it is not necessary to change this ranking even after we come to believe that both of these options with torture are better than not torturing either with or without remorse. Levi also claims that we should modify our antecedent commitments as little as is necessary, so we should not give up our original ranking of the two options with torture even after we come to believe that the best option includes torture. Although this is ingenious, it starts with and does not explain (or attempt to explain) why torture with remorse is better than torture without remorse even when torture is justified. My point is that this original ranking cannot be justified without in effect admitting that even justified torture violates what I call a moral requirement.

7 Cf. Foot, 'Moral Realism and Moral Dilemma' (1983), p. 382.

8 E.g. McConnell, 'Moral Dilemmas and Consistency in Ethics' (1978); Conee, 'Against Moral Dilemmas' (1982); Donagan,

'Consistency in Rationalist Moral Systems' (1984); and Feldman, *Doing the Best We Can* (1986), p. 203.

9 This approach is defended by Rawls, *A Theory of Justice*, p. 482, and Marcus, 'Moral Dilemmas and Consistency', p. 132. It is criticized in Greenspan, 'Moral Dilemmas and Guilt', (1983), pp. 122 and 124, n. 6, but I need not develop or defend a complete account of emotions here.

10 This point is argued in Phillips and Price, 'Remorse without Repudiation' (1967–8), pp. 18–20.

11 Cf. Strasser, 'Guilt, Regret, and *Prima Facie* Duties' (1987), pp. 133–46.

12 Walzer, 'Political Action: The Problem of Dirty Hands' (1971), p. 75.

13 Thomson, *Rights, Restitution, and Risk* (1986), pp. 41 and 40. See also pp. 66 ff; and Feinberg, 'Voluntary Euthanasia and the Inalienable Right to Life' (1978), p. 102.

14 Greenspan, 'Moral Dilemmas and Guilt', p. 124, n. 8, emphasizes apologies; and Nozick, 'Moral Complications and Moral Structures' (1968), mentions several kinds of moral residue.

15 Styron, *Sophie's Choice* (1980), p. 589. Greenspan, 'Moral Dilemmas and Guilt', pp. 118–19, and 'Sophie's Choices: More on Exclusive Requirement' (1986) argues that it makes a difference whether Sophie chooses which child will live or which child will die. I doubt this difference is important, but I will avoid this issue by using a version where Sophie must choose a child to be killed. The requirements might be even clearer if the guard told Sophie to kill one child herself, but I will stick closer to the original story.

16 Furthermore, the disjunctive moral requirement need not be stronger than the non-disjunctive moral requirements. We can change the case so that, if she refuses to choose, there is some chance that both children will be killed and some chance that the Nazi will repent, and we can adjust this chance until the disjunctive requirement neither overrides nor is overridden by the non-disjunctive requirements. In this case, the non-disjunctive requirements conflict and neither is overridden, not even by the disjunctive requirement.

17 A similar point is emphasized by Rawls, *A Theory of Justice*, p. 27.

18 Marcus, 'Moral Dilemmas and Consistency', p. 125. The twins can also be newborn in order to exclude any acquired differences.

19 This argument is suggested but not explicitly endorsed by Williams, 'Conflicts of Values' (1979), pp. 76 ff.

20 Aristotle, *Metaphysics* (1941), X 1053a 24–5.

21 Nagel, 'The Fragmentation of Value' (1979), p. 134. Nagel continues this line of argument in 'The Limits of Objectivity' (1980) and *The View from Nowhere* (1986). Notice that the view *sub specie aeternitatis* seems to correspond to both utility and perfectionist ends.

22 'The Fragmentation of Value', p. 128.

23 Ibid., p. 128.

24 Ibid., p. 135.

25 Cf. Guttenplan, 'Moral Realism and Moral Dilemmas' (1979–80), p. 72.

26 Marcus, 'Moral Dilemmas and Consistency', pp. 135–6, cites another case in which Forster and Worcester would choose differently if they had to choose between betraying a friend and betraying their countries. Marcus points out that different choices need not imply different moral rankings. I agree that this implication does not hold, but there are still cases where both choices and rankings are different. See also Levi, *Hard Choices*, ch. 6.

27 Snare, 'The Diversity of Morals' (1980), pp. 366–8. Even Hume, who often emphasizes that moral sentiments are universal, admits that some people approve of monkish or martial virtues more than others do. See Hume, *An Enquiry Concerning the Principles of Morals* (1902), pp. 254–5 and 270.

28 Cf. Firth, 'Ethical Absolutism and the Ideal Observer' (1952), pp. 343–4; and Rawls, *A Theory of Justice*, p. 139. Gert criticizes complete rankings in *Morality* (forthcoming), ch. 13.

29 I am indebted to Bernie Gert for this point.

30 This argument derives from de Sousa, 'The Good and the True' (1974), pp. 544–5. See also Raz, *The Morality of Freedom* (1986), p. 325. The argument does not depend on cardinal units. I use them only for illustration.

31 E.g. Ross, *Foundations of Ethics* (1939), p. 188. Levi, *Hard Choices*, p. 4, claims that, when moral reasons are incomparable, 'the agent does not know what ought to be done.' This is true if it means that he does not know which moral reason overrides which, since neither does. However, the fact that the agent does not know any ranking or equation does not imply that there is anything to be known that he does not already know. The agent

must decide, but that is not a matter of knowledge, as Levi himself emphasizes.

32 See Ross, *Foundations of Ethics*, p. 180 ff.

33 The possibility and limitations of weighted averaging are discussed in Levi, *Hard Choices*. His basic example is on pp. 11–13.

34 For more on incomparability, see references in notes 19, 21, 30 and 31 as well as Sen, 'Well-being, Agency, and Freedom' (1985); Wiggins, 'Weakness of Will, Commensurability, and the Objects of Deliberation and Desire' (1978–9); and Griffin, *Well-Being* (1986), ch. V.

CHAPTER 3 SOME OPPONENTS

1 J.S. Mill, *A System of Logic* (1884), Book VI, ch. XII, sec. 7.

2 Cf. W.D. Ross, *Foundations of Ethics* (1939), p. 173, and Marcus, 'Moral Dilemmas and Consistency' (1980), p. 125.

3 This disjunctive response can also be given by non-utilitarians. E.g. Donagan, 'Consistency in Rationalist Moral Systems' (1984), p. 307. Donagan might depend here on his principle of the least evil in *The Theory of Morality* (1977), p. 154. If so, this puts him in the same camp as utilitarians insofar as only the total counts. In any case, my criticisms still apply.

4 Cf. Rawls, *A Theory of Justice* (1971), pp. 27 ff. See Slote, 'Utilitarianism, Moral Dilemmas, and Moral Cost' (1985), p. 167, for an argument that some utilitarians can incorporate the distinctness of persons, but only in ways that introduce moral dilemmas.

5 Mill, *Utilitarianism* (1979), p. 11.

6 Moore gives the basic arguments in *Principia Ethica* (1903) and *Ethics* (1912). See also Nozick, *Anarchy, State, and Utopia* (1974), pp. 42–5; and Sen, 'Plural Utility' (1981) and 'Well-being, Agency and Freedom' (1985).

7 Hare, *Moral Thinking* (1981), ch. 2.

8 Cf. Gert, *Morality*, chs. 2–3; and Bond, *Reason and Value* (1983).

9 Cf. de Sousa, 'The Good and the True' (1974).

10 Cf. Levi, *Hard Choices* (1986), especially sec. 10.5.

11 For more on utilitarianism and moral dilemmas, see notes 4–10 and Nowell-Smith, 'Some Reflections on Utilitarianism' (1972–3); Bronaugh, 'Utilitarian Alternatives' (1975); and McConnell, 'Utilitarianism and Conflict Resolution' (1981).

12 Berkeley, *Passive Obedience* (1929), sec. 26; and Donagan, *The*

Theory of Morality. See Atkinson, *Conduct* (1969), ch. 2, on Kant.

13 Cf. Davidson, *Essays on Actions and Events* (1980), p. 59; but Davidson counts rest as a bodily movement.

14 This is a modification of an infamous example from Kant, 'On a Supposed Right to Lie from Altruistic Motives' (1949). My response to Kant is similar to that of Bradley, *Ethical Studies* (1927), p. 158. See also Hill, 'Moral Purity and the Lesser Evil' (1983), pp. 217–20; and Korsgaard, 'The Right to Lie: Kant on Dealing with Evil' (1986).

15 Kant, *Foundations of the Metaphysics of Morals* (1959) p. 39, n. The distinction based on enforcement by external law comes from 'the schools'.

16 Mill, *Utilitarianism*, p. 48.

17 These points come from Bennett, 'Morality and Consequences' (1981), especially sec. 3.

18 See Foot, *Virtues and Vices* (1978), p. 29.

19 Hare, *The Language of Morals* (1952), e.g., p. 54.

20 Donagan, *The Theory of Morality*, p. 154, tries to avoid dilemmas with a similar clause about impermissible means, but he never explains whether something is impermissible when it violates a non-overridden requirement or only when it violates an overriding requirement. See also my pp. 105–6 below.

21 Gewirth, *Reason and Morality* (1978), p. 237 (my emphasis). He gives a summary of his general ranking on pp. 341 ff.

22 Cf. Rawls, *A Theory of Justice*, pp. 42–3.

23 Gewirth, *Reason and Morality*, p. 352.

24 E.g., Prichard, 'Does Moral Philosophy Rest on a Mistake?' (1968) and Dancy, 'Ethical Particularism and Morally Relevant Properties' (1983), emphasize particular obligations; and even W.D. Ross, *The Right and the Good* (1930), p. 42, ranks some conflicting requirements by particular 'perception' rather than by any general rules or ranking.

25 E.g., Kant's distinction between grounds of obligation and obligations or duties in *The Metaphysical Elements of Justice* (1965), p. 25, although Donagan, 'Consistency in Rationalist Moral Systems', pp. 294–5, argues that Kant had something else in mind.

26 W.D. Ross, *The Right and the Good*, p. 19. Some morally relevant facts might not seem to generate kinds or properties of acts, but Ross also refers to 'an element' of the situation on p. 20.

27 W.D. Ross does mention related distinctions in his later book,

Foundations of Ethics, pp. 109 ff, but he does not see their importance for his definition of prima facie duties. See also Raz,
'Reasons, Requirements, and Practical Conflicts' (1974), pp.
30–5, who criticizes Chisholm for overlooking similar distinctions, and Chisholm's 'Reply to Comments' (1974), pp. 45–6.

28 My act of painting the house might not be an act of keeping a
promise if you told me not to paint it, but Ross cannot assume
that the only relevant kind is 'the keeping of a promise', since
his definition is supposed to help determine which kinds are
relevant.

29 E.g., W.D. Ross, *The Right and the Good*, p. 28.

30 This point and much of what follows derives from Searle, *'Prima
Facie* Obligations' (1980).

31 E.g., W.D. Ross, *The Right and the Good*, p. 20.

32 Ibid, pp. 28–9.

33 Ibid, p. 20.

34 Ibid, pp. 28–9. Ross does say that this analogy is imperfect, but the
only disanalogy that he explicitly admits is that 'prima facie' refers
to 'no relation that involves succession in time'.

35 E.g., Ibid, p. 28.

36 The notion of a prima facie duty is sometimes formalized in conditional deontic logics, but these technical developments provide
no new arguments against moral conflicts or dilemmas, since
various interpretations of prima facie requirements are paral-
leled by various interpretations of 'O(A/B)' which differ on
whether 'OA' can be detached from 'O(A/B)' given 'B', and on
whether incompatible alternatives can be morally required relative to the same total situation. A confusion between cancelling
and justifying is the source of Powers's paradox of John and Suzy
in 'Some Deontic Logicians' (1967). See also Searle, *'Prima Facie*
Obligations', who criticizes Hintikka's attempt in 'Some Main
Problems of Deontic Logic' (1971), to explain prima facie obligations by deontic implication.

37 Aquinas, *Summa Theologiae* (1964–75), I–II, Q. 19, art. 6, ad 3;
II–II, Q. 62, 2 obj. 2; III, Q. 64, art. 6 ad 3; and *de Veritate*
(1952–4), Q. 17, art. 4 ad 8. Von Wright, 'Deontic Logic' (1951),
p. 14, n. 1. Geach, *God and the Soul* (1969), p. 128. Donagan, *The
Theory of Morality*, pp. 143 ff; and 'Consistency in Rationalist
Moral Systems', pp. 305–6. See also McConnell, 'Moral Dilemmas
and Consistency in Ethics' (1978), p. 276. Zimmerman, 'Lapses
and Dilemmas' (unpublished), pp. 7 ff, rejects this position for

situations that are moral dilemmas on my definition but adopts a similar position for some related situations.

38 Cited by Donagan, *The Theory of Morality*, p. 144.
39 See Hamblin, 'Quandaries and the Logic of Rules' (1972).
40 Von Wright, 'Deontic Logic', p. 14, n. 1.
41 This claim is made by Marcus, 'Moral Dilemmas and Consistency'.
42 Donagan, 'Consistency in Rationalist Moral Systems', pp. 304–5. This third principle is strange, because even an insincere promisor believes that the promisee understands the promisor to believe that he can and may do as he promises. Also, the second part of the second principle could rule out moral requirement conflicts even without this third principle.

Chapter 4 The Argument from ' "Ought" Implies "Can" '

1 E.g., McConnell, 'Moral Dilemmas and Consistency in Ethics' (1978), pp. 271 ff, and Donagan, 'Consistency in Rationalist Moral Systems (1984), pp. 297 ff.
2 This defence is adopted by Williams, 'Ethical Consistency' (1973), pp. 181 ff; van Fraassen, 'Values and the Heart's Command' (1973), p. 13; and Marcus, 'Moral Dilemmas and Consistency' (1980), p. 134.
3 This defence is adopted by Lemmon, 'Moral Dilemmas' (1962), p. 150, n. 8, and 'Deontic Logic and the Logic of Imperatives' (1965), pp. 47–50; Trigg, 'Moral Conflict' (1971), p. 46; Nagel, 'War and Massacre' (1979), p. 74; and Rescher, *Ethical Idealism* (1987), pp. 34 ff (but see note 15 below).
4 Holly Smith Goldman suggested this in correspondence.
5 I am using 'true' and 'false' in a way compatible with both realism and anti-realism. See below, section 7.1, p. 190.
6 Some philosophers describe a kind of presupposition that is pragmatic, but, if this is the relation between 'ought' and 'can', it can be true that an agent ought to do what he cannot do, so this could not rule out moral dilemmas for the same reason as with conversational implication.
7 Cf. Austin, 'A Plea for Excuses' (1970), p. 176. Similar points apply to apologies which are not mere formalities uttered for extraneous purposes, etc.
8 This objection was raised by Martinich, 'Ought, Can and Conversational Implication' (1986). This issue is also relevant to the

debate about moral luck: e.g., Williams, 'Moral Luck' (1981); and Nagel, 'Moral Luck' (1979).

9 Cf. Hare, *Freedom and Reason* (1963), p. 56. Hare refers not to advice but to prescriptions and practical questions, but the same points apply.

10 I discuss this last example in detail in ' "Ought to Have" and "Could Have" ' (1985), pp. 44–8. Even more counterexamples arise if 'ought' has the same meaning in all contexts, since then 'ought' does not semantically imply 'can' unless it does so in every context. But 'ought' does not imply 'can' in many non-moral contexts. For example, I (prudentially) ought not to laugh at my boss's new haircut, but I cannot stop myself. And 'Everyone ought to be beautiful' can be true in an evaluative context, even though nobody can make everyone beautiful. Finally, it can be true that the train ought to be here soon, even if the train cannot be here soon because it fell off its tracks. These nonmoral uses of 'ought' show that moral uses of 'ought' do not entail 'can' if but only if 'ought' is univocal. My arguments in the text do not depend on this assumption, since they use 'ought' in moral contexts.

11 I derived my example from White, *Modal Thinking* (1975), p. 149. After I wrote this chapter, Michael Stocker informed me that he gave a similar example earlier in ' "Ought" and "Can" ' (1971), p. 314. I also give similar examples which do not depend on promising in 'A Resolution of a Paradox of Promising' (1987), p. 81.

12 E.g., Goldman, 'Dated Rightness and Moral Imperfection' (1976), pp. 449–87; and Zimmerman, 'Remote Obligation' (1987). Thomason, 'Deontic Logic and the Role of Freedom in Moral Deliberation' (1981), p. 180, claims this for 'the deliberative reading' of 'ought' but not for 'ought' in general.

13 This principle was mentioned by Kaplan as reported by Thomason, 'Deontic Logic as Founded on Tense Logic' (1981), p. 175. See also Stocker, ' "Ought" and "Can" ', p. 316.

14 Some opponents might respond that, whenever the helicopter in fact will arrive in time, it is true even before the helicopter arrives that Adams can meet Brown at 6.00. However, it does not seem that what the agent can do depends on future facts like these which the agent cannot know and cannot control. Even if 'can' can be used apart from such knowledge and control, this is not how it is used in the traditional principle that 'ought'

implies 'can', since the traditional view is that lack of knowledge and control removes blameworthiness and falsifies 'ought'
judgements. See Martinich, 'Obligation, Ability, and *Prima Facie
Promising*' (forthcoming) and my response in 'Promises which
Cannot be Kept' (unpublished).

15 Rescher, *Ethical Idealism*, p. 44, suggests that (in my terms) moral
   reasons do not imply 'can', but overriding moral reasons still
   imply 'can'. My examples use moral reasons which are overriding
   only because they do not conflict with anything. They thus leave
   open the possibility that overriding moral reasons imply 'can' if
   overriding is analysed so that a moral reason is not overriding
   unless it both conflicts with and is morally stronger than another
   moral reason. If we then add that two reasons conflict only if
   each can be followed, overriding moral reasons do entail 'can' on
   this analysis. However, this entailment is due to the analyses of
   overriding and conflict rather than to the moral reasons or their
   strengths. In any case, this principle could not be used to rule out
   moral dilemmas.

16 Hare, *Freedom and Reason*, pp. 53–4, defends presupposition.
17 Grice, 'Logic and Conversation' (1975), p. 67.
18 Ibid., p. 67.
19 Ibid., p. 69.
20 Ibid., p. 69. This test distinguishes conversational from conventional implications.
21 Ibid., p. 74.
22 Ibid., pp. 74–5.
23 Both quotations are from Williams, 'Ethical Consistency', p. 182.
24 Ibid., p. 182. He seems to have in mind Hare, *The Language of
   Morals* (1952).
25 A similar example is given by Swank, 'Reasons, Dilemmas, and
   the Logic of "Ought" ' (1985), pp. 113–4.

CHAPTER 5 THE ARGUMENT FROM 'OUGHT AND OUGHT NOT'

1 McConnell, 'Moral Dilemmas and Consistency in Ethics' (1978),
  p. 272–3; Hare, *Moral Thinking* (1981), pp. 27–8; and Conee,
  'Against Moral Dilemmas' (1982), pp. 87–8.
2 Greenspan, 'Sophie's Choices' (1986), denies closure except for
  overriding moral reasons. Doubts are expressed by Lemmon,
  'Deontic Logic and the Logic of Imperatives' (1965), pp. 65–6;
  Williams, 'Ethical Consistency' (1973), p. 180; Marcus, 'Iterated

Deontic Modalities' (1966); and Foot, 'Moral Realism and Moral Dilemma' (1983), p. 384.

3 E.g., Trigg, 'Moral Conflicts' (1971); van Fraassen, 'Values and the Heart's Command' (1973); and Marcus, 'Moral Dilemmas and Consistency' (1980).

4 If we define '$\boxed{c}$A' as '$-\diamondsuit - A$', (COC) becomes '$\boxed{c}(A \rightarrow B) \rightarrow$ (OA $\rightarrow$ OB)' which is closer in form to (COL). I use the formulation in (COC) because '$\boxed{c}(A \rightarrow B)$' has no natural expression in English.

5 This is emphasized by Marcus, 'Moral Dilemmas and Consistency'.

6 Alf Ross, 'Imperatives and Logic' (1941).

7 This is Grice's principle of quantity in 'Logic and Conversation' (1975), p. 67. This solution to Ross's paradox is also given by Follesdal and Hilpinen, 'Deontic Logic: An Introduction' (1971), p. 22.

8 Forrester, 'Gentle Murder, or the Adverbial Samaritan' (1984). Here I modify Forrester's paradox slightly to fit my terminology. A more complete discussion is in Sinnott-Armstrong, 'A Solution to Forrester's Paradox of Gentle Murder' (1985). The Good Samaritan paradox occurs first in Prior, 'The Paradoxes of Derived Obligation' (1954), and derives its name from his example.

9 Davidson, *Essays on Actions and Events* (1980), essay 6.

10 Cf. Jackson and Pargetter, 'Oughts, Options, and Actualism' (1986), pp. 247–9.

11 A critic might object that my reason not to borrow the book without returning it does not override my reason to bring the book and return it, since I *can* fulfil both reasons by both borrowing the book and returning it, so these reasons do not conflict. However, if we take it as settled that I will not return the book, this option is no longer relevant, and I must choose between the above reasons, so these reasons *do* conflict. On the other hand, if we do not take it as settled that I will not return the book, it is an option to bring it and return it, and then I *ought* to bring the book. This judgement seems false only if one assumes I will not return it. Thus, closure holds as long as we keep constant our assumptions about what is settled or which options are relevant. This is enough for moral dilemmas, since then it is not settled which alternative the agent will adopt, so both are relevant options.

12 Cf. Grice's rule of quantity in 'Logic and Conversation', p. 67.

13 Cf. Grice's rule of relevance in 'Logic and Conversation', p. 67.

14 A related objection is that my moving some air molecules would not be intentional. However, even if so, I have argued above that intentionality is not necessary to violate a moral requirement, if what is intentional is less than what is done knowingly and not accidentally.

15 Foot, 'Moral Realism and Moral Dilemma' (1983), p. 384.

16 My restriction is similar to Foot's restriction to means which must be possible in 'Moral Realism and Moral Dilemma', p. 384. Chris Gowans in correspondence suggested why it is necessary to include '$\Diamond$ B' as well as '$\Diamond$ A' in the antecedent of (RCOC*). (RCOC*) without '$\Diamond$ B' would be (1) (OA & $\Diamond$ A & $-$ $\Diamond$ (A&B)) $\rightarrow$ O$-$B. The problem is that there seems always to be some value of 'A' (e.g., not to kill everyone) such that (2) OA & $\Diamond$ A. (1) and (2) imply (3) $-$ $\Diamond$ (A&B) $\rightarrow$ O$-$B. Since (4) $-$ $\Diamond$ B $\rightarrow$ $-$ $\Diamond$ (A&B), we can derive (5) $-$ $\Diamond$ B $\rightarrow$ O$-$B. This claims that whatever cannot be done ought not to be done, and that seems wrong. Furthermore, if 'ought' is interpreted so as to refer to overriding moral reasons, then (6) OB $\rightarrow$ $-$O$-$B, but (5) and (6) imply (7) OB $\rightarrow$ $\Diamond$ B, which claims that this interpretation of 'ought' implies 'can'. All such conclusions are avoided by adding '$\Diamond$ B' to (1) to get (RCOC*).

17 Marcus, 'Iterated Deontic Modalities', pp. 581–2, gives two more examples, and they do refute the principle of extensionality she wants to refute but not the restricted principle of closure I defend.

18 E.g., McConnell, 'Moral Dilemmas and Consistency in Ethics', pp. 272–3, and Conee, 'Against Moral Dilemmas', pp. 87–8.

19 This is why advocates of this argument insist that they do not use this interpretation of 'ought'. McConnell, 'Moral Dilemmas and Requiring the Impossible' (1976), p. 409; Conee, 'Against Moral Dilemmas', p. 87.

20 It might seem more natural to interpret 'permitted' as 'not required not', but then, if 'ought' is defined in terms of moral reasons (including moral ideals), 'permitted' does not imply 'not ought not', as (8) claims, because there might be no moral requirement not to adopt an alternative, even if there is an overriding moral ideal not to adopt the alternative. Thus, such interpretations cannot save the argument from 'ought and ought not'.

21 A similar explanation is given by Foot, 'Moral Realism and Moral Dilemma', p. 385.

22 Grice, 'Logic and Conversation', p. 67. Searle also uses this maxim to show a related but different conversational implication in '*Prima Facie* Obligations' (1980), p. 88. See also Raz, 'Reasons, Requirements, and Practical Conflicts' (1974), p. 24.

23 Grice, 'Logic and Conversation', p. 74.

24 Van Fraassen, 'Values and the Heart's Command', p. 13. Another argument is that 'O(B&−B)' cannot be true, because 'ought' implies 'logically possible'. Cf. Hare, *Moral Thinking*, pp. 27–8. This premise might be true even if 'ought' does not imply 'can', but we need to see why it is true, and that is what van Fraassen's argument attempts to show.

25 This escape is adopted by Williams, 'Ethical Consistency', pp. 180 ff; Marcus, 'Moral Dilemmas and Consistency', p. 134; and van Fraassen, 'Values and the Heart's Command', p. 15.

26 Lemmon, 'Deontic Logic and the Logic of Imperatives', p. 47, and Trigg, 'Moral Conflicts', p. 46, deny (10.6) and claim that 'O(A&−A)' is possible, but it is not clear whether they deny (10.3) or (10.5).

27 McConnell, 'Moral Dilemmas and Requiring the Impossible', p. 412.

28 A similar result can be achieved by replacing material implication '→' with a stronger implication so that contradictions do not imply everything. Cf. da Costa and Carnieli, 'On Paraconsistent Deontic Logic' (1986). Notice also that I assume throughout that 'A' and 'B' stand for action sentences with the same agent, for the same reasons as with closure under 'can'.

CHAPTER 6 CONSISTENCY

1 Cf. Marcus, 'Moral Dilemmas and Consistency' (1980), pp. 128 ff.

2 Some defenders of moral dilemmas have also shown that it is possible to construct non-standard formal semantics which allow moral dilemmas. E.g., van Fraassen, 'Values and the Heart's Command' (1973); Schotch and Jennings, 'Non-Kripkean Deontic Logic' (1981); and Belzer and Loewer, 'Absolute Obligations and Lewis' Semantics of Deontic Logic' (1987).

3 Marcus emphasizes this in 'Moral Dilemmas and Consistency', pp. 128 ff.

4 Levi, *Hard Choices* (1986), p. 7.
5 Cf. Hamblin, 'Quandaries and the Logic of Rules' (1972), pp. 80 and 83; and Donagan, *The Theory of Morality* (1977), p. 148.
6 The basic idea of this argument was suggested in a letter by Geoff Sayre McCord.
7 E.g., Hare, *The Language of Morals* (1952), etc.
8 Marcus emphasizes this in 'Moral Dilemmas and Consistency', pp. 129 ff.
9 Cf. Brennan, *The Open Texture of Moral Concepts* (1977).
10 Cf. Woodruff, 'The Bystander Paradox' (1977), pp. 77–8.
11 I will argue in the next chapter that different personal rankings might make situations differ in morally relevant ways. Nonetheless, any theory which makes moral judgements independent of the agent still must claim that everyone must choose the same way in situations that are realistically similar. This applies not only to realism but also to views like Hare's, in which moral judgements depend on the principles of the judger but not the agent. And, even if the agent's personal rankings are relevant, the agent might not have any personal moral ranking, and then he would have to apply any judgement of moral wrongness or overridingness to other agents.
12 Teachability is emphasized by Rescher, *Ethical Idealism* (1987), pp. 50 ff. I will discuss more advantages of dilemmatic theories in chs. 7 and 8.

CHAPTER 7 MORAL REALISMS

1 Cf. Trigg, 'Moral Conflict' (1971), p. 42. Hare, *Moral Thinking* (1981), ch. 2, admits that his prescriptivism implies the impossibility of moral dilemmas, but he uses his theory to argue against moral dilemmas, whereas I argue for moral dilemmas to show that prescriptivism is not adequate for all moral language.
2 There are several arguments from moral dilemmas against moral anti-realism. Wiggins, 'What Would be a Substantial Theory of Truth?' (1980), p. 216, claims that moral conflicts and dilemmas give 'powerful phenomenological support for moral cognitivism or realism', because 'the competing claims present themselves as objective and real'. Guttenplan, 'Moral Realism and Moral Dilemmas' (1979–80), pp. 79 and 75–6, argues against moral anti-realists 'coping so well with the epistemological issues of' cases of 'the uncertain' in which 'no amount of deliberation convinces

[an agent] that one or the other course of action is required' (overridingly?). These arguments are right that moral anti-realists owe us explanations of why morality feels objective and of how moral beliefs can be known or rejected as false or doubted or uncertain. However, moral anti-realists have given many explanations of such aspects of morality. In any case, these issues are not peculiar to moral dilemmas but arise as well in situations that are not even moral conflicts. Platts, 'Moral Reality and the End of Desire' (1980), gives another argument, but it depends on a 'brute fact' (p. 79) that moral anti-realists can plausibly deny.

3 E.g., Wiggins, 'Truth, Invention, and the Meaning of Life' (1976), requires this. Such claims derive from Dummett, but I do not see why even extreme moral realists cannot accept that some moral judgements are neither true nor false in some cases.

4 E.g., Sturgeon, 'Moral Explanations' (1984), and Blackburn, *Spreading the Word* (1984), p. 257, emphasize explanation and causation, but such claims seem irrelevant to moral dilemmas.

5 This use of Tarski's theory of truth is made by Stevenson, *Facts and Values* (1963), pp. 214–20; and Nowell-Smith, *Ethics* (1954), p. 197.

6 Wiggins, 'Truth, Invention, and the Meaning of Life', p. 357.

7 Platts, 'Moral Reality and the End of Desire', pp. 69 and 73. The context suggests that Platts has in mind the desires of the judged agent.

8 Nagel, 'The Limits of Objectivity' (1980), pp. 100, 114, etc.

9 Blackburn, *Spreading the Word*, pp. 217–20, claims a moral anti-realist can be a 'quasi-realist' and agree that moral judgements have truth values that are independent of the mind. This position has problems, but, even if it works, all moral realists still must claim independence of the mind, and that is all that is necessary for my argument below.

10 Crispin Wright pointed out this distinction.

11 For example, Hare, *The Language of Morals* (1952), p. 70, claims dependence on the moral principles of the judger; Williams, 'Internal and External Reasons' (1981), p. 112, makes claims about reasons in general which imply that judgements about moral reasons depend on the motivations of the person whose acts are judged; and Harman, *The Nature of Morality* (1977), pp. 122–3, claims dependence on the motivations of both the judger and the judged.

12 E.g., Firth, 'Ethical Absolutism and the Ideal Observer' (1952).

Contrast Brandt, *Ethical Theory* (1959), pp. 265–9, who makes ideal reactions determine whether moral judgements are justified but not whether they are true. Thus, Brandt's theory, unlike Firth's, is compatible with moral realism.

13 Another reason why I define 'moral realism' so that it implies independence of even ideal states is because moral realism is supposed to claim that moral judgements are like scientific judgements, and scientific realists often claim that the truth values of scientific judgements are independent of even ideal theories. Cf. Putnam, *Meaning and the Moral Sciences* (1978), pp. 36 and 125. Further arguments that moral realism should imply independence of ideal states are given by Dancy, 'Two Conceptions of Moral Realism' (1986).

14 Moderate versions of moral realism are distinguished and discussed by Sayre McCord, 'The Many Moral Realisms' (1986), pp. 10 ff.

15 E.g., Wiggins, 'Truth, Invention, and the Meaning of Life', p. 370, claims that valuations are realistic, but practical judgements are not. See also Pettit, 'Reply: Evaluative "Realism" and Interpretation' (1981), pp. 219–23.

16 Such an error theory is defended by Mackie, *Ethics* (1977), p. 35.

17 Sartre, 'Existentialism is a Humanism' (1957), pp. 297–8.

18 Williams, 'Ethical Consistency' (1973), p. 172.

19 Foot, 'Moral Realism and Moral Dilemma' (1983), p. 387, points out that some belief conflicts leave a residue. For example, even if one alternative is more dangerous than the other, the less dangerous alternative is still dangerous, and this remaining danger is a ground for fear. Such residue does not imply that judgements of danger are not cognitive or realistic, so residue after moral conflicts also does not show that moral judgements are not cognitive or realistic.

20 Williams, 'Ethical Consistency', pp. 175–6.

21 Williams, 'Consistency and Realism' (1973), p. 204. Williams says that realists must deny that inconsistent moral judgements can be 'backed by the best possible reasons'. However, moral realists need not deny this, if they claim that what is backed by the best possible reasons might turn out to be false. Cf. Harrison, 'Ethical Consistency' (1979), pp. 32–5.

22 Williams, 'Consistency and Realism', pp. 187–92, draws this distinction, but he assumes moral realists are concerned only with

truth-inconsistency, whereas moral realists can recognize both kinds of inconsistency in moral judgements. Cf. Foot, 'Moral Realism and Moral Dilemma', pp. 390–1.

23 My argument is derived from Winch, 'The Universalizability of Moral Judgments' (1972); MacIntyre, 'What Morality is Not' (1978); and Wiggins, 'Truth, Invention, and the Meaning of Life'. Winch and MacIntyre direct their arguments against universalizability, but Wiggins shows how such arguments affect moral realism.

24 MacIntyre, 'What Morality Is Not', p. 98. See also Winch, 'The Universalizability of Moral Judgments', p. 165, on decisions; and Williams, 'Ethical Consistency', pp. 184–6, on the 'deliberative use of "ought" '.

25 Cf. Marcus, 'Moral Dilemmas and Consistency' (1980), pp. 135–6; and Kolenda, 'Moral Conflicts and Universalizability' (1975), pp. 464–5.

26 Cf. MacIntyre, 'What Morality Is Not', p. 99.

27 Geoff Sayre McCord raised this objection in correspondence. Similar points apply to obligations that arise from decisions to have children, etc.

28 Contrast Winch, 'The Universalizability of Moral Judgments', p. 153, and MacIntyre, 'What Morality Is Not', p. 98, who claim that their anti-realist judgements can be made only in the first person, since their interpretations depend on speech acts that can be done only in the first person.

CHAPTER 8 APPLICATIONS

1 Cf. Gert, *Morality*, ch. 12: 'Morality and Society'.

Bibliography

Ackermann, Robert, 'Consistency and Ethics', *Proceedings of the Aristotelian Society*, 69, (1968–9), pp. 73–86.

al-Hibri, Azizah, *Deontic Logic: A Comprehensive Appraisal and a New Proposal* (Washington, DC: University Press of America, 1978).

—— 'Conditionality and Ross's Deontic Distinction', *Southern Journal of Philosophy*, 11 (1980), pp. 79–87. *See also* Cox, A.A.

Anderson, Lyle, 'Moral Dilemmas, Deliberation, and Choice', *Journal of Philosophy*, 82 (1985), pp. 139–62. Criticizes Marcus, 'Moral Dilemmas and Consistency'; and criticized by McConnell, 'More on Moral Dilemmas'.

Aquinas, St Thomas, *de Veritate*, trs R. W. Mulligan, J. V. McGlynn and R. W. Schmidt (Chicago: H. Regnery Co., 1952–4).

—— *Summa Theologiae*, trs Thomas Gilby *et al.* (New York: McGraw-Hill, 1964–75).

Aristotle, *Metaphysics*, in *The Basic Works of Aristotle*, ed. R. McKeon, (New York: Random House, 1941), pp. 689–926.

Atkinson, R. F., 'Ethical Consistency', *Proceedings of the Aristotelian Society*, supp. vol. 39 (1965), pp. 125–38. Comments on Williams, 'Ethical Consistency'.

—— *Conduct: An Introduction to Moral Philosophy* (London: Macmillan 1969). See especially ch. 2: 'Conflicts of Duty'.

Austin, J. L., 'A Plea for Excuses', reprinted in *Philosophical Papers*, eds. J. O. Urmson and G. J. Warnock (New York: Oxford University Press, 1970), pp. 175–204. Second edition.

Barry, Brian, 'Tragic Choices', *Ethics*, 94 (1984), pp. 303–18. Review of Calabresi and Bobbitt, *Tragic Choices*.

Baumrin, Bernard H., and Lupu, Peter, 'A Common Occurrence: Conflicting Duties', *Metaphilosophy*, 15 (1984) pp. 77–90.

Beardsmore, R. W., *Moral Reasoning* (New York: Schocken Books, 1969).

Belzer, Marvin, and Loewer, Barry, 'Absolute Obligations and Lewis'

Semantics for Deontic Logic', read at the meetings of the Pacific Division of the APA, San Francisco, March 1987.

Benn, Stanley I., 'Private and Public Morality: Clean Living and Dirty Hands', *Public and Private in Social Life*, eds. S. I. Benn and G. F. Gaus (New York: St Martin's Press, 1983), pp. 155–81.

—— 'Persons and Values: Reasons in Conflict and Moral Disagreement', *Ethics*, 95 (1984), pp. 20–37.

Bennett, Jonathan, 'Morality and Consequences', in *The Tanner Lectures on Human Values*, ed. S. M. McMurrin (Salt Lake City: University of Utah Press, 1981), vol. 2, especially pp. 95–105.

Berkeley, Bishop, *Passive Obedience*, in *Berkeley: Selections*, ed. M. W. Calkins (New York: Scribner's, 1929), pp. 427–69. Originally published in 1712.

Berlin, Isaiah, *Four Essays on Liberty* (New York: Oxford University Press, 1969).

Blackburn, S. W., 'Moral Realism', in *Morality and Moral Reasoning*, ed. John Casey (London: Methuen, 1971), pp. 101–24.

—— *Spreading the Word; Groundings in the Philosophy of Language* (Oxford: Clarendon Press, 1984).

Bond, E. J., *Reason and Value* (New York: Cambridge University Press, 1983). Ch. 8 discusses Wiggins, 'Truth, Invention, and the Meaning of Life'.

Bradley, F. H., *Ethical Studies* (New York: Oxford University Press, 1927). Second edition.

Brandt, Richard B., *Ethical Theory* (Englewood Cliffs, NJ: Prentice-Hall, 1959).

Brennan, J. M., *The Open Texture of Moral Concepts* (New York: Barnes and Noble, 1977).

Bronaugh, Richard, 'Utilitarian Alternatives', *Ethics*, 85 (1975), pp. 175–8.

Calabresi, Guido, and Bobbitt, Philip, *Tragic Choices* (New York: Norton, 1978).

Carey, Toni Vogel, 'What Conflict of Duty is Not', *Pacific Philosophical Quarterly*, 66 (1985), pp. 204–15.

Castañeda, Hector-Neri, *Thinking and Doing: The Philosophical Foundations of Institutions* (Dordrecht: Reidel, 1975).

—— 'Conflicts of Commitments and Morality', *Philosophy and Phenomenological Research*, 38 (1978), pp. 564–74. Response to Cox, 'Castañeda's Theory of Morality'.

Chisholm, Roderick, 'Contrary-to-duty Imperatives and Deontic Logic', *Analysis*, 24 (1963), pp. 33–6.

——— 'Practical Reason and the Logic of Requirement', in Körner, *Practical Reason*, pp. 1–17, with comments by Anscombe, Raz, and Watkins, pp. 17–40.

——— 'Reply to Comments', in Körner, *Practical Reason*, pp. 40–53.

Conee, Earl, 'Against Moral Dilemmas', *Philosophical Review*, 91 (1982), pp. 87–97. Criticisms of Marcus, 'Moral Dilemmas and Consistency', and others.

Cox, A. A., 'Castañeda's Theory of Morality', *Philosophy and Phenomenological Research*, 38 (1978), pp. 557–63. Response in Castañeda, 'Conflicts of Commitments and Morality'. *See also* al-Hibri, Azizah.

da Costa, Newton C. A., and Carnieli, Walter A., 'On Paraconsistent Deontic Logic', *Philosophia* 16 (1986), pp. 293–305.

Dancy, Jonathan, 'Ethical Particularism and Morally Relevant Properties', *Mind*, 92 (1983), pp. 530–47.

——— 'Two Conceptions of Moral Realism', *Proceedings of the Aristotelian Society*, supp. vol. 60 (1986), pp. 167–87.

Davidson, Donald, *Essays on Actions and Events* (New York: Oxford University Press, 1980).

de Sousa, Ronald B., 'The Good and the True', *Mind*, 83 (1974), pp. 534–51.

Donagan, Alan, *The Theory of Morality* (Chicago: University of Chicago Press, 1977). Criticized in McConnell, 'Moral Absolutism and the Problem of Hard Cases'.

——— 'Consistency in Rationalist Moral Systems', *Journal of Philosophy*, 81 (1984), pp. 291–309.

Dworkin, Ronald, 'Is There Really No Right Answer in Hard Cases?', in *A Matter of Principle* (Cambridge, Mass.: Harvard University Press, 1985), pp. 119–145.

Feinberg, Joel, *Social Philosophy* (Englewood Cliffs, NJ: Prentice-Hall, 1973). See especially ch. 5.

——— 'Voluntary Euthanasia and the Inalienable Right to Life', *Philosophy and Public Affairs*, 7 (1978), pp. 93–123. Reprinted in Feinberg, *Rights, Justice, and the Bounds of Liberty*.

——— *Rights, Justice, and the Bounds of Liberty: Essays in Social Philosophy* (Princeton: Princeton University Press, 1980).

Feldman, Fred, *Doing the Best We Can* (Boston: Reidel, 1986). See especially ch. 9: 'Conflicts of Obligation'.

Firth, Roderick, 'Ethical Absolutism and the Ideal Observer', *Philosophy and Phenomenological Research*, 12 (1952), pp. 317–45.

Fogelin, Robert J., *Evidence and Meaning* (London: Routledge and

Kegan Paul, 1967), especially ch. vii.

Follesdal, D., and Hilpinen, R., 'Deontic Logic: An Introduction', in Hilpinen, *Deontic Logic*, pp. 1–35.

Foot, Philippa, *Virtues and Vices* (Berkeley: University of California Press, 1978).

—— 'Moral Realism and Moral Dilemma', *Journal of Philosophy*, 80 (1983), pp. 379–98. Responds to Williams, 'Ethical Consistency' and 'Consistency and Realism'.

Forrester, James W., 'Gentle Murder, or the Adverbial Samaritan', *Journal of Philosophy*, 81 (1984), pp. 193–7.

Frankena, William K., 'Recent Conceptions of Morality', in *Morality and the Language of Conduct*, ed. H.-N. Castañeda and G. Nakhnikian (Detroit: Wayne State University Press, 1963), pp. 1–24.

Geach, Peter, *God and the Soul* (London: Routledge and Kegan Paul, 1969).

Gert, Bernard, *Morality: A New Justification for the Moral Rules* (New York: Oxford University Press, forthcoming). A revised version of Gert, *The Moral Rules* (New York: Harper and Row: 1966).

Gewirth, Alan, *Reason and Morality* (Chicago: University of Chicago Press, 1978). See especially pp. 338–54: 'Conflicts of Duties'. Criticized in Raphael, 'Rights and Conflicts'.

—— 'Replies to My Critics', in Regis, *Gewirth's Ethical Rationalism*, pp. 192–255. Response to Raphael, 'Rights and Conflicts'.

Goldman, Holly Smith, 'Dated Rightness and Moral Imperfection', *Philosophical Review*, 85 (1976), pp. 449–87. *See also* Smith, Holly.

Gowans, Christopher W., 'The Logic of Moral Dilemma', delivered at the APA Central Division Meetings, St Louis, 2 May 1986.

—— 'Introduction: The Debate on Moral Dilemmas', in Gowans, *Moral Dilemmas*, pp. 3–33.

—— *Moral Dilemmas* (New York: Oxford University Press, 1987).

Greenspan, Patricia, 'Moral Dilemmas and Guilt', *Philosophical Studies*, 43 (1983), pp. 117–25. Reactions to Marcus, 'Moral Dilemmas and Consistency'.

—— 'Sophie's Choices: More on Exclusive Requirement', delivered at the APA Central Division Meetings, St Louis, 3 May 1986.

Grice, H. P., 'Logic and Conversation', in *The Logic of Grammar*, ed. D. Davidson and G. Harman (Belmont, Cal.: Dickenson Pub. Co., 1975), pp. 64–75.

Griffin, James, 'Are There Incommensurable Values?', *Philosophy and Public Affairs*, 7 (1977) pp. 39–59.

—— *Well-Being* (Oxford: Clarendon Press, 1986).

250 *Bibliography*

Guttenplan, Samuel, 'Moral Realism and Moral Dilemmas', *Proceedings of the Aristotelian Society*, 80 (1979–80), pp. 61–80. Discusses Wiggins, 'Truth, Invention and the Meaning of Life'.

Hamblin, C. L., 'Quandaries and the Logic of Rules', *Journal of Philosophical Logic*, 1 (1972), pp. 74–85.

Hampshire, Stuart, *Morality and Conflict* (Cambridge, Mass: Harvard University Press, 1983).

Hare, R. M., *The Language of Morals*, (New York: Oxford University Press, 1952).

—— *Freedom and Reason* (New York: Oxford University Press, 1963).

—— 'Moral Conflicts', in *The Tanner Lectures on Human Values*, ed. S. M. McMurrin (Salt Lake City: University of Utah Press, 1980), vol. 1, pp. 169–93.

—— *Moral Thinking: Its Levels, Method, and Point* (New York: Oxford University Press, 1981), especially part 1. Criticized by Primorac, 'Hare on Moral Conflicts'.

Harman, Gilbert, *The Nature of Morality* (New York: Oxford University Press, 1977).

Harrison, Ross, 'Ethical Consistency', in *Rational Action*, ed. R. Harrison (Cambridge: Cambridge University Press, 1979), pp. 29–45. Discusses Williams, 'Consistency and Realism'.

Hill, Thomas E., 'Moral Purity and the Lesser Evil', *Monist*, 66 (1983), pp. 213–32.

Hilpinen, Risto, *Deontic Logic: Introductory and Systematic Readings* (Dordrecht: Reidel, 1971).

—— *New Studies in Deontic Logic* (Dordrecht: Reidel, 1981).

Hintikka, Jaakko, 'Some Main Problems of Deontic Logic', in Hilpinen, *Deontic Logic*, pp. 59–104.

Hoag, Robert W., 'Mill on Conflicting Moral Obligations', *Analysis* 43 (1983), pp. 49–54.

Hook, Sidney, *Pragmatism and the Tragic Sense of Life* (New York: Basic Books, 1974). See especially pp. 3–25.

Howard, Kenneth W., 'Must Public Hands be Dirty?', *Journal of Value Inquiry*, 11 (1977), pp. 29–40.

Hume, David, *Enquiries Concerning Human Understanding and Concerning the Principles of Morals*, ed. L. A. Selby-Bigge (Oxford: Clarendon Press, 1902). Originally published 1752.

Jackson, Frank, 'Internal Conflicts in Desires and Morals', *American Philosophical Quarterly*, 22 (1985), pp. 105–14.

—— 'Davidson on Moral Conflict', in *Actions and Events: Perspectives on the Philosophy of Donald Davidson*, eds Ernest LePore and Brian P.

McLaughlin (New York: Basil Blackwell, 1985), pp. 104–15.

Jackson, Frank, and Pargetter, Robert, 'Oughts, Options, and Actualism', *Philosophical Review*, 95 (1986), pp. 233–55.

Kant, Immanuel, 'On a Supposed Right to Lie from Altruistic Motives', tr. L.W. Beck, in *Kant's Critique of Practical Reason and Other Writings in Moral Philosophy*, ed. L.W. Beck (Chicago: University of Chicago Press, 1949), pp. 346–50. Originally published 1797.

—— *Foundations of the Metaphysics of Morals*, tr. L. W. Beck (Indianapolis: Bobbs-Merrill, 1959). Originally published 1785.

—— *The Metaphysical Elements of Justice*, tr. John Ladd (New York: Bobbs-Merrill, 1965). Originally published 1797.

Kipnis, Kenneth, *Legal Ethics* (Englewood Cliffs, NJ: Prentice-Hall, 1986). See especially ch. 3: 'Conflict of Interest and Conflict of Obligation'.

Kolenda, Konstantin, 'Moral Conflicts and Universalizability', *Philosophy*, 50 (1975), pp. 460–5. Criticizes Winch, 'The Universalizability of Moral Judgments'.

Körner, Stephan, *Practical Reason* (New Haven: Yale University Press, 1974).

Korsgaard, Christine, 'The Right to Lie: Kant on Dealing with Evil', *Philosophy and Public Affairs*, 15 (1986), pp. 325–49.

Ladd, John, 'Remarks on the Conflict of Obligations', *Journal of Philosophy*, 55 (1958), pp. 811–19.

—— 'Moral Dilemmas'. Unpublished.

Lemmon, E.J., 'Moral Dilemmas', *Philosophical Review*, 71 (1962), pp. 139–58.

—— 'Deontic Logic and the Logic of Imperatives', *Logique et Analyse*, 8 (1965), pp. 39–71.

Levi, Isaac, *The Enterprise of Knowledge* (Cambridge, Mass.: MIT Press, 1980). See especially ch. 8: 'Value Conflict'.

—— *Hard Choices: Decision Making under Unresolved Conflict* (New York: Cambridge University Press, 1986).

MacIntyre, Alasdair, 'What Morality is Not', reprinted in *Against the Self-Images of the Age* (Notre Dame, Ind.: University of Notre Dame, 1978), pp. 96–108.

—— *After Virtue: A Study in Moral Theory* (Notre Dame: University of Notre Dame Press, 1981).

Mackie, J. L., *Ethics: Inventing Right and Wrong* (New York: Penguin, 1977).

—— *Persons and Values* (Oxford: Clarendon Press, 1985).

Mallock, David, 'Moral Dilemmas and Moral Failure', *Australasian*

Journal of Philosophy, 45 (1967), pp. 159–178.

Marcus, R.B., 'Iterated Deontic Modalities', *Mind*, 75 (1966), pp. 581–3.

—— 'Moral Dilemmas and Consistency', *Journal of Philosophy*, 77 (1980), pp. 121–36. Criticized by Anderson, 'Moral Dilemmas, Deliberation, and Choice'; Conee, 'Against Moral Dilemmas'; and Donagan, 'Consistency in Rationalist Moral Systems'.

—— 'More on Moral Dilemmas'. Unpublished.

Martinich, A. P., 'Ought, Can, and Conversational Implication', read at the meetings of the Central Division of the APA, St Louis, 3 May 1986.

—— 'Obligation, Ability, and *Prima Facie* Promising', *Philosophia* (forthcoming). Criticizes Sinnott-Armstrong, 'A Resolution of a Paradox of Promising'.

McConnell, T. C., 'Moral Dilemmas and Requiring the Impossible', *Philosophical Studies*, 29 (1976), pp. 409–13.

—— 'Moral Dilemmas and Consistency in Ethics', *Canadian Journal of Philosophy*, 8 (1978), pp. 269–87.

—— 'Moral Absolutism and the Problem of Hard Cases', *Journal of Religious Ethics*, 9 (1981), pp. 286–97. Criticizes Donagan, *The Theory of Morality*.

—— 'Utilitarianism and Conflict Resolution', *Logique et Analyse*, 24 (1981), pp. 245–57.

—— 'Moral Blackmail', *Ethics*, 91 (1981), pp. 544–67.

—— 'More on Moral Dilemmas', *Journal of Philosophy*, 83 (1986) pp. 345–51. Criticizes Anderson, 'Moral Dilemmas, Deliberation, and Choice'.

—— 'Interpersonal Moral Dilemmas', read at the APA Central Division Meetings, St Louis, 3 May 1986.

McDowell, John, 'Virtue and Reason', *Monist*, 62 (1979), pp. 331–50.

Melden, A. I., *Rights and Persons* (Berkeley: University of California, 1977).

Mill, John Stuart, *A System of Logic* (New York: Harper and Brothers, 1884). Originally published 1843.

—— *Utilitarianism* (Indianapolis: Hackett, 1979). Originally published 1861.

Moore, G.E. *Principia Ethica* (Cambridge: Cambridge University Press, 1903).

—— *Ethics* (New York: Oxford University Press, 1912).

Nagel, Thomas, 'War and Massacre', reprinted in Nagel, *Mortal Questions*, pp. 53–74.

___ 'Moral Luck', reprinted in Nagel, *Mortal Questions*, pp. 24–38.

___ 'The Fragmentation of Value', reprinted in Nagel, *Mortal Questions*, pp. 128–41.

___ *Mortal Questions* (New York: Cambridge University Press, 1979).

___ 'The Limits of Objectivity', in *The Tanner Lectures on Human Values*, ed. S. M. McMurrin (Salt Lake City: University of Utah Press, 1980), vol. 1, pp. 77–139.

___ *The View from Nowhere* (New York: Oxford University Press, 1986).

Nowell-Smith, P. H., *Ethics* (Baltimore: Penguin, 1954).

___ 'Some Reflections on Utilitarianism', *Canadian Journal of Philosophy*, 2 (1972–3), pp. 417–31.

Nozick, Robert, 'Moral Complications and Moral Structures', *Natural Law Forum*, 13 (1968), pp. 1–50.

___ *Anarchy, State, and Utopia* (New York: Basic Books, 1974).

___ *Philosophical Explanations* (Cambridge, Mass.: Harvard University Press, 1981). See especially ch. 5.

Nussbaum, Martha, *The Fragility of Goodness: Luck and Ethics in Greek Tragedy and Philosophy* (Cambridge: Cambridge University Press, 1986).

Parfit, Derek, *Reasons and Persons* (Oxford: Clarendon Press, 1984).

Pettit, Philip, 'Reply: Evaluative "Realism" and Interpretation', in *Wittgenstein: To Follow a Rule*, eds S. Holzman and C. Leich (Boston: Routledge and Kegan Paul, 1981), pp. 211–45.

Phillips, D. Z., and Mounce, H. O., *Moral Practices* (New York: Schocken, 1970). See espeically ch. 8: 'Moral Dilemmas'.

Phillips, D. Z., and Price, H. S., 'Remorse without Repudiation', *Analysis*, 28 (1967–8), pp. 18–20.

Pincoffs, Edmund, 'Quandary Ethics', *Mind*, 80 (1971), pp. 552–71.

___ *Quandaries and Virtues* (Lawrence, Kansas: University Press of Kansas, 1987).

Plato, *The Republic*, tr. Paul Shorey, in *The Collected Dialogues of Plato*, eds E. Hamilton and H. Cairns (Princeton: Princeton University Press, 1961), pp. 576–844.

Platts, Mark, *Ways of Meaning* (Boston: Routledge and Kegan Paul, 1979).

___ 'Moral Reality and the End of Desire', in *Reference, Truth, and Reality*, ed. M. Platts (Boston: Routledge and Kegan Paul, 1980), pp. 69–82.

Powers, L., 'Some Deontic Logicians', *Nous*, 1 (1967), pp. 381–400.

Prichard, H. A., 'Does Moral Philosophy Rest on a Mistake?', reprinted

254   *Bibliography*

in *Moral Obligation*, ed. W. D. Ross (New York: Oxford University Press, 1968), pp. 1–17.

Primorac, Igor, 'Hare on Moral Conflicts', *Analysis*, 45 (1985), pp. 171–5.

Prior, A. N., 'The Paradoxes of Derived Obligation', *Mind*, 63 (1954), pp. 64–5.

Putnam, Hilary, *Meaning and the Moral Sciences* (Boston: Routledge and Kegan Paul, 1978).

Quinn, Philip, *Divine Commands and Moral Requirements* (Oxford: Clarendon Press, 1978).

—— 'Moral Obligation, Religious Demand, and Practical Conflict', in *Rationality, Religious Belief, and Moral Commitment*, eds R. Audi and W. J. Wainwright (Ithaca, NY: Cornell University Press, 1986), pp. 195–212.

Rabinowicz, Wlodzimierz, 'Utilitarianism and Conflicting Obligations', *Theoria*, 44 (1978), pp. 19–24.

Raphael, D. D., 'The Standard of Morals', *Proceedings of the Aristotelian Society*, 75 (1974–5), pp. 1–12 and 12A–12E.

—— 'Rights and Conflicts', in Regis, *Gewirth's Ethical Rationalism*, pp. 84–95. Criticisms of Gewirth, *Reason and Morality*.

Rawls, John, *A Theory of Justice* (Cambridge, Mass.: Harvard University Press, 1971).

—— 'Kantian Constructivism in Moral Theory', *Journal of Philosophy*, 77 (1980), pp. 515–72.

Raz, Joseph, 'Reasons, Requirements, and Practical Conflicts', in Körner, *Practical Reason*, pp. 22–35.

—— 'Reasons for Actions, Decisions and Norms', in Raz, *Practical Reasoning*, pp. 128–43.

—— *Practical Reasoning* (New York: Oxford University Press, 1978).

—— 'Value Incommensurability: Some Preliminaries', *Proceedings of the Aristotelian Society* 86 (1985–6).

—— *The Morality of Freedom* (Oxford: Clarendon Press, 1986). See especially ch. 13: 'Incommensurability'.

Regis, Edward, *Gewirth's Ethical Rationalism: Critical Essays with a Reply by Alan Gewirth* (Chicago: Chicago University Press, 1984).

Rescher, Nicholas, *Ethical Idealism* (Berkeley: University of California Press, 1987). See especially ch. 2: 'Does *Ought* Imply *Can?*; On Inconsistent Obligations and Moral Dilemmas'.

Ross, Alf, 'Imperatives and Logic', *Theoria*, 7 (1941), pp. 53–71.

Ross, W. D., *The Right and the Good* (New York: Oxford University Press, 1930).

—— *Foundations of Ethics* (New York: Oxford University Press, 1939).

Routley, Richard, and Plumwood, Val, 'Moral Dilemmas and the Logic of Deontic Notions', in *Paraconsistent Logic*, eds G. Priest, R. Routley and J. Norman (Munich: Philosophia Verlag, 1987).

Sartre, Jean-Paul, 'Existentialism is a Humanism', tr. P. Mairet, in *Existentialism from Dostoevsky to Sartre*, ed. W. Kaufmann (New York: Meridian, 1957), pp. 287–311. Originally published 1946.

Sayre McCord, Geoff, 'Deontic Logic and the Priority of Moral Theory', *Nous*, 20 (1986), pp. 179–97.

—— 'The Many Moral Realisms', *Southern Journal of Philosophy*, 24 (1986), supplement, pp. 1–22.

Schotch, Peter, and Jennings, Raymond, 'Non-Kripkean Deontic Logic', in Hilpinen, *Deontic Logic*, pp. 149–62.

Searle, J. R., '*Prima Facie* Obligations', in *Philosophical Subjects: Essays Presented to P. F. Strawson*, ed. Zak van Straaten (Oxford: Oxford University Press, 1980), pp. 238–59. Shorter form in Raz, *Practical Reasoning*, pp. 81–90.

Sen, Amartya, *Collective Choice and Social Welfare* (San Francisco: Holden Day, 1970).

—— 'Choice, Orderings and Morality', in Körner, *Practical Reason*, pp. 54–67.

—— 'Plural Utility', *Proceedings of the Aristotelian Society*, 81 (1981), pp. 193–215.

—— 'Well-being, Agency, and Freedom: The Dewey Lectures', *Journal of Philosophy*, 82 (1985), pp. 169–221.

Sinnott-Armstrong, Walter, ' "Ought" Conversationally Implies "Can" ', *Philosophical Review*, 93 (1984), pp. 249–61.

—— ' "Ought to Have " and "Could Have" ', *Analysis*, 45 (1985), pp. 44–8.

—— 'A Solution to Forrester's Paradox of Gentle Murder', *Journal of Philosophy*, 82 (1985), pp. 162–8.

—— 'Moral Dilemmas and Incomparability', *American Philosophical Quarterly*, 22 (1985), pp. 321–9.

—— 'Moral Dilemmas and "Ought and Ought Not" ', *Canadian Journal of Philosophy*, 17 (1987), pp. 127–39.

—— 'Moral Realisms and Moral Dilemmas', *Journal of Philosophy*, 84 (1987), pp. 263–76.

—— 'A Resolution of a Paradox of Promising', *Philosophia*, 17 (1987), pp. 77–82. Criticized by Martinich, forthcoming.

—— 'Promises which Cannot be Kept'. Unpublished. Responds to Martinich, forthcoming.

Smith, Holly, 'Moral Realism, Moral Conflict, and Compound Acts', *Journal of Philosophy*, 83 (1986), pp. 341–5. Criticizes Tännsjö, 'Moral Conflict and Moral Realism'. *See also* Goldman, Holly Smith.

Snare, Frank, 'The Diversity of Morals', *Mind*, 89 (1980), pp. 353–69.

Steiner, Hillel, 'Moral Conflict and Prescriptivism', *Mind*, 82 (1973), pp. 586–91. Criticizes Trigg, 'Moral Conflict'.

Stevenson, Charles, *Facts and Values* (New Haven: Yale University Press, 1963).

Stocker, Michael, ' "Ought" and "Can" ', *Australasian Journal of Philosophy*, 49 (1971), pp. 303–16.

—— 'Dirty Hands and Conflicts of Values and of Desires in Aristotle's Ethics', *Pacific Philosophical Quarterly*, 67 (1986), pp. 36–61.

Strasser, Mark, 'Guilt, Regret, and *Prima Facie* Duties', *Southern Journal of Philosophy*, 25 (1987), pp. 133–46.

Sturgeon, Nicholas, 'Moral Explanations', in *Morality, Reason, and Truth*, eds D. Copp and D. Zimmerman (Totowa, NJ: Rowman and Allanheld, 1984), pp. 49–78.

Styron, William, *Sophie's Choice* (New York: Bantam Books, 1980).

Swank, Casey, 'Reasons, Dilemmas, and the Logic of "Ought" ', *Analysis*, 45 (1985), pp. 111–16.

Tännsjö, Torbjörn, 'Moral Conflict and Moral Realism', *Journal of Philosophy*, 82 (1985), pp. 113–17. Criticized by Smith, 'Moral Realism, Moral Conflict, and Compound Acts'.

Taylor, Charles, 'The Diversity of Goods', in *Utilitarianism and Beyond*, eds A. Sen and B. Williams (New York: Cambridge University Press, 1982), pp. 129–144.

Thomason, Richmond, 'Deontic Logic as Founded on Tense Logic', in Hilpinen, *New Studies in Deontic Logic*, pp. 165–76.

—— 'Deontic Logic and the Role of Freedom in Moral Deliberation', in Hilpinen, *New Studies in Deontic Logic*, pp. 177–86.

Thomson, Judith Jarvis, *Rights, Restitution, and Risk*, ed. W. Parent (Cambridge, Mass.: Harvard University Press, 1986).

Trigg, Roger, 'Moral Conflict', *Mind*, 80 (1971), pp. 41–55. Criticized by Steiner, 'Moral Conflict and Prescriptivism'.

Urmson, J. O., 'A Defense of Intuitionism', *Proceedings of the Aristotelian Society*, 75 (1974–5), pp. 111–19.

Vallentyne, Peter, 'Two Types of Moral Dilemmas', *Erkenntnis* (forthcoming).

—— 'Prohibition Dilemmas and Deontic Logic'. *Logique et Analyse* (forthcoming).

van Fraassen, Bas, 'Values and the Heart's Command', *Journal of Philosophy*, 70 (1973), pp. 5–19.

von Wright, G. H., 'Deontic Logic', *Mind*, 60 (1951), pp. 1–15.

Walzer, Michael, 'Political Action: The Problem of Dirty Hands', *Philosophy and Public Affairs*, 2 (1972), pp. 160–80.

Wertheimer, Roger, *The Significance of Sense* (Ithaca, NY: Cornell University Press, 1972).

White, Alan R., *Modal Thinking* (Ithaca, NY: Cornell University Press, 1975).

Wiggins, David, 'Truth, Invention, and the Meaning of Life', *Proceedings of the British Academy*, 62 (1976), pp. 331–78. Discussed in Guttenplan, 'Moral Realism and Moral Dilemmas'; and Bond, *Reason and Value*. Reprinted in Wiggins, *Needs, Values, Deliberation and Truth*.

—— 'Weakness of Will, Commensurability, and the Objects of Deliberation and Desire', *Proceedings of the Aristotelian Society*, 79 (1978–9), pp. 251–77.

—— 'What would be a Substantial Theory of Truth?', in *Philosophical Subjects: Essays Presented to P. F. Strawson*, ed. Zak van Straaten (Oxford: Oxford University Press, 1980), pp. 189–221.

—— *Needs, Values, Deliberation and Truth* (Oxford: Basil Blackwell, 1987).

Williams, Bernard, 'Ethical Consistency', reprinted in Williams, *Problems of the Self*, pp. 166–86.

—— 'Consistency and Realism', reprinted in Williams, *Problems of the Self*, pp. 187–206. Criticized by Foot, 'Moral Realism and Moral Dilemma'; and Harrison, 'Ethical Consistency'.

—— *Problems of the Self* (London: Cambridge University Press, 1973).

—— 'Moral Luck', reprinted in Williams, *Moral Luck*, pp. 20–39.

—— 'Conflicts of Values', reprinted in Williams, *Moral Luck*, pp. 71–82.

—— 'Internal and External Reasons', reprinted in Williams, *Moral Luck*, pp. 101–13.

—— *Moral Luck* (New York: Cambridge University Press, 1981).

—— *Ethics and the Limits of Philosophy* (Cambridge, Mass.: Harvard University Press, 1985).

Winch, Peter, 'The Universalizability of Moral Judgments', reprinted in *Ethics and Action* (London: Routledge and Kegan Paul, 1972), pp. 151–70. Criticized by Kolenda, 'Moral Conflicts and Universalizability'.

Woodruff, Paul, 'The Bystander Paradox', *Analysis*, 37 (1977), pp. 74–8.

—— 'Justification or Excuse: Saving Soldiers at the Expense of Civilians', *Canadian Journal of Philosophy*, supp. vol. 8 (1982), pp. 159–76.

Zimmerman, Michael J., 'Remote Obligation', *American Philosophical Quarterly*, 24 (1987), pp. 199–205.

—— 'Lapses and Dilemmas'. Unpublished.

Zwicky, A., and Sadock, J., 'Ambiguity Tests and How to Fail Them', in *Syntax and Semantics*, ed. J. P. Kimball (New York: Academic Press, 1975), vol. 4, pp. 1–36.

Index